The World of
the Forsytes

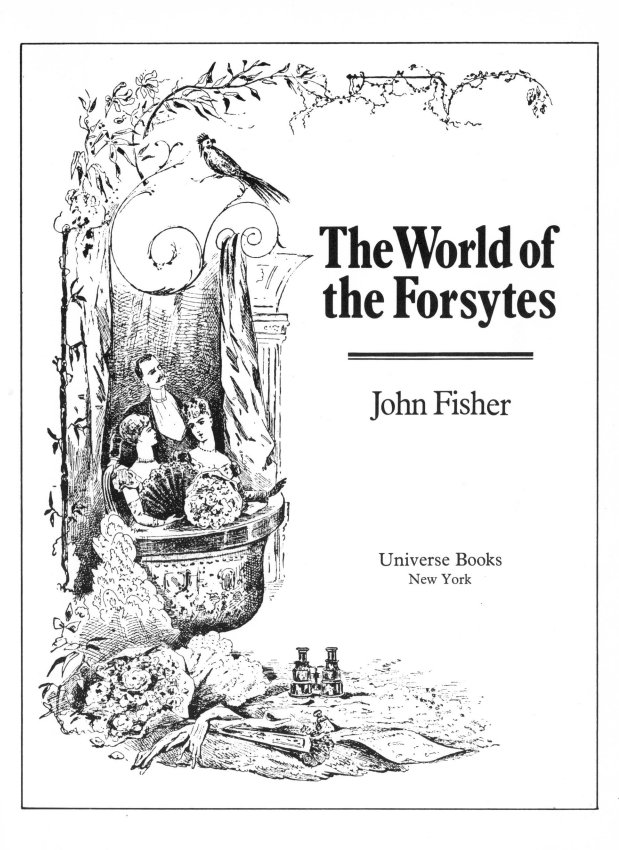

The World of the Forsytes

John Fisher

Universe Books
New York

Published in the United States of America in 1976
by Universe Books
381 Park Avenue South, New York, N.Y. 10016

Library of Congress Catalog Card Number: 76-8803
ISBN 0-87663-244-4

This book was designed
and produced by George Rainbird Limited,
36 Park Street, London W1Y 4DE

Picture researcher: Mary Anne Norbury
Designer: Pauline Harrison
Indexer: Myra Clark

Text set by Jarrold and Sons Ltd,
Norwich, Norfolk
Book printed and bound by
Dai Nippon Printing Co. Ltd,
Tokyo, Japan

Contents

Color Plates

6

Author's Acknowledgments

In writing of the fictional Forsytes, I have not been compelled to guard my language to spare the feelings of surviving relatives. But I should not have been able to write nearly so freely without generous help from a number of unexpected sources.

It was fortunate that, while I was still writing the book, the BBC chose to re-run their version of *The Forsyte Saga*, the twenty-six episodes of which provided both a welcome re-appearance of the Forsytes in human form and a timely reminder of the Saga's dramatic essentials.

I am extremely grateful to Miss Susan Hampshire, who played Fleur Forsyte on the television screen, for giving me her meticulous analysis of Fleur's character, and also to Mr Eric Porter, to whom I talked at some length about Soames.

The Staff of the London Library have, as ever, been indefatigable in providing literary treasures; and I should also like to express my appreciation of the kindness shown by two specialist libraries: the Library of the Royal College of Physicians and the Library of the Institute of Practitioners in Advertising. Miss Betty Medd, Principal of the Norland Nursing Training College, kindly gave me permission to consult the records on the training of children's nurses seventy years ago.

My warmest thanks are due to Messrs William Heinemann and Charles Scribner's Sons, who have been good enough to allow me to quote at length from *The Forsyte Saga* and from other of Galsworthy's writings.

I should also like to express my thanks for permission to quote from the following copy-right works, with acknowledgments to: The Rt Hon. The Lord Greville for the quotations from *The Gentlewoman in Society* by Lady Beatrice Violet Greville; Macdonald and Jane's Publishers and Penguin Books Ltd for the quotation from *Sinister Street* by Compton Mackenzie; Mrs Dorothy Cheston Bennett, George H. Doran Company and Doubleday and Company for the quotation from *Books and Persons 1908–1911* by Arnold Bennett; Mrs Nicolete Gray and The Society of Authors, on behalf of the Laurence Binyon Estate, for the quotation from 'Men of Verdun' from *The Collected Poems of Laurence Binyon*; A. D. Peters and Company Ltd for the quotation from 'Third Ypres' from *The Poems of Edmund Blunden*; The Owen Estate, Chatto and Windus Ltd and New Directions Publishing Corporation for the quotation from 'S.I.W.' from *The Collected Poems of Wilfred Owen*, edited by C. Day Lewis; G. T. Sassoon and The Viking Press for the quotations from 'Good Friday Morning' and 'Does it Matter?' from *The Old Huntsman and Other Poems* by Siegfried Sassoon; and William Heinemann Ltd for the quotation from *Sir Patrick Hastings* by H. Montgomery Hyde.

I have had every encouragement from Mr John Hadfield, Deputy Chairman of the Rainbird Publishing Group, and from his highly professional staff. I also owe much to Miss Ann Hoffmann for her researches into matters of detail which must, at times, have seemed to amount to literary pointillism, and to Mrs Charles Fisher and Mrs Irene Thrower who have retyped some lavishly amended drafts.

Introduction

The Forsytes are surely the best-known English upper-middle-class family in the Western world. *The Man of Property*, the novel which first introduced Soames Forsyte to his public, has already been reprinted more than sixty times, and the Forsytes have also achieved lasting success on the television screen. When *The Forsyte Saga* was first shown on BBC2 in 1967 an average of 700,000 viewers watched, despite the fact that, in those days, few homes could receive the service. More than twenty times as many (15,950,000) saw the first re-run on BBC1 in 1968/9, and 9,000,000 the second re-run a year later. A fourth successful BBC showing – matinées only – took place in 1974.

Abroad, the Forsytes have won friends on both sides of the Iron Curtain. Certainly the twenty-six part BBC serial of *The Forsyte Saga* achieved immediate success not only in Britain but in places as far apart socially as the Far West and the Soviet Union. Donald Wilson, who persuaded the BBC that the Forsytes would be good material, and dramatized the television series, ascribed its phenomenal popularity to the fact that it dealt with primary emotions and appetites:

The people and the way they were presented touched a chord in everybody. It didn't matter who they were, whether they were Yugoslavs or Russians or Americans. There's something about what happens to these people and what they do which is basic to humanity: desires and needs and conflicts which everybody recognizes in themselves.

A family chronicle as such is universally interesting, including eventually the breakdown in the family which so many people have seen happen within their own knowledge. Galsworthy's theme, which really does go right through to the end of *Swan Song*, of beauty as a disruptive element in society, one which overrules all laws and all conventions, is also something which has universal appeal.

The Russians particularly saw the serial as something to explore and look at and satirize the follies of the bourgeois. Equally the people in California were able to say, 'Yes. This is us. We recognize ourselves.'

Yet *The World of the Forsytes* is not intended as a family album of prints to be viewed through the eyes – some would say blinkers – of Soames Forsyte, or Fleur, or any other Forsyte relatives. There are good reasons for this.

The main Forsyte era stretches from the year 1886, almost on the eve of Queen Victoria's Golden Jubilee, when London was the centre of the world's wealthiest and most powerful empire, to the year 1926, when Britain, disrupted by the near-civil-war of the General Strike, stood divided and unsure of herself. To describe it we draw on the three books of Galsworthy's *Forsyte Saga* and the subsequent trilogy, published as *A Modern Comedy*, as also on the family sketches of the Forsytes, first published in 1930 under the title *On Forsyte 'Change*. The curtain falls on Soames's death in 1926. During such a period, many disturbing events occurred even in the privileged parish of the Forsytes which they did not perceive or preferred to ignore.

Therefore *The World of the Forsytes* must be a synthesis which includes not only the adventures in society of the Forsytes themselves, but also the changing world around them which caused them to act and react as they did.

You will not find here any suggestions as to whether Galsworthy's portrait of the class into which he was born was fair or biased. But many English families have recognized themselves and their relatives in the portraits which Galsworthy painted. Young Jolyon, who often seems to have represented Galsworthy's thinking, once gave his views on the whole Forsyte tribe to Philip Bosinney:

'A Forsyte . . . is not an uncommon animal. There are hundreds among the members of this Club. Hundreds out there in the streets; you meet them wherever you go!'

'And how do you tell them, may I ask?' said Bosinney.

'By their sense of property. A Forsyte takes a practical – one might say a common-sense – view of things, and a practical view of things is based fundamentally on a sense of property. A Forsyte, you will notice, never gives himself away.'

'Joking?'

Young Jolyon's eye twinkled.

'Not much. As a Forsyte myself, I have no business to talk. . . .'

'You talk of them,' said Bosinney, 'as if they were half England.'

'They are,' repeated young Jolyon, 'half England, and the better half, too, the safe half, the three per cent half, the half that counts. It's their wealth and security that makes everything possible; makes your art possible, makes literature, science, even religion, possible. Without Forsytes, who believe in none of these things, but turn them all to use, where should we be? My dear sir, the Forsytes are the middlemen, the commercials, the pillars of society, the cornerstones of convention; everything that is admirable! . . . The great majority of architects, painters, or writers have no principles, like any other Forsytes. Art, literature, religion, survive by virtue of the few cranks who really believe in such things, and the many Forsytes who make a commercial use of them. At a low estimate, three-fourths of our Royal Academicians are Forsytes, seven-eighths of our novelists, a large proportion of the Press. Of science I can't speak; they are magnificently represented in religion; in the House of Commons perhaps more numerous than anywhere; the aristocracy speaks for itself. But I'm not laughing. It is dangerous to go against the majority – and what a majority!'

He fixed his eyes on Bosinney: 'It's dangerous to let anything carry you away – a house, a picture, a – woman!'

Opinions are still divided on whether Galsworthy was fundamentally an impartial chronicler (as he himself liked to maintain) or a subversive critic (as he sometimes disclosed himself to be) or a reluctant admirer (as he may eventually have unconsciously· become) of the Forsyte philosophy.

This is something that the reader will have to decide for himself.

*   *   *

The illustrations to this book, which attempt to give a representative view of upper-middle-class life in England between the eighteen-eighties and the mid-nineteen-twenties, include some photographs of people, known or unknown, chosen as 'prototypes' of members of the world of the Forsytes. They are not intended as exact representations of characters in *The Forsyte Saga* – or of the actors and actresses who portrayed these characters in the television series. It is hoped, however, that they will indicate how deeply-rooted Galsworthy's characters were in the real life of the times.

Riot Warning for the Forsytes

It might seem inappropriate for John Galsworthy to have picked 1886 as the opening year of *The Man of Property*, the first book in *The Forsyte Saga* trilogy, because on Monday 8 February of that year a vicious and explosive riot raged through the highways and by-ways of fashionable London, seriously threatening the world of the Forsytes.

The Duke of Wellington's windows were broken, as were those of the Duke of Cambridge. Marshall and Snelgrove claimed £80 damages from the County of Middlesex for its failure to maintain law and order, and Peter Robinson, another department store, put in for £90. Queen Victoria herself wrote a letter to Messrs Thomas Goode, the china shop in South Audley Street, expressing 'sincere sympathy with all the sufferers in the recent riots'. W. H. Smith, of bookstall fame, who was then Member of Parliament for Westminster and Leader of the House of Commons, declared it to be 'almost incredible that, for at least an hour, the most frequented streets in the west end of London should be entirely at the mercy of a mob' such as he had not seen within his recollection.

The event was enough to astonish the weak nerves of the stoutest Forsyte. A number of different organizations, one of which was the revolutionary Social Democratic Federation, had arranged to hold a meeting in Trafalgar Square to discuss the plight of the unemployed (there were as yet no government labour exchanges), and, as *The Times* reported:

About noon in the thoroughfares leading to Trafalgar Square were seen parties of workers from the suburbs, chiefly men engaged in the building trades directing their steps towards this central part of London.

Their numbers were increased by a very great many of the idle class – of that large body in London who are spoken of by workers themselves as the class who want no work to do.

By two o'clock there were probably between fifteen and twenty thousand massed together, mainly on the southern side of Trafalgar Square round Nelson's Column. A few police were present and endeavoured to prevent would-be speakers from climbing the stonework on the level with Landseer's lions. But the leaders of the Social Democratic Federation, headed by John Burns, an engineer who was also parliamentary candidate for Nottingham, swarmed on to the disputed vantage point and rallied the throngs of people round him by waving a red flag. Police who tried to dislodge the invaders were pelted with flour, which presumably had been specially brought by the demonstrators. Soon afterwards the red flag, which had vanished from the vicinity of Landseer's lions, reappeared on the roadway in front of the National Gallery, where speakers resumed business. By then the whole of the square, including the area round the fountains, was densely packed with people. So were the roadways on each side and the steps of St Martin-in-the-Fields.

The crowd cheered as the man with the red flag clambered on to the stonework overlooking

'The demonstrators in turn availed themselves of fresh ammunition from St James's Street, where the road had been dug up for macadamizing'

the square. Burns undoubtedly had a good carrying voice. He told his audience that the House of Commons was composed of capitalists who had fattened upon the labour of the working man and that its membership was made up of landlords, railway directors and employers, who were no more likely to legislate in the interests of the working man than were wolves to labour for the lambs. To hang these people, he said, would be a waste of good rope, and, as no good to the people was to be expected from these 'representatives', there must be a revolution to put an end to this state of affairs. This was heady stuff from a man who himself wanted to enter Parliament – he eventually joined the Cabinet of a Liberal Government – but the crowd nevertheless listened in silence.

The chairman of the meeting, seeing that the crowd was becoming impatient, tried to wind up the proceedings. But the mob surged forward and the platform with its burden of speakers – and reporters – collapsed, spreading confusion and disorder. The 'heavies', as the

Henry Hyndman, sometimes called the founder of British Socialism but distinguishable from most other Socialists in so far as he played county cricket for Sussex and wore a top hat when selling his left-wing weekly *Justice*, was later tried at the Old Bailey (and acquitted) for his part in the riot. He said in his defence that the trouble did not start until the procession was further down Pall Mall and was provoked by the staff of the Reform Club, who threw missiles in the shape of old nailbrushes and shoes at the crowd. The demonstrators in turn availed themselves of fresh ammunition from St James's Street, where the road had been dug up for macadamizing. Hyndman noted with some satisfaction that among the institutions whose windows were broken was the New University Club, from which he had been expelled a short while earlier for speaking on behalf of the unemployed.

Cobbles, directed perhaps with the straight arm of cricketing enthusiasts (Burns was also one), produced highly satisfactory results in St James's Street. At Arthur's Club all the windows in the morning room were broken. At Brooks's Club forty large panes of glass were smashed. At the Devonshire Club eight or nine windows were shattered, and about the same number at Boodle's.

The crowd was now getting very close to Forsyte territory. But they poured on into Hyde Park, turning the fashionably dressed men and women out of their carriages – in one case stripping the coachman of his livery and jumping up on the box in his place. There was a further foray into Grosvenor Square and North Audley Street before the mob, feeling that it had made its point, dispersed. The Forsytes had been warned.

But as the plebs stream away eastwards, we can recross the frontier back into the territory of the Forsytes, to meet some of the tribal elders of this still well-preserved family, men of property whose way of life was totally different from that of the agitators.

toughs were then called, set upon those bystanders who seemed worth robbing. Hats, especially top hats, were tossed in the air and the crowd poured out into the open space where Northumberland Avenue, Whitehall, Cockspur Street and the Strand converge.

Pall Mall was handy, and stones were thrown at several of the clubs there. At the Carlton Club the crowd, which had now swelled to several thousand, stopped, and several of the Socialist leaders climbed on to the railings, one of them waving a red flag. After another harangue the crowd threw stones at the club windows, several of which were broken.

2

The Forsytes in Person

'Old Jolyon' Forsyte, aged eighty, twelve years a widower, and head of the family, would have been one of those most affected by the rioting, for his house lay in Stanhope Gate, that short gully running out of South Audley Street into Park Lane.

At the party given in that summer of 1886 to celebrate the engagement of June Forsyte, his granddaughter, to Philip Bosinney, old Jolyon is described as standing in the centre of the room under the chandelier, as became a host:

with his fine, white hair, his dome-like forehead, his little, dark grey eyes, and an immense white moustache, which drooped and spread below the level of his strong jaw, he had a patriarchal look, and in spite of lean cheeks and hollows at his temples, seemed master of perennial youth.

Even so, it must have been difficult to believe that he had once been a schoolboy packed off each term to Epsom, travelling up from Dorset on the box of a coach, fortified with a mutton pie and a flask of Cherry Brandy.

What old Jolyon thought of unemployed rioters is not precisely stated in *The Man of Property*, the opening volume of *The Forsyte Saga*, but we are given a clue in Galsworthy's sketch 'A Portrait' in his miscellany *A Motley*, which was said to be based on his father, from whom old Jolyon was also drawn.

(*opposite*) '"Old Jolyon" Forsyte, aged eighty, twelve years a widower' . . .

He might pity [malefactors] as well as condemn them, but the idea that the society to which he belonged was in any way responsible for them, would never have occurred to him. His sense of justice, like that of his period, was fundamentally based on the notion that every man had started with equal, or at all events, with quite sufficient opportunities and must be judged as if he had. But, indeed, it was not the custom in his day to concern oneself with the problems outside one's own class.

Here Galsworthy over-simplified social history. It is true that the Victorian middle classes did not feel towards the poor the same obligations that the owners of some great estates in the country felt towards their tenantry. But a considerable number of the aristocracy had devoted themselves to good works – preferably in favour of the deserving poor (that is, the clean, respectful and attentive-in-church poor) – and had even turned charity into a fashionable cult. For example, there was Angela Burdett-Coutts, who had devoted the fortune she inherited from her mother, the Duchess of St Albans (formerly Harriot Mellon the actress), to improving working-class housing. She was created a baroness in her own right. And had not Rear Admiral His Royal Highness the Duke of Edinburgh volunteered in 1880 to serve with the relief squadron engaged in distributing seed potatoes to the distressed peasants of Mayo and Galway?

George Peabody, the American-born philanthropist and banker, who spent half a million dollars on working-class homes, had been

(*above left*) 'The poor in bulk were considered the concern of the Poor Law'
(*above right*) William Booth
(*right*) Peabody Square, Westminster

offered – and, moreover, had refused – a baronetcy. And William Booth had won credit for himself with the Salvation Army, founded in 1878.

But it was probably true to say that, in the world of the Forsytes, the poor in bulk were considered the concern of the Poor Law and in no sense the responsibility of the individual citizen.

Old Jolyon's son 'young Jolyon', known in the family as 'Jo', did not closely resemble his father, nor did he conform to the normal world of the Forsytes. By the standards of the time he was the scape-grace of the family. He ran away with a half-Austrian governess to have one child out of wedlock, and later, after his second wife had died, begot a second illegitimate child before marrying as his third wife, his cousin Soames's ex-wife, Irene. He had already been in trouble at Cambridge where he lost money at cards, ran up bills with the tradesmen and got into the hands of a money-lender, without having the courage to come to

his father for help. Like the prodigal son, he was eventually forgiven.

He ends up by living in Soames's former house with Soames's former wife and wrecking the prospects of his son's marriage to the girl he loves. He had become a willing slave to the woman who had broken up the engagement of his elder daughter June. At the time of old Jolyon's reception he was living off the beaten track in St John's Wood, then a district much favoured by those who could afford to build cottages for their mistresses.

James Forsyte, old Jolyon's younger brother by five years, must, however, have heard the rioters, for his house lay in Park Lane itself. He is described as tall and very lean, with a

(*opposite*) Young Jolyon, 'Jo' (Kenneth More), Irene (Nyree Dawn Porter) and Soames (Eric Porter)

(*above left*) John Welsh as James Forsyte, old Jolyon's younger brother by five years
(*above right*) Hens and a white rooster in a farm yard, by Melchior de Hondecoeter

permanent stoop, and at the family reception we see him brooding over the scene, his grey eyes having 'an air of fixed absorption in some secret worry, broken at intervals by a rapid shifting scrutiny of surrounding facts'. 'I'm very well in myself,' he proclaimed, 'but my nerves are out of order. The least thing worries me to death.'

A born ulcer-man and parsimonious to boot, he once spent £25 on a Dutch painting, by Hondecoeter, of hens and a white rooster in a farm yard. He considered it a bargain, especially as it measured eleven feet by six feet. There

(*opposite*) Soames (Eric Porter) at dinner

was a place for it on the stairs of his house, where it would not be too closely examined. Unfortunately it proved too heavy to be hung, and was consigned by popular demand of the family to the lumber room. When, after James's death, it came out to be sold, it went to a designer of posters working for a poultry firm, for £5.

Soames Forsyte, solicitor and company director, and only son of James Forsyte, is the central figure not only in the three books which make up *The Forsyte Saga* but also in the three following volumes constituting *A Modern Comedy*.

He is first described as having a 'habitual sniff' on his face and as being 'pale and well shaved, dark-haired, rather bald' – he was already thirty-one – and 'carrying his nose with that aforesaid appearance of "sniff", as though despising an egg which he knew he

could not digest'. He was also 'flat-shouldered, flat-cheeked, flat-waisted, yet with a something round and secret about his whole appearance'. On various occasions he 'muttered', or 'snarled' his observations, and he 'moused' rather than walked along the street.

Some people considered that the Soames they met in the television adaptation of *The Forsyte Saga* was a more attractive character than the original Soames in *The Man of Property*. They were right. But as Eric Porter, who played the part, pointed out, he had to allow for the undoubted fact that the written Soames becomes progressively more human as time goes by. The probable explanation for the change is that in the earlier stages of the story Galsworthy, to some extent, used young Jolyon (Jo) as his personal mouthpiece, and when, because of the demands of the plot, Jo had to die, Galsworthy was left with no one through whom to speak. It was then that he began to soften towards Soames and to transfer to him some of his own sympathetic personality.

In the later volumes, in which Soames and his daughter Fleur are the main characters, Soames even becomes slightly pathetic, with his almost slave-like adoration of Fleur, who receives from him all the frustrated affection that he had hoped to lavish on Irene, his first wife, in their house in Montpelier Square.

Soames is indeed at his most human in the World War I sketch 'Soames and the Flag' which Galsworthy wrote about him several years after he had finished *A Modern Comedy*. In it we see a Soames who refuses to add to the panic at the outbreak of war by selling his shares, who finds himself breaking in on a conversation at the next table at his club in order to get the latest war news (and he even tipped the club waiter in another unheard-of breach of club etiquette). We find him surreptitiously helping Fräulein Schulz,

(*opposite*) 'Soames Forsyte, solicitor and company director' . . .

Fleur's German governess, with money and a letter of support to the authorities, after Annette, Soames's French wife, had insisted she should be immediately dismissed.

Soames even demurred at conscientious objectors being harassed by their own countrymen, although he did not agree with their views. He cared about Britain more than he himself realized. His first reaction on Armistice Day was that it would be vulgar to celebrate the occasion in the streets, so he goes into his house, slams the door and sits in an armchair with his back to the world, tears of relief streaming down his face.

At the Club; drawing by George Du Maurier

Of Soames's sister Winifred there is little to be said except that she lived in Green Street, Mayfair, and was kind-hearted, worldly and smart. She suffered deeply from her marriage to Montague Dartie, an 'outside broker' on the Stock Exchange (today he would probably have been cast as a secondhand car salesman).

Over against the piano at the family reception a man of bulk and stature was wearing on his wide chest two waistcoats and a ruby pin instead of the single satin waistcoat and diamond pin of more usual occasion, and his shaven, square old face, the colour of pale leather, with pale eyes, had its most dignified look, above his satin stock. This was Swithin Forsyte, twin of James.

Very little can be said in his favour. He was

vain, gross and self-centred, and in his later years was followed by his valet Adolf carrying an air cushion for his greater comfort. His family had named him Four-in-Hand Swithin in token of his desire to be taken for a dashing driver, although in fact he had never managed more than a pair. He lived in rooms in Hyde Park Mansions.

Roger Forsyte was exceptional among the older Forsytes in being completely clean-shaven – even Swithin had a little tuft of beard on his chin. (We do not know if he used one of those safety razors because, although the Star Safety Razor was endorsed by Oliver Wendell Holmes and by Teddy Wick, the champion barber who had shaved ten men with it in one minute fifty-eight seconds, 'safeties' were considered at first to be slightly effeminate.) Roger also possessed a grey top hat. He was a property developer and a resident of Prince's Gate, Kensington, and it was during a dance at his house – rather a skimped affair – that June Forsyte, granddaughter of old Jolyon, perceived that Irene had taken her fiancé, Philip Bosinney, from her.

Nicholas Forsyte, youngest but one of the six brothers, had made money in mines, railways and house property and was said to be one of the cleverest of the family. But he was outwitted by his wife Elizabeth ('Fanny') who refused to have more than six children and walked out of his house, living in hotels and pawning her jewellery until he agreed to settle an allowance of £500 on her.

Timothy Forsyte, the youngest brother, 'had not thought it wise' to come to the reception 'with so much of this diphtheria about'; he was 'so liable to take things'. He remained a bachelor, never having had the courage to propose marriage to the rumbustious Miss Hatty Beecher after he had seen her arrive back from the opera in a cab alone with a rival suitor. Timothy lived in a red-brick house in the Bayswater Road in an area which was then just becoming fashionable, and provided shelter in it for three Forsyte 'Aunts'. It was there, on Forsyte 'Change, to use the family catch-phrase, that the family tended to meet for tea on Sunday afternoons – it was before the era of weekends – for the purpose of relating their experiences to those present and gossiping about those who were not.

Of the female Forsytes, Aunt Ann was the remembrancer of the family, with her square chin and corkscrew curls. Being the eldest of a family of ten, she had felt bound after her mother died to look after her father and the younger children and to reject her only suitor.

Ann's sister, Hester Forsyte, had, like Ann, remained unmarried and was usually discovered with a book in her hand by the fireside. But once upon a time while touring the Rhine with friends she had slipped out of her hotel

Family group, about 1886

(*opposite*) 'Winifred was kind-hearted, worldly and smart'; painting by Whistler
(*opposite, above right*) 'Montague Dartie, an "outside broker" on the Stock Exchange' . . .; cartoon by Spy

(*left to right*) Fay Compton as Aunt Ann, Fanny Rowe as Emily, Nora Swinburne as Aunt Hester and Nora Nicholson as Aunt Juley in episode two of *The Forsyte Saga*

room for a night of torrid romance with a German army officer.

Then there was a third sister, 'Aunt Juley', née Forsyte, widow of Septimus Small, an architect, who, encouraged by his success at a family river picnic (lobster salad, pigeon pie, tipsy cake, raspberries and champagne), proposed to her soon afterwards on the esplanade at Brighton. But Septimus was delicate – he had a distressing cough which caused the younger members of the family to nickname him the Cough-Lozenge. When he died, Julia went to live, like Ann and Hester, with Timothy, and reverted in effect to spinster status.

Juley's only gesture of independence seems to have ended in a tearful scene after she was followed home by a small white Pomeranian dog and struggled, against the objections of the family, to be allowed to keep it. In any family discussion she could be depended on, with the best of intentions, to ask the questions that must never be asked and to make the comments that should never be heard.

Although they were a brood of ten, the Forsytes were not, in their day, an exceptionally large family. In times of high infant mortality only a plentiful supply of children could ensure the survival of the race and the Empire it had created; and when houses were spacious and servants abundant large families were happy families.

Birth control, of a kind, existed, but it was not

until late in the 1870s that the rubber 'French Letter' began to replace the older type of sheath made of sheep-gut. Such matters were not spoken of in polite society; and Annie Besant, one of the most attractive-looking feminists of her century (she was an atheist once married to the vicar of Sibsey, Lincolnshire), had as late as 1877 been prosecuted for publishing details of birth control methods which, she hoped, would save women from being condemned to perpetual childbearing, amid conditions in which so many died.

William Whiteley, the Universal Provider, included a contraceptive device in his catalogue of 1885, but in 1886, the year of June Forsyte's engagement to Philip Bosinney, Dr H. A. Allbutt was struck off the Medical Register for having recommended a quinine pessary perfected by W. J. Rendell, a chemist of 26 Great Bath Street, Farringdon Road, London, as an effective device for birth control.

Ignorance prevailed in Forsyte circles about many other facts of life. Menstruation, the cause of which was not fully understood until 1895, was regarded either as an undesirable abnormality, or as a sign of displeasure visited from on high and directed towards the sexually inclined. The new revolutionary sanitary towels, which could be burned after use, were already in existence, although till the 1890s there was some hesitation about advertising the fact.

A high moral tone prevailed in most upper-class Victorian – even late Victorian – homes, and the richer bourgeoisie, having no titles or landed estates which would distinguish them from the common people, endeavoured to create their own distinction by assuming a pervasive nobility of purpose and an exaggerated refinement of expression. In the middle years of Victoria's reign it was considered bad form to mention the fact that a woman had legs or was to have a baby (babies, as carefully explained to the children of the family, were habitually discovered under gooseberry

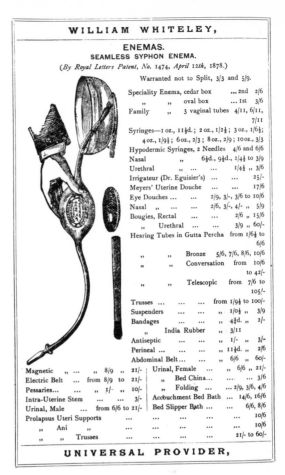

William Whiteley, the Universal Provider, included a contraceptive device in his catalogue of 1885

bushes, and women having them were said to be unwell, or 'not going about just now'); Susan Hayman, née Forsyte, the youngest of the four sisters, scandalized her relatives when she proclaimed, during a discussion on dress, that her husband liked her best without any clothes on.

A curtain of silence separated the known activities of fathers, uncles and brothers within the family circle, which were conducted in an atmosphere of the highest rectitude, from less well-known activities outside the family in which no moral standards of any kind were recognized. Prostitutes were in almost permanent occupation of Piccadilly, Coventry

Street, Haymarket and the Strand in the evening, and had been so in the Burlington Arcade almost since its completion by Samuel Ware in 1819. The police reckoned that five hundred prostitutes were normally to be found in Lower Regent Street alone. Some were girls who had been lured from the provinces for a day's outing in London, had been induced with the help of drink to miss the last train home, and had then been 'taken to some nice lodgings' for the night. Others, servants perhaps, had been marked down as likely material during their walks in the park by women who first befriended them and then prepared their downfall. Other harlots were recruited from hat or dress shops, and some were even bred by their mothers for the trade.

In the early 1880s it was far from safe for women to walk unescorted even in Bond Street; and only those aged under sixteen were protected by the Abduction Laws. Up until 1885 procuration was no offence, and the 'age of consent' at which it was assumed that a girl knew her own mind when she said, 'Yes', was fixed at thirteen. It was not raised to sixteen until after W. T. Stead, Editor of the *Pall Mall Gazette* had shown, the year before, how easily children could be bought and sold in the London pleasure market.

Attempts to check prostitution were resisted not only by those who profited from it – the brothel keepers and the prostitutes themselves – but by all males, who regarded any exposure of their extra-marital activities as an intrusion into their private life. Even the reformers feared that the honour of respectable women might be at risk if the 'safety valve' of prostitution were removed.

Endeavours to control the spread of venereal disease, for example, by the provisions of the Contagious Diseases Act of 1864, which provided free hospital treatment for sufferers, were strenuously resisted by feminists like Josephine Butler, Harriet Martineau and Florence Nightingale, who declared in a

manifesto that it was wrong for the State to afford what amounted to a convenience for the vicious. Josephine Butler stoutly rejected the male argument that in such traffic the women were more to blame than the men since by exacting payment they were turning a natural male impulse into a commercial transaction.

Women heavily outnumbered men in Victorian Britain, yet few careers other than that of teaching or acting as a paid companion were open to single women, a state of affairs which established the nineteenth century as the age of the English spinster. Even so, the right to work, that is the right to a livelihood independent from marriage on the one hand or of promiscuity on the other, was hotly contested.

As early as 1870 Victoria was writing:

The Queen is most anxious to enlist every one who can speak or write to join in checking this mad, wicked folly of Women's Rights with all its attendant horrors, on which her poor feeble sex has been forgetting every sense of womanly feeling and propriety. God created man and woman different – then let them remain each in their own position. Woman would become the most hateful, heartless and disgusting of human beings were she allowed to unsex herself, and where would be the protection which man was intended to give to the weaker sex?

In the end male vanity rather than the promptings of humanity helped to raise women to a state of social grace. As men became better educated they felt the need for better educated wives. Lady Margaret Hall and Somerville, still two of the leading Oxford colleges, were established in 1879, and in 1881 women at Cambridge were allowed to take part in the examinations for university degrees. Oxford followed suit three years later.

Soon women, having received a superior education, were insisting on putting it to use. They invaded the fields of medicine and journalism in which Lady Florence Dixie, younger sister of the Marquis of Queensberry –

(*left*) Lady Florence Dixie
(*centre right*) Somerville
College, Oxford
(*below*) 'The advent of the
typewriter helped to pro-
cure women their latchkeys'

famous for the Queensberry rules and the
Oscar Wilde case – showed the way in her
dispatches to the *Morning Post* from Zululand.
She had also written of her travels in Patagonia.
Mrs Gordon-Cumming had explored the
banks of the Ganges and the Fiji Islands, and
Miss Muriel Dowie had described mountain
climbing in the Carpathians.

Women Art Students at the Slade School of
Art demanded and, in 1881, obtained male
models willing to pose for them.

As industry and commerce expanded, the
need arose for women who could work in
offices – preferably at lower wages than men.
The advent of the typewriter helped to procure
women their latchkeys, and in 1883 the first
machine appeared on which it was possible to
see what one had typed without opening up
the apparatus. An advertisement in William
Whiteley's 1885 catalogue recommended the
typewriter, especially to clergymen who prepared their own sermons, since it would give
them the advantage of having a clearly
printed address to read at less than half the
labour and expense of preparing a written one.

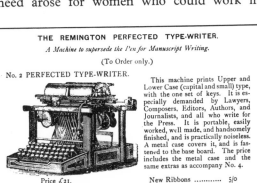

THE REMINGTON PERFECTED TYPE-WRITER.

A Machine to supersede the Pen for Manuscript Writing.

(To Order only.)

No. 2 PERFECTED TYPE-WRITER.

This machine prints Upper and
Lower Case (capital and small) type,
with the one set of keys. It is especially demanded by Lawyers,
Composers, Editors, Authors, and
Journalists, and all who write for
the Press. It is portable, easily
worked, well made, and handsomely
finished, and is practically noiseless.
A metal case covers it, and is fas-
tened to the base board. The price
includes the metal case and the
same extras as accompany No. 4.

Price £21.
CAPITALS AND SMALL LETTERS.

New Ribbons 5/0
Red-inking 1/6
Portable Copy-holder ... 10/0

A Discount of 7½ per cent. allowed off the above prices.

Traces of the new women were also to be found even among the younger Forsytes, in Francie, daughter of Roger Forsyte, for instance. Francie had first shown signs of independence at the age of twelve, when she ran away from home in protest against the dismissal of her favourite butler. When Francie grew up she was a further source of amusement and surprise to the family. 'If she did not precisely suggest the Keltic twilight, she had dark hair and large grey eyes, composed music, wrote stories and poems, and played on the violin', said Galsworthy's sketch of her in *On Forsyte 'Change*. 'For all these reasons she was allowed a certain licence by the family, who did not take her too seriously, and the limit of the licence granted is here recorded.' (In the sketch her father stepped in to save her from marrying an Italian violin player by secretly giving him £500 and a first-class boat ticket to New York.)

Thin, rather tall, intense and expressive, Francie had a certain charm, together with the power, engrained in a daughter of Roger, of marketing her wares, and at the age of thirty she had secured a measure of independence. She still slept at Prince's Gate, but had a studio in the purlieus of Chelsea. For the period she was advanced, even to the point of inviting to tea there her editors, fellow writers, musicians, and also those young men with whom she danced in Kensington, generally christened 'Francie's lovers' by her brother George. At Timothy's in the Bayswater Road, they would say to her at times: 'Do you think it's quite nice, dear, to have young men to tea with you?' And Francie would answer: 'Why not?', which always stopped further inquiry, for the aunts felt that it would be even less nice to put a finer point on it, and, after all, dear Francie was musical. It was believed in the family, rather than known, that she was always in love with someone, but that seemed natural in one of her appearance and was taken to be spiritual rather than bodily. And this

diagnosis was perfectly correct, such was the essential shrewdness underlying the verbal niceties on Forsyte 'Change.

George Forsyte, Francie's brother mentioned above, was perhaps one of the few members of the family who saw the Forsytes as they really were and was not afraid to say so. He was the humorist of the family although the targets for his wit rarely appreciated his jokes.

George was a rebel Forsyte, too, but not an artistic rebel. He had failed for the army, and then became an apprentice farmer at Plumtree Park in Bedfordshire. There he rode other people's horses, shot other people's pheasants, and fell in love with Flora Basset, whose landowning husband was a major with the militia. But during a long hot summer George succeeded only once in pleasuring Mrs Basset before the major returned from his military manoeuvres to resume his civilian occupations.

June Forsyte, the bride never-to-be, became a protector of 'lame ducks'. She had started protecting them even at school and brought back a Cockney child, Susie Betters – who had been bullied in the playground – to have lessons at the Forsyte home. But June and Susie ended up fighting when Susie ill-treated her doll and had to be sent home again.

There were, of course, other Forsytes standing in the wings or to be called later on stage.

June Barry as June

(*opposite*) 'Traces of the new women were also to be found even among the younger Forsytes, in Francie, daughter of Roger Forsyte, for instance' . . .

27

But just what was the strength of the cement holding the family together? According to Galsworthy, the visitor to the family reception for June's engagement would have

gleaned from a gathering of this family – no branch of which had a liking for the other, between no three members of whom existed anything worthy of the name of sympathy – evidence of that mysterious concrete tenacity which renders a family so formidable a unit of society, so clear a reproduction of society in miniature. . . . The Forsytes were resentful of something, not individually, but as a family; this resentment expressed itself in an added perfection of raiment, an exuberance of family cordiality, an exaggeration of family importance, and – the sniff. Danger – so indispensable in bringing out the fundamental quality of any society, group, or individual – was what the Forsytes scented; the premonition of danger [the consequences of June's engagement to the unknown architect Philip Bosinney] put a burnish on their armour. . . . Never had there been so full an assembly, for, mysteriously united in spite of all their differences, they had taken arms against a common peril. Like cattle when a dog comes into the field, they stood head to head and shoulder to shoulder, prepared to run upon and trample the invader to death.

But there were family rows, too, and secrets.

Hitherto [before Soames became a Man of Property] there had been between these six brothers no more unfriendly feeling than that caused by the secret and natural doubt that the others might be richer than themselves; a feeling increased to the pitch of curiosity by the approach of death – that end of all handicaps – and the greater 'closeness' of their man of business, who, with some sagacity, would profess to Nicholas ignorance of James's income, to James ignorance of old Jolyon's, to Jolyon ignorance of Roger's, to Roger ignorance of Swithin's, while to Swithin he would say, most irritatingly, that Nicholas must be a rich man.

So, within the family, the Forsytes did not love each other to distraction. Yet, outside in the world at large, they were not insensitive to charms and were at times susceptible to worldly temptations.

(*below*) Family reception; drawing by George Du Maurier

3

The Forsytes in Love

There is no doubt that the Forsytes appreciated beauty when they saw it. And *The Forsyte Saga* and its sequels deal largely with the disturbances that ensue when beauty disarranges a materialist world

Most of the Forsytes had encountered romance of a kind in their day. Swithin, for instance, while holidaymaking in the years back, had found himself caught up with a girl militant in the Hungarian independence movement. But the beauty that chiefly disturbed the characters of *The Man of Property* was, of course, Soames's wife, Irene.

The gods had given Irene dark brown eyes and golden hair, that strange combination provocative of men's glances, which is said to be the mark of a weak character. And the full, soft pallor of her neck and shoulders, above a gold-coloured frock, gave to her personality an alluring strangeness.

Soames's courtship of Irene had opened in 1881, while he was developing property in the neighbourhood of Bournemouth, and a musical tea was given in his honour.

Late in the course of this function, which Soames, no musician, had regarded as an unmitigated bore, his eye had been caught by the face of a girl dressed in mourning, standing by herself. The lines of her tall, as yet rather thin, figure showed through the wispy, clinging stuff of her black dress, her black-gloved hands were crossed in front of her, her lips slightly parted, and her large, dark eyes wandered from face to face. Her hair, done low on her neck, seemed to

gleam above her black collar like the coils of shining metal. And as Soames stood looking at her, the sensation that most men have felt at one time or another went stealing through him – a peculiar satisfaction of the senses, a peculiar certainty, which novelists and old ladies call love at first sight.

During his courtship Soames had to wait patiently, 'watching Irene bloom, the lines of her young figure softening, the stronger blood deepening the gleam of her eyes, and warming her face to a creamy glow'. And then, when they were married:

He had never met a woman so capable of inspiring affection. They could not go anywhere without his seeing how all the men were attracted by her; their looks, manners, voices, betrayed it; her behaviour under this attention had been beyond reproach.

At first, at any rate.

But the most detailed description of Irene's beauty occurs when she has already strayed somewhat from the path of duty. And she is here seen through the eyes of young Jolyon, who would one day marry her. He had taken to painting, and was making some studies in the Botanical Gardens, then in Regent's Park.

He saw a rounded chin nestling in a cream ruffle, a delicate face with large dark eyes and soft lips. A black 'picture' hat concealed the hair; her figure was lightly poised against the back of the bench, her knees were crossed; the tip of a patent leather shoe emerged beneath her skirt. . . . Her face was not the face of a sorceress, who in every look holds out to men the offer of pleasure; it had none of the 'devil's beauty' so highly prized among the first Forsytes of the land; neither was it of that type, no less adorable, associated with the box of chocolate; it was not of the spiritually passionate, or passionately spiritual order, peculiar to house-decoration and modern poetry; nor did it seem to promise to the playwright material for the production of the interesting and neurasthenic figure, who commits suicide in the last act.

In shape and colouring, in its soft persuasive passivity, its sensuous purity, this woman's face reminded him of Titian's 'Heavenly Love', a reproduction of which hung over the sideboard in his dining-room. And her attraction seemed to be in this soft passivity, in the feeling she gave that to pressure she must yield.

Nyree Dawn Porter
as Irene

She was waiting of course for Philip Bosinney, though Soames had not yet given up hope that the affair would come to nothing.

Like most novel readers of his generation (and Soames was a great novel reader), literature coloured his view of life; and he had imbibed the belief that it was only a question of time. In the end the husband always gained the affection of his wife. Even in those cases – a class of book he was not very fond of – which ended in tragedy, the wife always died with poignant regrets on her lips, or if it were the husband who died – unpleasant thought – threw herself on his body in an agony of remorse.

Yes. That indeed was the kind of thing that occurred in so many of the sagas written by the Victorian women novelists whose works circulated in ever-widening ripples through Victorian society; their heroines and the way they behaved exerted an influence on readers not only in the Forsyte circle but on historians writing later on the social life and tastes of the period.

Euphemia Forsyte, who would then have been about twenty-five, was, we are told, eager to borrow the Revd Mr Scoles's latest work entitled *Passion and Paregoric*. By no means all of such novels were written for the servants' hall or for frustrated spinsters. Margaret Oliphant Wilson, for instance, specialized in plots based on every-day life in a country parish. Charlotte M. Yonge's offerings were especially wholesome because of the moral principles she proclaimed, and were warmly approved of not only by ladies in the parlour but even by soldiers fighting in the Crimea. Few men could have shown greater virtue than Sir Guy Morville, the hero of her best-known work *The Heir of Redclyffe*.

Mudie's, the very successful circulating library which had been established in 1842 (and now had several million volumes out on loan), exercised a strict moral supervision over the works it issued (George Meredith's *Ordeal of Richard Feverel* was among the many it refused to handle).

Mrs Humphry Ward, a granddaughter of Dr Arnold, the famous headmaster of Rugby School, was an untiring advocate, in her novels, of social service as a career for heroines, and Mr Gladstone, the Liberal leader, personally reviewed her novel *Robert Elsmere*, which strongly attacked the evils of unbelief.

But there were other Victorian novelists less preoccupied with the moral well-being of their readers, and more, much more, concerned with entertaining them. Their works were nonetheless thought worthy of binding in leather, and so they survive even today on many an old library shelf. Their very titles show the way the world was going. *Only a Girl Wife* came

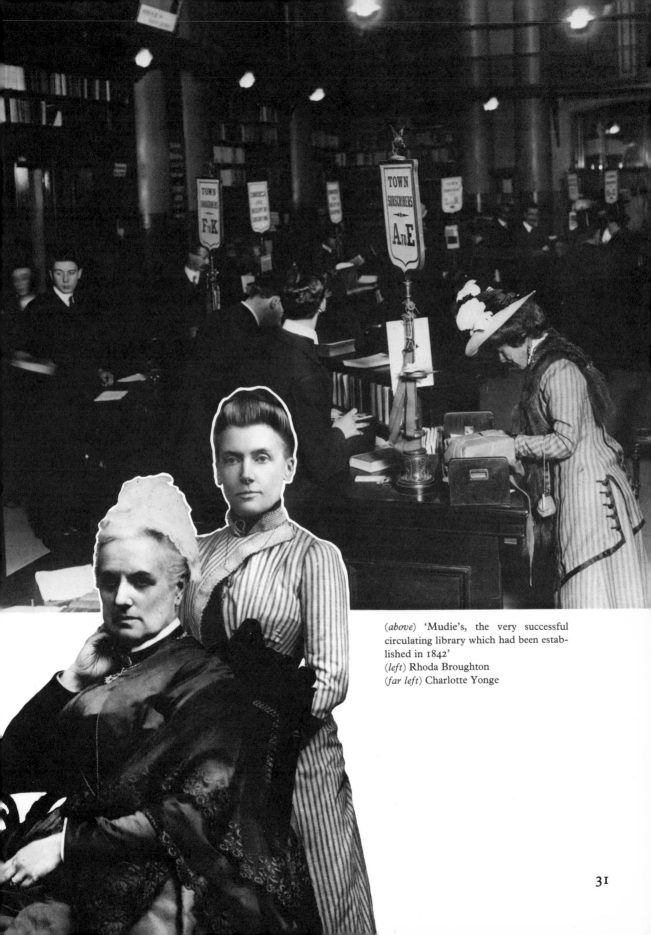

(*above*) 'Mudie's, the very successful
circulating library which had been established in 1842'
(*left*) Rhoda Broughton
(*far left*) Charlotte Yonge

from the pen of Ruth Lamb, one of the more successful women writers of her day. *A Passion in Tatters* was the title of a story by Annie Thomas, Mrs Pender Cudlip in private life. And Rhoda Broughton, daughter of a Welsh parson, whose lyrical racy prose captured more readers than almost any other of her tribe, produced *Red as a Rose is She, Not Wisely but Too Well, A Fool in her Folly* and *Goodbye Sweetheart*.

The class of heroine was also changing. Clearly the outdoor athletic type was coming into favour, and red hair, freckles and a snub nose were becoming acceptable in an atmosphere which was growing more and more permissive . . . and more explicit. Cycling was becoming a recognised recreation for women, and advertisements for cycles emphasized the freedom and glamour that was attached to this new escape from tradition.

In the earlier Victorian novels, which aimed at the assertion of a moral principle, there was little time for kissing. But later novel-readers evidently asked for more, and in this respect Rhoda Broughton was one of the most liberal providers. In *Cometh Up as a Flower*, published in 1867, for example, as the happy ending draws near, the hero rains on the heroine's lips kisses 'as thick as leaves in autumn or the whirling Simois'.

But this was kids' stuff compared to what happened *after* marriage. For example, Mrs Hungerford, a well-established woman novelist whose books were published by Chatto & Windus, leaves little to the imagination in her novel *A Modern Circe* which includes a torrid extra-marital love affair.

What would actually happen, as far as young people were concerned, was rather different. For instance, it would have been unthinkable for a young man to take a young girl out to dinner alone. No girl of self-respect would compromise herself by allowing a young man to incur expense on her behalf. She could not allow herself to be seen in public in such circumstances.

A standard work on etiquette warned young men that if, when riding, they met a girl they knew who was on foot, they should dismount and walk with her in the direction she was going, for no nice girl could be seen standing in the street talking to a young man.

And as late as March 1894 in *The Nineteenth Century* – the same periodical which published Mr Gladstone's review of Mrs Humphry Ward's novel – we find an article by Kathleen Cuffe, still demanding that young girls be allowed the privilege of walking alone or going to a tea party unaccompanied, in short of abolishing chaperons on all possible occasions. The anomaly was that while their married but, to the naked eye, indistinguishable sisters were afforded comparative freedom, unwedded girls were not allowed even to go to church unaccompanied, let alone a matinée or concert.

Nor were they permitted any great freedom of choice in the clothes they wore on such occasions.

(*opposite*) 'The freedom and glamour of cycling for women'; poster of 1899 by J. Ramsdell

4

Safety in Stays

When Oscar Wilde declared fashion to be 'a form of ugliness so absolutely unbearable that we have to alter it every six months', he should have been thinking of the bustle. This abomination, an artificial protuberance clamped on to the feminine bottom, had first made its appearance around 1870, had temporarily disappeared eight years later, but had returned in an even more extreme form in the mid-1880s. As C. Willett and Phillis Cunnington record in their *Handbook of English Costume in the Nineteenth Century*, it jutted out like a shelf on which a good-size teatray might have been carried, and at times wobbled from side to side in a ridiculous manner.

Day dresses often had a separate bodice and skirt, the skirt falling from the bustle in swathes across the front, waterfall fashion, the sleeves of the bodice kicking up

(*above*) The bustle, 27 February 1886

(*opposite*) Latest Paris fashions of April 1886

slightly above the shoulder to suggest the quill of an angel's wing or perhaps more directly the *en gigot* sleeves that were to follow.

The famous battle between bonnets and hats was not yet over, as is apparent in the issue of *The Queen* ('The Lady's Newspaper and Court Chronicle') dated 10 July 1886:

There is certainly a great deal that is new, and not a little extraordinary, in the present modes, more especially as regards millinery. When you examine fashionable bonnets in the hand they seem almost too bizarre to wear, but they prove becoming when on, and by no means so out of the common as to verge on the grotesque. A grey coarse-plaited straw bonnet, with two points to the crown, like a couple of gables side by side. Another was in the thatched cottage style; it was composed of the husks of wheat and straw sewn closely together, and covering the whole shape, with just a knot of red poppies in front, and red tulle strings. A white bonnet of

33

PARIS FASHIONS
SPRING HATS AND BONNETS.

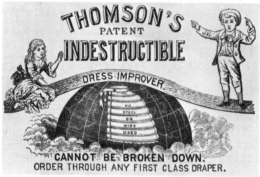

(*top*) 'There is a great deal that is new, and not a little extraordinary, in the present modes, more especially as regards millinery'
(*above*) Advertisement for the 'artificial protuberance'

crinoline plait, beaded with pearls, was still more unique, for it was made with one point like a Phrygian cap, caught down and hidden among the roses, and loops of ribbon at the top.

Young girls wear hats in London on almost all occasions and the present styles are, as a rule, becoming. Sailor hats have large bows carried on to the crown in front, and the brim inside is covered with soft tulle, which is wonderfully becoming. Other hats have crowns as high as it is possible to make them, the brims turned up and lined, hardly any two alike. [So high did crowns become that *Punch* suggested that hansom cabs should be modified to allow them to protrude through the roof.] Huge clusters of ostrich plumes appear at the side, as many as seven distinct feathers sometimes. Rush hats, coarsely plaited and of mixed colourings, are much worn. A few trifles quite new are worth mentioning.

A small lion's head and tail, made in fur for the front of a hat; a fringe of West Indian silver-grey seeds, known as Job's tears, mixed with steel beads; large steel balls for the ends of bows and brass dress buckles. All these require to be applied with skill, and then are novel additions to a well-thought-out costume.

In the end the hat ousted the bonnet and flat crown hats won the contest against high-crowns. Veils were popular during the closing years of the century and Mr Lee, the Court Veiler of Wigmore Street, exploited the trend for spotted veils with his Nell Gwynne model which had on it only two black beauty spots.

Bracelets and jewelled 'dog collars' were in vogue and about 1888 wrist watches (for women only) began to appear. Parasols were dome-shaped, like those seen ninety years later; they were often trimmed with ribbon and sometimes decorated on top with an artificial bird.

The tea gown – a loose-fitting dress, often of velvet, had been taken up in the late 1870s by married women who preferred eating their sandwiches and cake at home in comfort; in the eighties it was worn by younger women as well.

But this was of course only in preparation for the far more exacting toilette of the evening. The more fashionable had their evening- and, for that matter, their day-dresses made, if not in Paris, at least by a Court dressmaker, one of the many small establishments whose name was passed round by personal recommendation among those who moved in such circles. Later the big department stores set up their own dressmaking section for women who did not know or were not sufficiently sophisticated to get to know any Court dressmaker, yet were too fashionable to have their clothes made by their local seamstress. Ready-to-wear dresses

(*opposite*) 'Sailor hats have large bows'

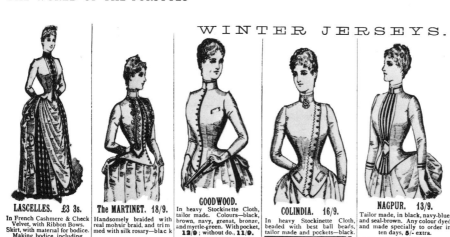

WINTER JERSEYS.

LASCELLES. £3 3s.
In French Cashmere & Check Velvet, with Ribbon Bows. Skirt, with material for bodice. Making bodice, including linings, &c., **15/-** extra.

The MARTINET. 18/9.
Handsomely braided with real mohair braid, and trimmed with silk rosary—black

GOODWOOD.
In heavy Stockinette Cloth, tailor made. Colours—black, brown, navy, grenat, bronze, and myrtle-green. With pocket, **12/9**; without do., **11/9.**

COLINDIA. 16/9.
In heavy Stockinette Cloth, beaded with best ball beads, tailor made and pockets—black.

NAGPUR. 13/9.
Tailor made, in black, navy-blue, and seal-brown. Any colour dyed and made specially to order in ten days, **5/-** extra.

The NAUTILUS. 15/9.
In black, navy-blue, and seal-brown. Any colour dyed and made to order in ten days, **5/-** extra.

WARRINGTON.
In Foulé Cloth, panel. Skirt and with braided col Making bodice, inc &c., 15/-

NEW CORSET WAIST, 1s 6d. EXTRA.

Ready-to-wear dresses, from *The Lady*, 1886

were also imported from Paris. They were originally draped on stands but were later shown by 'models' dressed underneath in rigid black satin who were thus no more than moving dummies. Yet the days were soon to come when such models not only acquired a personality of their own but were paraded at select receptions in the salon, watched by such celebrities as Ellen Terry, Lillie Langtry and the Duchess of Westminster. Later still they reached a wider public by parading in the restaurants of the well-known department stores while lunch was being served to the patrons.

In the mid-1880s of which we are speaking the décolletage of an evening gown could be square, round or V-shaped. It had dropped considerably since the early years of the century. The Marchioness of Londonderry, in a sketch taken of her about this time, appears in an evening dress the neck-line of which starts from below the shoulder to proceed like an inverted Cupid's bow across her breast to just below the other shoulder. The aristocracy had less need for inhibitions than the middle classes. The Marchioness's eyebrows are perhaps heavier than we should see today and there is no discernible lipstick. She wears a necklace of two rows of pearls and carries an ostrich fan. The eighties was of course the great period for fans, and they had become larger than ever. *The Lady's World* in 1887 talks of ostrich feather fans mounted on tortoiseshell, and here and there a distinct Japanese influence could be noticed. Some of the more daring were transparent which precluded any uninhibited yawns.

Generally the dresses were simple but a glittering or luxurious effect was aimed at. Lace was in favour: Irene at one of her own dinners had 'adorned the bosom of her dress' with a cascade of it. Boas and shawls – relics of the days when you could not put on a coat over a crinoline – were still in use, but fitted sealskin jackets had now become popular as evening wraps.

The hair in this period was dressed close to the head with the ears uncovered and it was secured in a bun at the nape of the neck; there was often a short fringe in front. The general effect tended to be Grecian. But for the evening it was often brushed up and secured on top of the head – disclosing, perhaps even unconsciously, a faint Japanese influence.

Underclothes, generally referred to as *lingerie*, were becoming less unmentionable, though, in order to avoid undue suggestiveness, advertisements for women's underwear often showed the garments only, without the lady wearer inside. And even Francie Forsyte

| | MALVERN. £1 19s. 6d. | ABERDARE. £5 5s. | CLARENDON. £4 4s. | FANCY MUFF DEPARTMENT. | MELTON. £2 12s. 6d. | CRAVEN. £1 15s. 9d. | GRANVILLE. 16/9. | SOUTHSEA. 8/11 |

D. 8/11. s shape, pa-cloak, with back, one convenient worn. asure, 50, 52, inches.

MALVERN. £1 19s. 6d. In Navy Estamine Serge, trimmed with Bretonne braid. Skirt, with material and braid for bodice. Making bodice, including linings, &c., **15/-** extra.

ABERDARE. £5 5s. Costume of Black Spanish Lace, with handsome beaded panel and jet ornaments. Skirt, with length for bodice. Making bodice, including linings, &c., **15/-** extra.

CLARENDON. £4 4s. Costume of plain and spotted Brussels Net, trimmed with ribbons. Skirt and length for bodice. Making bodice, including linings, &c., **15/-** extra.

FANCY MUFF DEPARTMENT. A large variety in all the Newest Shapes, in Black and Coloured, from **2/11** to **35/-**. Ladies are respectfully invited to write for our New Illustrations, sent Post Free.

◆◆◆◆◆◆◆◆◆◆◆◆◆

PATTERNS AND ESTIMATES POST-FREE.

◆◆◆◆◆◆◆◆◆◆◆◆◆

Ladies can forward Pattern Bodice, from which a PERFECT FIT is guaranteed.

MELTON. £2 12s. 6d. Costume of Nun's Veiling and Satin Mevveilleux. Skirt, and length for Bodice. Making bodice, including linings, &c., **15/-** extra.

CRAVEN. £1 15s. 9d. Costume in black lace, trimmed with satin ribbons. Skirt, with length for bodice. Making bodice, including linings, &c., **15/-** extra.

GRANVILLE. 16/9. Spence's new shape waterproof rubber cloak, with sling sleeves and box pleats fitting to the waist. Sizes, back measure, 52, 54, 56, 58 inches.

SOUTHSEA. 8/11 Circular Cloak, with patent untearable armhole, superior quality rubber and good Canton back. Sizes, back measure, 50, 52, 54, 56, 58 inches.

would not yet have worn the transparent nightdress which was to come in during the nineties. Corsets, however, had become positively daring. For example, *The Graphic* of 30 January 1886 carries a corset advertisement for: 'The Gladys, A charming Mantle for Summer Wear, made in Ottoman Bengaline or Broche Silk, very fully trimmed with Lace, Jet Passementerie and Ribbon Bows.' And, in the end, you could get away with almost anything if it was classical. For instance, an advertisement in the *Illustrated London News* of February 1896 for Vogeler's Curative Compound claiming success in the treatment of hysteria, languor and ringing noises in the head, showed a young woman, 'The Queen of Health', who had just climbed dripping out of the Fountain of Health, her wet muslin robe clinging to most of her figure except for a beautifully-shaped left breast which was uncovered. Aloft in her hand she held a bottle of the elixir.

Elsewhere there were already signs that the more fantastic and exaggerated features of Victorian women's dresses – the high-boned collars, stiff stays, tight gloves and buttoned boots – the symbols of law and order in the social world, were on the way out. Queen Victoria had strongly objected to the absurdities of the crinoline, and in 1881 Viscountess Harberton founded the Rational

'The hair was dressed close to the head with ears uncovered . . . but for the evening it was often brushed up and secured on the top of the head'

'Advertisements for women's underwear often showed the garments only, without the lady wearer inside'

Dress Society and organized the Hygienic Wearing Apparel Exhibition the following year in Kensington Town Hall. She held the view that petticoats were unhealthy, dangerous, and, because they dragged on the floor, dirty, and appeared on public platforms corsetless in black satin Turkish trousers, a white waistcoat and velvet black jacket. Her followers, equally corsetless, favoured divided skirts, or knickerbockers under a loose skirt which could be lifted up if necessary. Her 'Dual Garmenture', portrayed in the Rational Dress Society's *Gazette*, was in fact a divided petticoat, and to this extent less revolutionary than Amelia Bloomer's bifurcated unmentionables had been in 1849. Mrs Ada Ballin agreed with Lady Harberton in her work, *The Science of Rational Dress*, published in 1885, in which she said that bloomers had been too radical and that future reforms would have to be more gradual. Two years later the students of Girton and Newnham, the two Cambridge women's colleges, perfected a design for a boneless corset, known as the *Corset sans Arrête* in appreciation of the newly marketed boneless sardine.

There were revolutionary trends in the material from which clothes were made as well as in their structure. For example, Arthur Lasenby Liberty, who had founded Liberty's store in 1875, discarded from his shelves the hard cottons and stiff brocades which had hitherto delighted the Victorians, in favour of softer styles (and colour dyes) used in the Orient. Soon, the drooping figures and pale and interesting faces of the Pre-Raphaelites appeared in flimsy loose-sleeved open-necked dresses of the Liberty type which clung to the figure in an appealing medieval or neo-Grecian way. William Morris, Thomas Carlyle, Ruskin, Burne-Jones, Millais and the Aesthetes, some more precious than others, also flocked to 218a Regent Street to buy Liberty fabrics for house furnishings. Some aesthetes went into knee breeches, velvet jackets and loose-knotted ties.

But Liberty had a rival. As far back as 1870

'Corsets had become positively daring'

'A Women's Archery Association had existed since 1864'

Bernard Shaw ordered himself a complete woollen suit.

But the orthodoxies of dress design were under assault from feminine athletes, as well as reformists and faddists. A Women's Archery Association had existed since 1864, and in 1871 ladies were already being taught to swim off the Brighton beach. *Punch* in 1884 reported several women's cricket matches, and in 1886 fencing was noticeably popular; 1894 saw the first women's intervarsity hockey match.

Then there was the tricycle. In Court circles Princess Mary, Duchess of Teck, took the initiative by riding one, and Queen Victoria presented a tricycle to her young granddaughter, the Princess of Hesse. So how could it be wrong for middle-class people to ride tricycles too? And how could it be wrong, when tricycles were replaced by the much more manageable and compact bicycle, for women to ride these as well, though they were not at first equipped with bell, front and rear brakes, or skirt guard? It became fashionable to go bicycling in Battersea Park – sending the servants ahead with the bicycles and arriving oneself in the carriage. Then: coffee and rolls, a brisk bike-ride and 'Home, James' again in the carriage.

For a long time no suitable dresses existed for women who wanted to take up sport for its own sake. Ladies in London were unwilling to dispense with long skirts even when bicycling down Sloane Street, and Mrs Williams, the editor of *The Onlooker*, caused a sensation in October 1900 when she appeared in the Park with a device allowing her to hook up her skirt, leaving both hands free. Paquin, the French couturier, whose word was then law, insisted that even if he raised skirts as much as two inches off the ground, they would still need to be held up by hand in wet weather. To clear the ground completely, they would need to be six inches from it, and this would be unthinkable.

Tennis was popular, yet the long dresses sold

Dr Gustave Jaeger of Stuttgart had been advocating wool as the natural fabric for wearing next to the body, and his theories had won the approval of Field Marshal Count Helmuth von Moltke, Chief of the General Staff of the Prussian Army, as well as of dress reformists in Britain. Jaeger specified that the wool should be natural and undyed and advised that socks should be knitted with a separate compartment for each toe. Both Oscar Wilde and his wife (who was an active member of the Dress Reform Society) were Jaeger enthusiasts, and

for it were totally unsuitable and made their wearers look like 'swans waddling across a bowling green', as one observer noted. Not until 1885 was serge beginning to be advertised as the correct material for bathing costumes in place of flannel, which when soaked became heavy and inconvenient. (Straw hats were also recommended for bathing, indicating that the head was not normally ducked.)

Queen Victoria, with her travels, described in

(*above*) 'It became fashionable to go bicycling in Battersea Park'
(*right*) 'Tennis was popular'
(*below*) 'For a long time no suitable dresses existed for women who wanted to take up sport for its own sake'

Leaves from the Journal of my Life in the Highlands, and her disregard of the weather at Balmoral (balls were given there even when rain was blowing into the marquee) created a demand for outdoor wear. For although the Fox Frame umbrella had been patented in 1850, and the Aquascutum had been worn by officers in the Crimean War, few women of fashion had hitherto ventured outside their houses in bad weather. Perhaps the fact that non-smelling mackintoshes in bright colours were not available until late in the century may have had something to do with their reluctance.

Anyway in the end women got used to wearing Tam-o-Shanters, Norfolk jackets with waistcoats, shirts and ties, and deer-stalker hats; peaked jockey caps as well as sailor hats were seen on the sports field, and a pair of stockings of red silk, studded with swallows was noted by a fashion reporter in 1887. Around the turn of the century toupees, or transformations as they were called, were recommended not least by Mrs Henrietta Stannard who had edited *Winter's Weekly* and was soon to become President of the Society of Women Journalists. There need be no more disarranged curls, no more frowsy fringes at the damp seaside and no more caps for ladies past fifty, she said. Mrs Stannard, author of a best seller, *Bootle's Baby*, written under the pseudonym of John Strange Winter, was then fifty-four.

Blue serge was also recommended as the correct women's costume for yachting, and John Morgan, the Cowes outfitter, opened a branch in London, thereby helping to popularize the English 'tailor-made' costume.

The men of the Victorian age were, as might be expected, more cautious and less receptive than their womenfolk to new ideas in fashion, but their wardrobe was nevertheless very extensive. A man of fashion would often change three or four times a day according to whether he was to be working in the city, parading in Hyde Park, riding, looking in at a music hall, or attending the opera.

The frock coat was going out of general use and the *Gentleman's Magazine of Fashion* noted in 1887 that 'solicitors and doctors hardly ever wear frock coats, always morning coats'. It was also reported that almost every one who went to the Queen's Golden Jubilee Garden Party at Buckingham Palace had to place a special order for a new frock coat, so little were they worn under normal circumstances.

The morning coat which replaced the frock was, however, originally a good deal more severe than the swallow-tail we know today, being buttoned almost up to the throat. It was not worn open until the latter half of the 1880s.

The lounge suit had also arrived, and could be either dittos (that is, with the coat matching the trousers) or non-matching separates. The

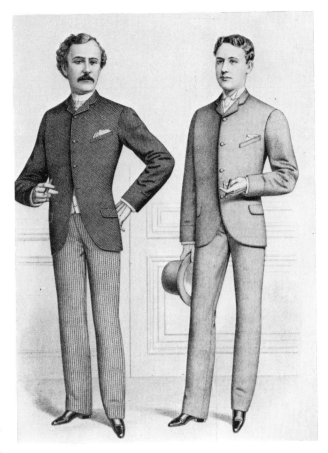

The morning coat and lounge suit. The heads were those of two newly elected MPs, Mr F. Otter (Lincolnshire South) and Mr H. L. W. Lawson (West St Pancras)

latter were becoming fashionable towards the end of the decade. A 'jockey' waistcoat with the points almost square and about two inches apart was often worn on informal occasions, and the Prince of Wales later set the fashion for knitted jackets with lounge suits. The trousers were cut narrow and well up at the front to show off the pointed shoes. Light-coloured bowlers were worn in summer.

For evening wear tails, white (or black) waistcoat and white tie knotted round a chimney pot collar turned down only very slightly at the top were worn. Swithin Forsyte, during a whole evening, was seen in consequence not to have been able to turn his head sideways more

(*above left*) Dressing gown
(*left*) Smoking jacket
(*above*) 'For evening wear tails'; drawing by Everard Hopkins
(*opposite*) Norfolk jacket
(*opposite above right*) Norfolk jacket with knickerbockers

than twice. Customers preferred the tails of the dress coat to be on the short side, considering that only waiters and servants wore them longer. Dinner jackets, for dinners and informal evening parties, had become general by the 1890s and were worn with a single-breasted

white waistcoat, without points. Later a cummerbund sash of crimson or black silk was wound round the waist in place of a waistcoat.

A smoking jacket was something else again. It was worn with a cap while in the smoking-room in order to protect the clothes and hair from the objectionable odour of tobacco. (Queen Victoria had gone even further, and, until after Princess Beatrice's marriage to

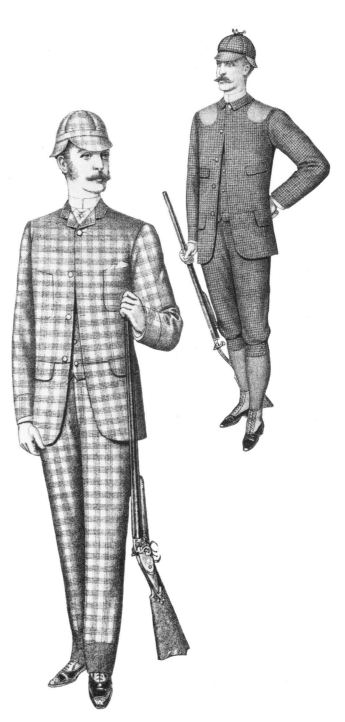

Prince Henry of Battenberg, banned all smoking in any royal residence.)

Precise evidence as to how far the Forsytes, when first introduced to us, observed the rules of fashion is not easily come by. We know that old Jolyon, on the night following the reception that he had given for June, decided that he would dine at his club and go on to the opera, and changed for the purpose into full evening dress, which would have included a collapsible opera hat. We know that Swithin Forsyte wore two waistcoats, and can guess that, if he had been driving a carriage and pair, he might have worn one of those Inverness greatcoats

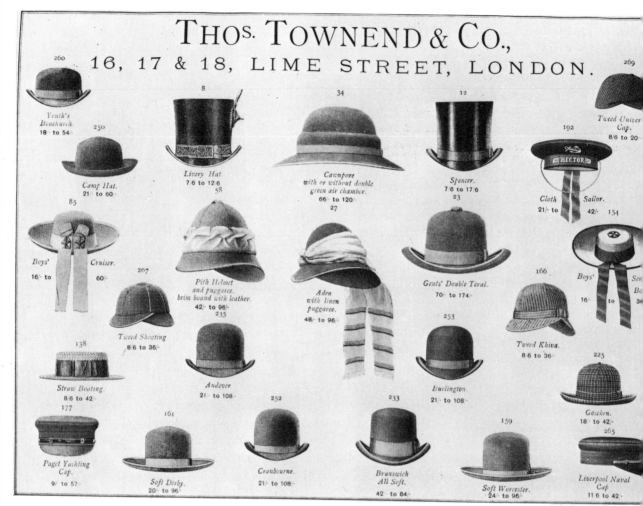

THOS. TOWNEND & CO.,
16, 17 & 18, LIME STREET, LONDON.

260 *Youth's Bonchurch.* 18/- to 54/-

250 *Camp Hat.* 21/- to 60/-

8 *Livery Hat.* 7/6 to 12/6

34 *Cawnpore* with or without double green air chamber. 66/- to 120/-

12 *Spencer.* 7/6 to 17/6

269 *Tweed Univer Cap.* 8/6 to 20/-

192 *Cloth Sailor.* 21/- to 42/-

85 *Boys' Cruiser.* 16/- to 60/-

58 *Pith Helmet and puggaree,* brim bound with leather. 42/- to 96/-

27 *Aden with linen puggaree.* 48/- to 96/-

23 *Gents' Double Terai.* 70/- to 174/-

166 *Tweed Khiva.* 8/6 to 36/-

154 *Boys'* 16/- to

207 *Tweed Shooting* 8/6 to 36/-

235 *Andover* 21/- to 108/-

253 *Burlington* 21/- to 108/-

138 *Straw Boating* 8/6 to 42/-

225 *Goschen.* 18/- to 42/-

177 *Paget Yachting Cap.* 9/- to 57/-

161 *Soft Derby.* 20/- to 96/-

252 *Cranbourne.* 21/- to 108/-

233 *Brunswick All Soft.* 42/- to 84/-

159 *Soft Worcester.* 24/- to 96/-

265 *Liverpool Naval Cap* 11/6 to 42/-

Hats of 1887

having an additional false cape in front covering the chest and sleeves. We can imagine that George, in the country, might have worn knickerbockers and a Norfolk jacket and perhaps in winter even one of those short covert coats that had become so popular. Soames we know was fastidious. He possessed a fur coat and used silk handkerchiefs. But there is a certain vagueness as to how exactly the Forsyte women were dressed. Aunt Ann, Aunt Hester and Aunt Juley are described at old Jolyon's reception as holding fans in their hands (well and good), and it was noted that each had some touch of colour, some emphatic feather or brooch, which testified to the solemnity of the occasion. Only later, at a family dinner at Swithin's, do we hear that Juley was 'sombrely magnificent in black bombazine with a mauve front cut in a shy triangle, and crowned with a black velvet ribbon round the base of her thin throat', black and mauve for evening wear being esteemed very chaste by nearly every Forsyte. We also know that Irene Forsyte stood at the reception 'her hands gloved in French grey, crossed one over the other', but we do not know much about her clothes except that the family said on Forsyte 'Change that they must have cost Soames a great deal too much. Indeed we know far more about Forsyte furniture than about Forsyte clothes.

5

Forsyte Furniture

In the drawing room, we had the same kind of monotony, only perhaps in a different colour; a green carpet with peaceful lilies intertwining with each other; a hearthrug, with a Bengal tiger ill at ease, with his back to the fire, and his face to the lilies; and a footstool, covered with Berlin wool, representing the pet dog of the period, very much astonished at his proximity to the aforesaid tiger; green curtains, with a Greek fret or honeysuckle border in yellow or gold; a gigantic valance with deep fringe worked into knots over turned wool beads.

In this passage, Robert Edis, Victorian lecturer and writer on interior decoration, whose best-known work, *The Decoration and Furniture of Town Houses*, was first published in 1881, is talking of the style of the 1860s. But was it just a coincidence that Timothy Forsyte and his coterie of aunts did in fact entertain upstairs in a drawing-room with green curtains patterned with red flowers and ferns? And could it have been free from the faults of most other Victorian salons?

One corner of Timothy's green drawing-room was decorated with 'a plume of dyed pampas grass in a light blue vase', and it is not too difficult to visualize the waxen grapes, and the flowers made of shells, at rest under a glass dome or 'shade' as it was called in the furniture trade.

We can see the walls crowded with pictures and the massive curtains providing a perfect trap for the dust, the occasional tables crowded with miniatures, draped with dark red cloth reaching to the ground. The mantel-shelf would be cluttered with vases placed unsuitably round a French marble clock. There would also be whatnots (those three- or four-tiered stands with open shelves placed each above the other, resting on pillars twisted like sticks of barley sugar).

There was a crimson silk sofa, and sofa tables which could be drawn up to it, and certainly an excessive number of beaded stools, including fender stools, made, some people thought, expressly to be tripped over. There was a Boudoir grand piano, carefully dusted but never played. There was also a firescreen, having a shield of worked crewel (worsted yarn) provided probably by industrious Forsyte fingers.

There would be armchairs covered with 'antis' to prevent the upholstery being smirched by masculine macassar oil hair dressing. There was a mahogany cupboard full of knick-knacks behind glass and an inlaid marquetry cupboard containing family treasures such as Hester's first fan and three bottled scorpions.

Since a coal fire was the main source of heat the room had usually only one really comfortable chair, the one nearest the fire, and in general the better the fire burned, the greater the draught in the rest of the room. There was a regular trade in draught-excluders – velvet serpents filled with sawdust which were positioned automatically or by hand along the bottom of the closed door by those who preferred warmth to fresh air.

'The mantel-shelf would be cluttered with vases'

We get some clues about the Forsyte decoration on the day after June's engagement party, when we meet old Jolyon having tea in his 'gloomy little study, with the windows of stained glass to exclude the view'. The study was 'full of dark green velvet and heavily carved mahogany'.

In the rich brown atmosphere peculiar to back rooms in the mansion of a Forsyte, the Rembrandtesque effect of his great head, with its white hair, against the cushion of his high-backed seat, was spoiled by the moustache, which imparted a somewhat military look to his face. An old clock that had been with him since before his marriage fifty years ago kept with its ticking a jealous record of the seconds slipping away for ever from its old master.

He had never cared for this room, hardly going into it from one year's end to the next, except to take cigars from the Japanese cabinet in the corner.

(For that matter he never went into the enormous billiard room either.) Other heads of household, however, made a good deal more use of their study, which would be furnished with a really solid desk, comfortable chairs, books of reference, bound volumes of *Punch*

and the *Illustrated London News* and, of course, a magnificent silver inkstand, letter scales, blotters, penwipers, sticks of sealing wax and tapers to melt them with, and a taper-snuffer to extinguish the flame afterwards.

If old Jolyon had not been so abstemious, there would also have been a tantalus, a trio of decanters in an open frame stand from which they could not be removed, except by unlocking the top bar of the frame, or sliding out the bottom tray.

Clearly old Jolyon, being a widower, felt free to smoke anywhere he liked in his house, but in many houses in the earlier years of Victoria's reign, he would almost certainly not have been; as late as 13 February 1886 we find Sir Pompey Bedell, a favourite character of the *Punch* artist George du Maurier, poking the fire in his *new* smoking-room and saying, 'This wretched chimney has got into a most objectionable way of smoking! I can't cure it.' Bedell Junior suggests the remedy: 'Just give it a couple of your cigars, Governor! – It'll never smoke again!'

We learn more about old Jolyon's house when he brings back young Jolyon for a night-cap of tea in the dining-room:

Young Jolyon looked round the room. It was peculiarly vast and dreary, decorated with the enormous pictures of still life that he remembered as a boy – sleep-

'A trio of decanters in an open frame stand from which they could not be removed'

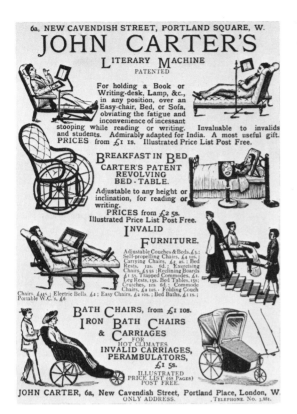

'In his great chair with the book-rest sat old Jolyon'

ing dogs with their noses resting on bunches of carrots, together with onions and grapes lying side by side in mild surprise. . . . In his great chair with the book-rest sat old Jolyon.

Except for the reading chair – and perhaps old Jolyon had no one to talk to at meal times except when June was at home – the dining-room sounds fairly typical of its day.

At the time when old Jolyon first set up house, the dinner table would have been laid with a white cloth, and the dishes of fish, meat, poultry or game that were to be eaten were placed on the table and served from there. Then, after the cheese had been eaten the whole table, cloth and all, was cleared and dessert was served.

In the latter half of the century the centre of the table was used for elaborate floral decorations arranged round an epergne in sparkling crystal. It is highly probable that one of these would have been standing on old Jolyon's table, or ready to take its place there. The table would have been a heavy mahogany one, capable of being extended by placing leaves in the middle for larger dinner parties.

Then there would have been a massive sideboard designed perhaps to look like a kind of shrine, elaborately decorated with mouldings and mirrors and smothered with ornaments. There would be drawers in front for napkins, knife-rests and other table paraphernalia. Many sideboards had a cellarette in which the bottles of wine and spirits needed for refilling the decanters were temporarily stowed.

There would probably have been a large folding screen shielding the door leading to the servants' quarters.

At the time when father Jolyon and son Jo arrived in the dining-room we are told that the gas had been turned low. Presumably, this would have been the gas light rather than the gas fire which would have been too much an innovation for old Jolyon, and unnecessary in a house with so many servants to lay coal fires. Gaslight in 1886 meant a gas jet issuing from a Bunsen burner – a device which shaped the flame into a kind of up-pointed moustache, thus displaying the light more effectively. The glare was further softened through being shielded behind an opalescent glass globe. It was not until 1887 that Carl Auer von Welsbach exhibited his patent gas mantle (a cylinder of woven cotton previously soaked in a metallic solution) which helped to diffuse the flame still further.

If the gas had been turned down low in Stanhope Gate that night, this was not necessarily for reasons of economy. There were many complaints about the smell of gas and also about the fact that it contained impurities that stained the wall-paper and ceilings. It was noisy, inconstant in its illumination, and at times dangerous.

Gaslight in 1895

Electric light, of course, was cleaner and safer, and, as early as 1881, Mr Richard D'Oyly Carte had installed in his theatre, the Savoy, the new kind which gave light from a filament instead of from pieces of carbon. It had proved itself, too, in railway stations such as Paddington, Charing Cross and Liverpool Street, as well as on public buildings, but the Electric Lighting Act, passed to encourage the development of electric light by private enterprise, did not become law until 1888, and Galsworthy probably dead-heated with the starter's pistol, if he did not jump the gun, in reporting that it had been installed at Stanhope Gate during the summer of 1886, though it is only fair to say that Lord Salisbury was experimenting with it in Hatfield House in 1880, and that by December that year Sir William Armstrong, the armaments manufacturer, had a complete electrical system working at his house, Crag-side, near Newcastle.

Other details are far from precise. For example, in old Jolyon's house in June 1886, the butler who doubled as a valet 'came to the ring of his [old Jolyon's] bell'. This could have been a hand bell with a clapper (Queen Victoria used a gold one), or it could have been a bell jangled by a wire reaching from the study to the butler's pantry. The bells would be mounted on a board indicating the room with which each of the bells was connected. Electric bells were coming into use around 1888 but one would not have thought that old Jolyon would have been one of the pioneers in this branch of campanology. Wrong again! For when old Jolyon returns from visiting Jo later in the summer of 1886 and falls asleep before dinner in his own dining-room, the butler *presses* the bell for dinner to be brought in from the kitchen, as arranged, at 7 p.m.

Old Jolyon showed no signs of possessing a telephone. Graham Bell's device had been shown at a British Association meeting in Glasgow in 1876. Long-distance telephoning was being tried out in London in 1877 and two private telephone companies – the Telephone Company Limited and the Edison

Joseph O'Conor as Jolyon adjusts his Edison Home Phonograph

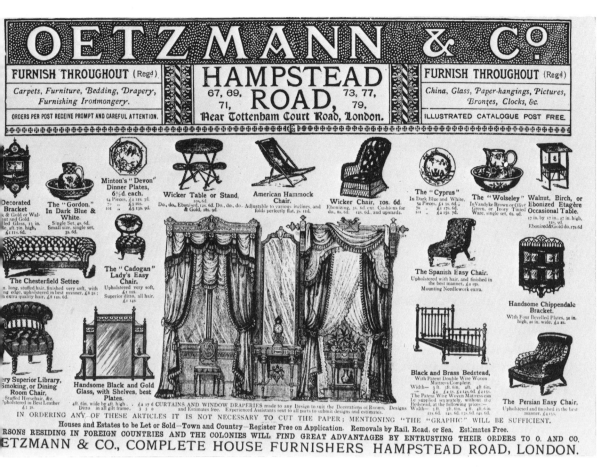

'Swithin preferred the European continental style'

Telephone Company Limited – were founded, the former in 1878, the latter in 1879. They were compelled to lease Post Office lines. The first official Telephone Exchange was set up in London in 1879 and was used by institutions like the House of Commons and the Law Courts. Private owners would come later still, with Lord Salisbury, who, according to his daughter, could be heard at Hatfield testing the apparatus by intoning nursery rhymes into the mouthpiece.

The Japanese cigar cabinet from which old Jolyon drew his supplies indicated the interest which Victorians took in the newly emergent East. But there was nothing oriental about Swithin's rooms in Hyde Park Mansions. He preferred the European continental style:

A cut-glass chandelier filled with lighted candles hung like a giant stalactite above [the dining table's] centre, radiating over large gilt-framed mirrors, slabs of marble on the tops of side-tables, and heavy gold chairs with crewel-worked seats.

Lighted candles were still an attraction, and a danger to be encountered in most houses when entertainment was afoot. They could be white, pink, green or red. They could be transparent. Some were guaranteed not to smell after being put out. There were specialized candles for use at the altar, on the piano, in the kitchen or at the bedside. Some were claimed as being dropless. Most were tapered at the lower end to allow them to be fitted snugly into any holder of equal or smaller diameter.

But what else was there about Swithin's rooms?

Everything betokened that love of beauty so deeply implanted in each family which has had its own way to make into Society, out of the more vulgar heart of Nature. Swithin had indeed an impatience of simplicity, a love of ormolu [imitation gold made from copper zinc and tin used for ornamenting furniture] which had always stamped him amongst his associates as a man of great, if somewhat luxurious, taste; and out of the knowledge that no one could possibly enter his rooms without perceiving him to be a man of wealth, he had derived a solid and prolonged happiness such as perhaps no other circumstance in life had afforded him.

During dinner Swithin claimed to have given £400 for a

group of statuary in Italian marble, which, placed upon a lofty stand (also of marble), diffused an atmosphere of culture throughout the room. The subsidiary figures, of which there were six, female, nude, and of highly ornate workmanship, were all pointing towards the central figure, also nude, and female, who was pointing at herself; and all this gave the observer a very pleasant sense of her extreme value. Aunt Juley, nearly opposite, had had the greatest difficulty in not looking at it all the evening.

Soames's house and the decorations inside it were of an entirely different nature from Swithin's; as Galsworthy points out, he was one of the 'enlightened thousands of his class and generation in this great City of London, who no longer believe in red velvet chairs, and know that groups of modern Italian marble are *vieux jeu*'.
His house had a green-painted front door,

a copper door knocker of individual design, windows which had been altered to open outwards, hanging flower-boxes filled with fuchsias, and at the back (a great feature) a little court tiled with jade-green tiles, and surrounded by pink hydrangeas in peacock-blue tubs. Here, under a parchment-coloured Japanese

sunshade covering the whole end, inhabitants or visitors could be screened from the eyes of the curious while they drank tea and examined at their leisure the latest of Soames's little silver boxes.

The inner decoration favoured the First Empire and William Morris (which since Morris was the apostle of simplification in design, divorced, alas, from industry and devoted to the revival of individual craftsmanship, constituted a totally unsuitable partnership). 'For its size, the house was commodious; there were countless nooks resembling birds' nests, and little things made of silver were deposited like eggs.'
Coal fires still heated the house. Soames, we are told, hated sunshine, and we can assume that his hall was not so very much lighter than Timothy's in which short-sighted Aunt Hester had mistaken Philip Bosinney's grey hat, resting on the hall table, for a strange cat.
The house, we know, was still gas-lit – Soames was breakfasting by gaslight that November – but the hanging lamp under which Bosinney said goodnight to Irene after dining at 62 Montpelier Square could have been an oil one. The hall also contained a carved rug-chest on top of which rested a porcelain bowl containing the visiting cards of those who had called to see the Forsytes. The front door had been fitted with a gilt wire cage into which the letters fell as the postman pushed them through the slit in the front door several times a day (with a delivery arriving even after dinner). It was not specified whether the cage was provided, as some were, with a lock, or whether it remained free, but the evidence suggests the latter was more likely.
There was a gong placed in the hall so that all at home would know when they were expected to assemble for meals. The gong could have been Burmese or rustic, or polished, or it might even have been a group of several gongs of different sizes, tuned to sound harmoniously together. Soames and Irene, we are told, dined

(*above*) Soames (Eric Porter) and Irene
(Nyree Dawn Porter)
(*right*) 'Irene's bedroom'

51

PEARS' SOAP

A SPECIALTY FOR CHILDREN.

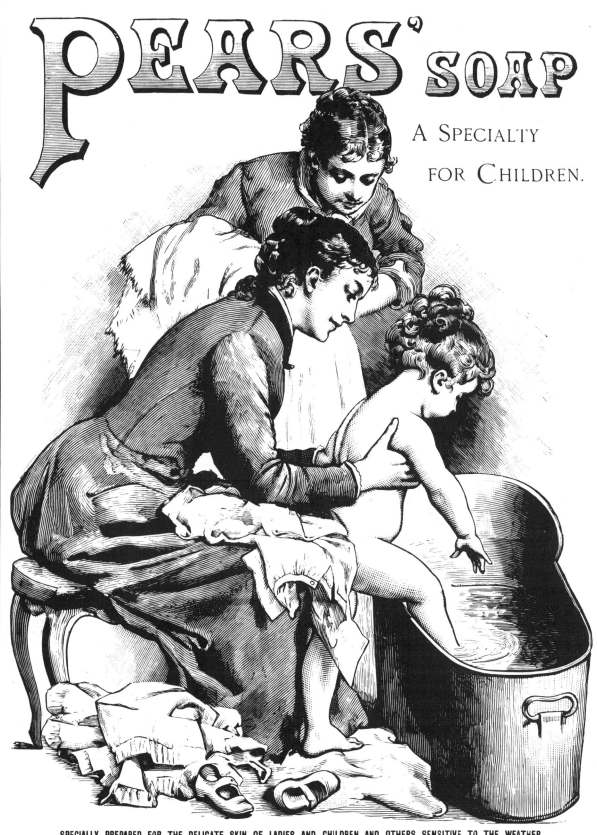

SPECIALLY PREPARED FOR THE DELICATE SKIN OF LADIES AND CHILDREN AND OTHERS SENSITIVE TO THE WEATHER.

PEARS' SOAP makes the Hands White and Fair, the Complexion Bright and Clear, and the Skin Soft and Smooth as Velvet.

at a handsome rosewood table without a cloth – 'a distinguishing elegance' – under a rose-shaded lamp which enhanced the ruby-coloured glass and 'quaint silver furnishing': silver pheasants were popular table ornaments and silver vine branches could be designed to be an excellent toast rack.

Because of the fact that Irene and Soames were already sleeping in separate bedrooms, hers had become even more elegant than might otherwise have been expected. The double-bed was apparently of the modern type, not shielded from public view by four posts and curtains; and Soames, when he went into the bedroom on the night when Irene had walked out of the house, could see at a glance that the bed was covered with its lilac silk quilt and that the sheets had been properly turned down at the head, as though nothing unusual had occurred. (We do not know whether either Soames or Irene used one of the hot-water bottles which first came into vogue around 1875.)

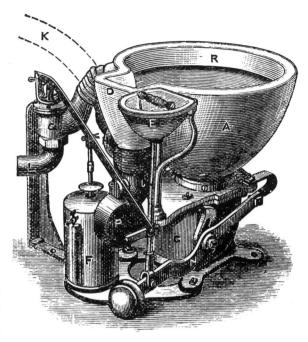

A patent optimus valve water-closet

Apart from the bed, the main piece of furniture in the room would have been the dressing table. This might have been of cream-painted wood decorated with pink or lilac moulding with two pillars of drawers on top and a swinging mirror between them, which could be adjusted and held in the desired position. On the dressing table there would have been many once-familiar objects: hair-pin boxes, china ring-stands, pin-cushions, glove-stretchers, hat-pin holders, scent bottles disguised as eggs – curiosities which sell well in the antique shops today. The room would also have contained a wardrobe, and possibly a chaise longue, an ottoman or blanket chest and perhaps a chiffonier for smaller clothes.

There would, of course, have been a bath-room, probably with hot water from a gas water-heater, and it might therefore have been possible to do without the irredeemably ugly wash-hand stand to be found in many Victorian bedrooms. Water-closets had been devised early in the Victorian era and water 'traps' to shut off the drains below, from the house above, had been introduced during the latter half of the century.

Unless there had been more than one bath-room, the servants would have had to make do with hip baths downstairs, and they would have had washstands, jugs and basins and chamber pots upstairs. Later we shall consider the entertainments which the Forsyte family were able to offer their guests, but, before doing so, we must follow some of their servants up and down the back stairs.

(*opposite*) 'The servants would have had to make do with hip baths downstairs'

6

Downstairs, Upstairs

The inadequacies of the servants furnished a topic of absorbing interest to the older members of the Forsyte circle, who treated the shortcomings of their domestic staff as an occasion for indignation or regret rather than for the patronizing ribaldry to be seen in *Punch*.

A high degree of obedience, reliability and endurance was indeed, essential; for the Forsyte residences, though not of a size that would require the gong for lunch, dressing time, and dinner, to be sounded separately every day in every corridor, as happened, for instance at Belvoir Castle, had their own built-in disadvantages.

Almost all supplies that came into the house, including casks of inflammable oil, had somehow to be transported down the steep area-steps. Coal could, in some cases, be discharged into the cellar direct through a diminutive manhole in the pave-ment or front doorstep, but this merely added to the amount of dusty slack which had to be taken into the house later. And, despite the boot-scrapers to be seen outside most front doors, a good deal of mire from the streets found its way into the front hall, across the door step or steps – which of course had to be scrubbed first thing every morning.

'Cleaning inside a house, such as was lived in by old Jolyon Forsyte or his brother James, was exceedingly laborious'

Cleaning inside a house, such as was lived in by old Jolyon or his brother James, was exceedingly laborious. Flue brushes were required, and hearth brushes, marble brushes, crumb brushes, billiard-table brushes, mattress brushes, telescopic brushes for curtains, banister brushes, and wardrobe brushes, in addition to the usual brushes for scrubbing the floors, cleaning boots and shoes, and the like. Silver had to be polished, sheets and table linen washed, starched and ironed. Fires had to be laid, and ornate coal grates cleaned,

'Fires had to be laid, and ornate coal grates cleaned, 'black-leaded' and polished'

'black-leaded' and polished. Scuttles of coal had to be taken up to the bedrooms – naturally by the back stairs.

Indeed Old King Coal was a far greater tyrant than the most inconsiderate mistress or house-keeper. True, oil stoves for heating were already in use in the 1890s, and were claimed to be odourless and 'fit for use in any drawing room', and a typical one was described as 'a very handsome ornamental cast-iron stove of pentagonal shape, with effective openwork panels and top, the five sides being fitted with ruby glass panes, having a very cheerful and effective appearance when burning'. But few Forsytes would have parted readily from something as traditional as the open hearth.

Primitive forms of oil-fired hot-water radiators were on sale, too, in the nineties for 'small greenhouses, porch conservatories, etc.', and there was a patent hot-air radiator which could be stationed in halls and passages; but we do not hear of their use in any Forsyte household. A gas bath-water-heater, alleged to be capable of raising the temperature of two gallons of water from sixty degrees Fahrenheit to 110

degrees in one minute was on sale in 1895, but the general shortage of hot water in the nineties was proclaimed by the variety of foot baths, leg or knee baths, hip baths still in use and, in most older houses, water for them had to be carried upstairs in brass cans and down again later in pails. In many cases the kitchen fire had to be kept on full blast twenty-four hours a day, winter and summer, in order to provide enough hot water.

Food, like the coal and the hot water, might have to be carried (on trays) up kitchen stairs to the dining-room, drawing-room, nursery or schoolroom as the case might be – and down again. And early morning tea was often served in the principal bedrooms as well.

Oil lamps, still in use long after the arrival of gas and electricity, were labour-intensive too. There were dire warnings of what might happen if the lamps were improperly used. No lamp, the manufacturers insisted, should be used if there was a chance of the oil coming into contact with the flame. If the lamp had not been used for some time, it must be given a thorough clean-out. The bowl had to be drained, cleaned, and filled with fresh oil and a clean wick put in. Special heed had to be paid to the size of the wick. It should exactly fit the

(above left) and *(above right)* 'Oil lamps were labour intensive too'
(above centre) 'Oil stoves for heating were already in use in the 1890s'

be added that such lamps could be supplied in electro-brassed metal 'having the appearance of real silver or richly polished brass' with the shine supplied by the housemaid.

As far as possible all cleaning had to be carried out below stairs, and in a larger house, a housemaid plumping up the cushions in the drawing-room would be expected to vanish if her mistress came into the room. Except when on special duties, a servant would not enter the same room as her mistress unless rung for. Upstairs, the parlourmaid would never appear without her uniform – a coronet of frilled linen, high starched collar and cuffs, dark blue or black blouse and a starched apron supported by patterned shoulder-straps.

Entertaining might have proved more arduous for the staff of a smaller house, not possessing its own separate still-room, store-room, china closet, knife-room, scullery and butler's pantry, than it would have been amid the stone corridors of a duke's residence. Elaborate kitchen equipment appeared to be needed even for small dinner parties. Any cook worth her salt would require a copper *bain-marie*, a braising pan and plate, cheese ovens, an omelette pan, a meat screen, a fish kettle, a sauté pan, patty pans, a broiler with hooks, saucepans, stewpans and steamers. In addition she would need trifles such as paper cutlet frills, sardine boxes, spoon warmers, jelly moulds, timbole (sic) moulds (presumably for Timbale, a dish of fowl or fish pounded and mixed with white of eggs and poured into a mould), border moulds – for building borders of rice round minced or other forms of meat – pie moulds, cake moulds, and vegetable moulds for shaping mashed potato into an eight-pointed star.

Some progress towards saving labour was being made, particularly on the Continent, and

burner, but be able to move up and down easily, and yet not loosely. It should be soft and not too tightly plaited. There were new perils to be surmounted when the moment came for putting out the lamp. It should not be turned down so far that the charred wick could fall into the bowl of the lamp. It was better to blow out the flame, turn down the wick to 'very low' and leave the glowing end to go out of its own accord.

The more advanced models included a patent lifting arrangement and an extinguisher which allowed the lamp to be lit or put out without removing the chimney. It need hardly

(opposite) 'A parlourmaid would never appear without her uniform – a coronet of frilled linen, high starched collar and cuffs'

HARROD'S STORES, Limited, Brompton. 223
IRONMONGERY AND TURNERY.
No. 10 DEPARTMENT—*FIRST FLOOR.*

BAKING DISHES—*continued.*

BAKING DISHES, Stamped,
oblong .. 10 in. 0/7, 11 in. 0/8,
12 in. 0/10, 13 in. 1/0,
14 in. 1/2, 15 in. 1/4,
16 in. 1/6

Oblong Baking Dish.

Oblong—
12 in. × 9 in. 3/
13 in. × 10 in. 3/3
14 in. × 10 in. 3/6
15 in. × 11 in. 3/11
16 in. × 11½ in. 4/6

Square—
12 in. × 12 in. 3/6
14 in. × 14 in. 4/6
15 in. × 15 in. 5/3
16 in. × 16 in. 5/11
17 in. × 17 in. 6/9
18 in. × 18 in. 7/11

Double Oven Pan.

Oblong Baking Plate. *Round Baking Plate.*

BAKING PLATES, tin round *(as design)*, 10 in. 1/5, 11 in. 1/6, 12 in. 1/9, 13 in. 2/6,
14 in. 2/9
Do.   do.   tin oblong *(as design)* ..   .. 14 in. 1/9, 15 in. 2/3, 16 in. 2/6
Do.   do.   wrought iron, round ..   .. 10 in. 2/2, 12 in. 2/6, 14 in. 3/0
Do.   do.   do.   oblong 12 in. 2/11, 14 in. 3/4, 16 in. 4/2, 18 in. 5/3
Do.   ao.   copper, round ..   .. 10 in. 3/10, 11 in. 4/7, 12 in.
Do.   do.   do.   oblong ..   .. 11 in. 4/8, 13 in. 6/3, 15 in.

Bain Marie Pans.

BAIN MARIE PANS, copper, best London made *(as design)*—
14 × 11, with 7 vessels, 67/3, 16×12½, with 9 vessels, 79/9, 18 × 14, with 11 vessels
99/6, 20×15, with 12 vessels, 113/0.
BAIN MARIE PANS, wrought iron pan and vessels, 7 vessels, 45/0, 9 vessels, 52/6
"   "   planished tin, 9 vessels, 27/0, 12 vessels, 31/6

(left) 'Any cook worth her salt would require a copper *bain-marie*'

(below left) 'Except when on special duties, a servant would not enter the same room as her mistress unless rung for'

(below) 'Cook'

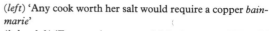

(*right*) Barnes' Patent Clothes Drier
(*below left*) Bradford's Vowel Washing Machine
(*below right*) A refrigerator of 1895

a surprising number of new inventions had appeared at the Vienna International Exhibition in 1883. The list included electric kettles, electric hot plates and electric blankets. Embryonic electric vacuum cleaners and dishwashers had already been devised.

Washing, of course, was seldom sent to a laundry. In Britain, Bradford's Vowel Washing Machine, so called because its various models were distinguished from each other in the catalogue by vowels, was on sale in the 1890s. It was worked by winding a handle geared to a cogwheel which caused the washing to turn over at a somewhat deliberate pace inside a closed chamber. The largest model could take twenty-four shirts at a time. But it had to be filled up first with hot water and later with rinsing water. Barnes' Patent Clothes Drier was a wooden frame, let down on pulleys from the ceiling and pulled up there again when the clothes had been hung over it. They had presumably already been squeezed through a mangle, the most expensive of which, listed as 'Ye Tudor', was decorated with a cast-iron top-piece representing the battlements of a castle.

Both refrigerators and freezers were on sale in the nineties. Refrigerators needed packing with ready-made ice if they were to cool food. Freezers, on the other hand, could produce solid bars of ice – or ice-cream – with the help of chemicals.

If servants were imposed on, so were their employers. Counterbalancing the authority which masters and mistresses exercised over their staff was the tyranny which servants exercised over their employers – not merely in the nursery or schoolroom, but everywhere.

No man is a hero to his valet, they say, and a wife who depended on a lady's maid to iron her dresses, tend her hair, and lace and unlace

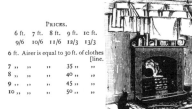

her corset, soon found that she had few secrets of her own. One of Elinor Glyn's heroines – who thought, mistakenly, when she saw her torn petticoat that she had been raped – believed that even though she might be able to conceal the whole affair from her friends, yet her maid would be bound to know, and disgrace would surely follow. Furthermore when a mistress joined a house party, it was just as important for her to maintain the reputation and standing of her maid in the Servants' Hall as it was to safeguard her own social position above stairs.

The duties of a servant in the Forsyte households were not too precisely defined. Smither, who served Timothy Forsyte and the aunts at The Bower, began the day in the role of lady's maid, by handing Aunt Ann her false curls and turning away discreetly while they were put on. But she also performed parlourmaid's duties by making the tea for Timothy's tea parties

and was doubtless capable of folding table-napkins at the luncheon table into 'mitres' or 'Noah's Arks' when occasion demanded. She also performed the duties of footman by taking notes to Park Lane to inquire after the health of James and to Winifred's house in Green Street.

Adolf, who was Swithin's German valet, also waited at table. And old Jolyon's butler, 'a large man with a beard, a soft tread, and a peculiar capacity for silence' (and for contempt for his employer), was also his valet.

Soames endeavoured to keep up the standards. Early in married life he insisted, it will be recalled, on the servants providing a hot dinner on Sundays as they had 'nothing to do but play the concertina'. Perhaps he was contrasting the carefree atmosphere which sometimes prevailed 'downstairs' with the more serious atmosphere which enveloped a Victorian master and mistress.

'The duties of a servant in the Forsyte household were not too precisely defined'

Forsyte Manners
and Menus

'Society', according to one rebel Victorian, 'is an elaborate, tiresome structure raised for the purpose of increasing needs and needlessly complicating life, inventing daily duties which do no good to anybody, and fostering in its hot, luxurious rooms, mean, ambitious and dangerous desires.' Few Forsytes, except perhaps the red-headed, quick-tempered June, would have agreed.

But if there were needless obligations, surely the morning social call, the overture to a Forsyte's day, was probably the most burdensome of them all.

'"Morning Calls" are a great test of individual capabilities for making small talk,' wrote 'A Member of the Aristocracy', the anonymous author of *Society Small Talk*, published in 1879, 'since a morning call signifies neither more nor less than a quarter of an hour's conversation with a person called on.'

When the call is made and the visitor is ushered into the drawing room, and the hostess has risen to shake hands, the usual salutation would be, 'How do you do?' The abbreviation of 'How do you do?' into 'Howdy do?' is supposed by some to be the height of good manners, whereas it sounds affected and is rather in bad taste than not. . . . The salutation 'How do you do?' should simply be regarded as a salutation only, and not as a personal inquiry after the health of the individual to whom it is addressed; and this formula of 'How do you do?' should be answered with the like formula of 'How do you do?'

Judged by these standards, the Forsytes would

have come out middling. Most of them say 'How are you?' to each other – which is understandable between members of the family – but the greeting means no more than if they had said 'How do you do?' for they none of them really wanted to be bored by accounts of each other's complaints. Swithin, welcoming the guests to his party says, 'Well, James, well, Emily! How are you, Soames? How do you do?'

But to get back to our morning call, we also learn that if tea was brought during the visit the hostess would probably say, 'May I give you some tea?' or 'Will you have some tea?' But she would not say, 'Will you allow me to offer you a cup of tea?' or 'Will you take a cup of tea?':

Drinking tea or not at a morning call is so thoroughly immaterial and unimportant a matter that no persuasion should be employed in the offering of it, and if visitors decline it, it is unnecessary to induce them to alter their minds.

It would also be out of place at this or any other purely formal call to offer cake or produce the family photograph album.

Entertainment (so-called) of the type favoured by the Forsytes at other times of the day would be far less unassuming. Indeed it was the quickest way of showing one's friends how much money one possessed. Even those who had little money entertained. 'It is wise to let your cook know your estimate of what the week's feeding ought to cost', wrote Marie de

Joncourt in a cookery book which ran to at least six editions and was often consulted by middle-class hostesses;

From twelve to fourteen shillings per head a week is ample and you ought to be able to live exceedingly well on that. This is the calculation for a London household, where you have to buy even parsley. If the weekly books are higher than they should be, it is quite as often the fault of the mistress as of the cook.

Another author, Lady Greville, in her book *The Gentlewoman in Society* which, despite its odious title, contains some shrewd comment, declared that:

The poorest young couple can manage a luncheon, and in this way dispense some kind of mild hospitality; while for cosmopolitan and mixed gatherings, such a meal is infinitely preferable [to dinner]. It is a pity young couples do not confine themselves entirely to luncheons composed of single dishes, where claret cup, cider or beer can be drunk, instead of attempting bad and expensive dinners with a profusion of champagne.

Lady Greville

This advice might well have been suitable for June Forsyte had she married Philip Bosinney, the struggling architect, but their circle of acquaintanceship would have been different from that of the Forsyte family as a whole. And it is hard to imagine June going through the laborious process of leaving visiting cards on families whose acquaintance she had no desire to make. Yet paying afternoon calls was another of society's most pressing obligations. The rule in those days was that the mistress of the family left cards for her husband and herself. If the person called on was not 'at home', that is, either out or unwilling to receive visitors, she had to leave three cards, one for herself and two for her husband (one from him to the husband and one from him to the wife). If the person called on was at home she had, nevertheless, to leave two of her husband's cards. If the mistress of the house had a grown-up daughter or daughters, she was obliged to turn down one corner of the card (usually the right) to include the daughters. (But diplomats the world over used a similar device to indicate that they had left calling cards in person and had not sent them by a servant.) If the mistress of the house was at home, the caller should, as in the case of the morning call, follow the servant into the drawing-room.

If the husband or any young man were paying a call, it was considered very bad taste for him to leave his hat in the hall, for only a member of the family living in the house would do that.

This was one reason why Philip Bosinney, who left his hat in the hall when paying a formal call on the Forsyte aunts during the season, made such a poor impression on his intended in-laws. Men also took their opera hats into the ballroom at a private dance.

If there were no afternoon calls to be paid, there might be a garden party, with lawn tennis in the background. Tea, coffee, sherry and claret cup would be served either in the house or in a marquee erected for the purpose. And, as Lady Greville wrote:

Music at garden parties is usually confined to the braying of a military brass or the wild harmonies of a Hungarian band, the loud tones of which accord with the freedom of the open air and the want of attention likely to be given to the music. In shady nooks, or behind bushes, you may tumble upon Tyrolese singers, or ringers of handbells, surrounded by little groups of listeners which rapidly melt away.

At the time of which we are writing none of the Forsytes had the necessary acreage to give a garden party, though they may possibly have attended one or two. Straight tea was more in their line, with the tea-kettle simmering over the spirit lamp, rock cakes, and scones kept hot on a plate over a bowl filled with hot water. We know, too, that muffins were much favoured by the Forsytes (James was found to have eaten the last on an occasion when Soames turned up late for tea at Timothy's). Forsyte muffins were, of course, toasted in the home kitchen and not bought ready-made from the itinerant muffin man who toured the streets about tea-time ringing his bell.

This was a family tea as distinct from tea as entertainment. Some hostesses offered both 'at homes' on certain days of the week, when anyone of their circle of acquaintanceship was welcome to call, and five o'clock teas for those individually invited.

Often some entertainment was provided, perhaps by one of the guests, or by a struggling music teacher, brought along by one of them, who would play without fee in the hope of attracting new pupils. Sometimes a professional musician was hired, in which case the invitation card would probably bear the warning 'Music' written at the bottom. Offenbach, Bizet, or perhaps Sullivan would be among the composers whose pieces were most often selected. Soames, as we know, first met his future wife at a musical tea. But normally few men could be found willing to attend such functions.

Dinner was where the Forsytes came into their own. At an early stage in *The Man of Property* we have two examples of their menus, the first being at Swithin's 'rooms'.

Family dinners of the Forsytes observe certain traditions. There are, for instance, no *hors d'œuvres*. The reason for this is unknown. Theory among the younger members traces it to the disgraceful price of oysters; it is more probably due to a desire to come to the point, to a good practical sense deciding at once that *hors d'œuvres* are but poor things. The Jameses alone, unable to withstand a custom almost universal in Park Lane, are now and then unfaithful.

Nothing is said about the general Forsyte attitude towards soup and fish, which normally preceded the entrée, but we are told that 'a silent, almost morose, inattention to each other succeeds to the subsidence in their seats, lasting well into the first entrée'. So there may have been two entrées at Swithin's served, it is implied, in succession. Then came the main

Tea-kettle with spirit lamp

dish, the crowning point of a Forsyte feast —
'the saddle of mutton'. Each of the Forsyte
elders claimed to be a connoisseur of mutton,
old Jolyon swearing by Dartmoor, James by
Welsh, and Swithin by Southdown, while
Roger, being 'original', had found a shop
selling German mutton for more than anyone
else paid.

The eating habits of Britons, including the
Forsytes had undergone marked changes
since the beginning of the century. The original
custom in early Victorian times was to place the
dishes that were to be eaten on the table. Each
guest helped himself and his neighbours from
the dish placed before him, and, if he fancied
anything that was beyond his reach, he asked
a servant to bring it to him. In general it was
none too easy to distinguish a regular progres-
sion between one course and another.

There was general agreement that soup
(usually two kinds, one white, one brown,
served at the same time) came first, and, when
it had been consumed, the tureens were
removed from the four corners of the table
and replaced by joints of beef, mutton or veal
placed one at each end of the table, and
generally referred to as the remove, equivalent
to the French term *relevé*. If, however, the
host wished to follow the orderly French habits
more closely, the soup, when removed, was
immediately followed by fish as the second
part of the first course, in which case the fish
was described as a remove.

The French added a number of other
refinements such as the *entremets*, a term which
referred originally to a dish served between
courses but was later monopolized by the
pastrycooks for their confections. There were
also *hors d'œuvres*, originally known as *assiettes
volantes* because they were handed round by
the servants and not left on the table.

In the latter part of the century when it
became fashionable to dine *à la Russe*, the
dishes were not put on the table but were
handed round by the servants in a set order and

in strict rotation to the guests either from the
kitchen or the sideboard. As a result, the
guests' choice of food was severely restricted,
and, since they were served one by one, the
meal took much longer. The fact that the
plates were changed with each course bore
hardly on those who had only one set of gold
plate, but, on the other hand, the guests, not
being pre-occupied with helping one another,
had more time to talk.

With *à la Russe* meals and no dishes on the
table, there could be no remove, and the entrée,
a made-up dish from the kitchen, tended to be
the first meat dish. This had advantages and
disadvantages. Many people disliked the old
habit of serving guests with a substantial
helping which exhausted their appetite before
they had a chance to savour what was to come.
Others, on the other hand, felt that the entrée,
being often a dish with piquant sauces, should
not be served before the more delicately
flavoured roast.

Apart from this, Swithin's dinner progressed
in an orderly manner with the still more
strongly flavoured ham touched up with West
India rum immediately before the strawberries
and cream.

Some of the younger members, we are told,
would have done without a joint altogether,
preferring guinea-fowl, or lobster salad —
something which appealed to the imagination
and had less nourishment — but these were
females; or, if not, had been corrupted by
their wives, or by mothers, who, having been
forced to eat saddle of mutton throughout their
married lives had passed a secret hostility
towards it into the fibre of their sons.

Dinner at Soames's, so far as one could tell,
deferred to this new trend. According to
James, it was 'nothing heavy and not too
Frenchified'. One menu, we learn, included
thick soup, Dover sole, cutlets, spring chicken,

(*opposite*) What the Forsytes were aspiring to. Detail from
'Dinner at Haddo House', 1884, by Alfred Edward Emslie

Jelly of 2 Colours.

Macedoine of Fruits with Jelly.

Lemon Cream.

Victoria Sandwiches.

Meringues.

Grape Jelly.

Chocolate Cream.

Trifle.

Iced Oranges.

Stewed Pears.

Tipsy Cake.

Rout Cakes.

Crystalized Fruits.

Nougat Almond Cake.

Apples à la Parisienne

Blanc-Mange à la Vanille.

apple Charlotte, Russian caviare and German plums. It would not have been out of place at this time to have served bananas for dessert, for they originally arrived from the Canaries each individually wrapped in protective cotton wool. The barrow-banana, brought from the West Indies in cold storage by Elder Dempster did not reach London in any quantity until after 1900.

Most of the Forsyte tribe would have had their own family recipes preserved as carefully as their other family traditions. But they were in the hands of their cooks and, in the pretentious prosperity of the mid-Victorian age, felt compelled to order dishes with a fine-sounding or foreign title, which were preferred to good plain cooking. Thus Dorset Apple Cake, that dish preserved for us in Florence White's classic work *The Good Things in England*, and for which Aunt Ann would no doubt have had a recipe, was ousted at Soames's dinner table by apple Charlotte.

Forsyte dinners, when not given for the family alone, would perhaps be more elaborate, with a table plan of the seating placed in the hall and place cards on the table, and each guest might be given, on arrival, a hand-painted envelope with a distinctive design to match that of his or her dinner partner.

Dinner parties were usually 'on strictly reciprocal principles', or 'cutlet for cutlet' as Lady Greville said:

Here again, no enjoyment is expected or received; a duty to society is simply fulfilled. So many people have dined or danced you; so many people must be dined in return. The guests are thrown together, anyhow, just taking care to divide the couples; but few girls are asked for they only take up room; a couple of young men, who are stuffed in anywhere, provide for the wants of the stray widow or the girl in question. The food at these repasts is stereotyped, the wine, invariably Champagne, more or less sweet, more or

(opposite) Jellies, Creams and Sweet Dishes, from *Beeton Household Management*, 1888

less well-iced; only in the host's high sense of honour lies your chance of escaping without a headache on the morrow.

Those hostesses who took a personal interest in their own cooking had no need to rely exclusively on Mrs Beeton for their menus. Charles Elmé Francatelli, who had been Maître d'Hôtel and Chief Cook to the Queen and had also served for seven years as Chef de Cuisine at the Reform Club, had written the five-hundred-page *Cook's Guide and Housekeeper's and Butler's Assistant: a Practical Treatise on English and Foreign Cookery in all its Branches*. It was first published in 1862 and within the following six years 23,000 copies had been printed. It was up to date in having a separate section for American drinks, among which it included Gin Sling (to be taken through a straw), Mint Julep, and the Knickerbocker ('a shillingworth of lemon ice from the confectioner mixed with half a pint of Madeira and a pint of iced Seltzer water'). The recipe given for a 'Cock-tail' included 'three lumps of sugar in a tumbler with a dessert spoonful of Savory & Moore's essence of Jamaican ginger, and a wineglassful of brandy, to be filled up with hot water'. The book contained 1058 recipes of various kinds and ninety different sauces with menus for small and large dinners throughout the year.

There were illustrations, too, of how the dishes should be presented: how the radishes should be arranged (in rows like the rays of the sun), how anchovies could be interlaced with each other in basket-weave style, how olives could be ranked like fish-scales. Butter pats were 'impressed' with leaf patterns or made to resemble sea-shells.

Francatelli by no means despised popular dishes such as Pigs Fry, Toad-in-the-Hole, Baked Tripe or Bubble-and-Squeak. And he does not mention caviare. Nevertheless his was perhaps a dangerous as well as a valuable book for it tempted hostesses to urge their

'Straight tea was more in their line with the tea-kettle simmering over the spirit lamp'

cooks to attempt dishes they could not manage.

Giving dances was the activity in which the Forsyte desire to receive value for money clashed most strongly with the guests' hopes of enjoying themselves. For example:

Roger's house in Prince's Gardens was brilliantly alight. Large numbers of wax candles had been collected and placed in cut-glass chandeliers, and the parquet floor of the long, double drawing-room reflected these constellations. . . . In a remote corner, embowered in palms, was a cottage piano with a copy of the 'Kensington Coil' [Francie's own composition] open on the music-stand.

Roger had objected to a band. He didn't see in the least what they wanted with a band; he wouldn't go to the expense, and there was an end of it. Francie (her mother, whom Roger had long since reduced to chronic dyspepsia, went to bed on such occasions) had been obliged to content herself with supplementing the piano with a young man who played the cornet, and she so arranged with palms that anyone who did not look into the heart of things might imagine there were several musicians secreted there. She made up her mind to tell them to play loud — there was a lot of music in a cornet if the man would only put his soul into it. . . .

Roger, indeed, after making himself consistently disagreeable about the dance, would come down presently, with his fresh colour and bumpy forehead, as though he had been its promoter; and he would smile, and probably take the prettiest woman in to supper; and at two o'clock, just as they were getting into the swing, he would secretly go up to the musicians and tell them to play 'God Save the Queen', and go away.

The hired butler had been told to put out only a dozen bottles of champagne. When that was gone they would have to make do with a champagne cup.

There, in a few words are set out most of the faults that could be found in such entertainments. The idea of collecting large numbers of candles in order to have a blaze of lights was the first mistake, for it created a bright light unflattering to women and was not conducive to romance. Furthermore the candles deprived the rooms of fresh air and produced a heat that rendered the atmosphere insufferably heavy; yet it was impossible to open all the windows that should have been opened without causing an uncomfortable draught on

'Dinner parties were usually "on strictly reciprocal principles", or "cutlet for cutlet" as Lady Greville said'

those sitting near them, and even a half-open window could set the candles flickering and dropping grease on the clothes of the guests beneath. The large blocks of ice, the best cooling device before the invention of air conditioning, seem to have been absent from Roger's dance.

Then there was the band. A form of cylinder gramophone had been seen in London as far back as 1878 but its tiny volume and unreliable tone – and the necessity of winding up the machine if not actually turning the cylinder by hand – made it unsuitable for any Forsyte dance. So one had to have a band of sorts. The charge in those days for a cornet player and a pianist was from one and a half guineas. But a string band could have been hired for £1 a man or less, and would have proved very much more suitable for the waltzes which, we learn, were danced during the greater part of the evening.

There were also risks when one hired a butler,

(*above*) 'Whether a shortage of small talk in Victorian homes led to after-dinner music or the after-dinner music led to a shortage of small talk is not clear'

(*left*) 'The charge in those days for a cornet player and a pianist was from one and a half guineas'

as Roger had, especially if he was provided by the caterer. Such men were often slow, awkward and inattentive, and liable to mistake a used glass for a clean one. Some had even been known to raid the supper table before the last guests had departed, as well they might if the menu included, as it should have done, some cold chicken, salmon, lobster, game pie and sandwiches.

And clearly the drink allowance was on the small side. *Party Giving on Every Scale*

recommended five dozen bottles of champagne as well as other wines for a dance of one hundred and fifty people, and it can hardly be assumed that Roger had invited only thirty guests.

At dances, as elsewhere, the Forsytes were short on small talk, and when they opened their mouths it was usually to refute a fact, inquire the price of some material possession or air a prejudice. Their prejudices covered most fields of endeavour including human relationships – especially within the family – and, at times, affairs of state. Few remarks were made without a purpose, and fewer still, except perhaps by George Forsyte, for the purpose of entertaining the listener.

The Forsytes did not need small talk. A very few words sufficed to tell a Forsyte whether the person he was addressing was of the same social standing as himself. In style, Forsyte usage was strictly in tune with the kind advocated in etiquette books of the day. For example, according to a contemporary guide to manners,

When a man makes use of an adjective describing a lady, he almost invariably calls her a woman; thus he would say, 'I met a rather agreeable woman at dinner last night'; but he would not say, 'I met an agreeable lady'; but he might say, 'A lady, a friend of mine, told me,' etc., when he would not say, 'A woman friend of mine told me,' etc. Again, a man would say, 'Which of the ladies did you take in to dinner?'; he would certainly not say 'Which of the women, etc.'

Thus Roger correctly said (as indeed we should correctly say today if we saw her) that Soames's wife was a 'good-lookin' woman'.

Whether a shortage of small talk in Victorian homes led to after-dinner music or the after-dinner music led to a shortage of small talk is not clear, but on most occasions someone was expected to sing for their supper, and someone else had to accompany the singer. The discovery of the upright piano, although it may not have been accepted in any Forsyte household, enabled many less fortunately placed families to engage in a musical soirée. Whoever said that 'Life would be tolerable were it not for its pleasures' could well have been thinking of such occasions. There was little difficulty in suiting the songs which the accompanist could play to those the singer knew, as they were almost invariably the same. Indeed some of them had been perpetrated in drawing-rooms for at least fifty years. For instance, the lines 'Mid pleasures and palaces though we

may roam, Be it ever so humble, there's no place like home', written by John Howard Payne, an American who was afterwards United States Consul in Tunisia, were first sung in 1823 in 'Home, Sweet Home' with music by Henry Bishop. The song 'Hearts of Oak' ('Come cheer up my lads, 'Tis to glory we steer') had been written in 1756 by David Garrick and was set to music by William Boyce. 'I Dreamt that I Dwelt in Marble Halls' was first heard in 1843 in *The Bohemian Girl* by Balfe.

On the whole the more sentimental – we should probably say morbid – themes had the greatest success in Forsyte and similar circles. An outstandingly popular 'number' for after-dinner use was 'The Lost Chord', composed by Arthur Sullivan to words written by Adelaide Proctor. Published in 1877, it was said to have sold half a million copies in the next twenty-five years. The last four lines read:

> It may be that Death's bright Angel
> Will speak in that chord again,
> It may be that only in Heav'n
> I shall hear that grand Amen!

Even more popular was 'Alice, Where Art Thou?', written by Wellington Guernsey, with words by Joseph Ascher. 'One year back this even, and thou wert by my side', the singer lamented, and eventually consoled himself by looking heavenward as he knew that was where Alice would be found.

Francie Forsyte, we are told, composed songs with titles such as 'Breathing Sighs' or 'Kiss Me, Mother, ere I Die' as well as the waltz 'Kensington Coil'. They were especially acceptable to her relatives when she was able to market them.

But neither Victorian sentiment nor Victorian pleasures were confined to the home, and Forsyte tastes and preferences were, as we shall see, exhibited publicly as well as in private.

8

The Forsytes at Play

Hyde Park was the nearest centre of relaxation for the Forsytes, since most of them lived close to its borders. The park was then more exclusive – it had tall and handsome iron railings round it – and much more fashionable than it is today.

'The Dromios' (as the Forsytes called Giles and Jesse Hayman after the twin servants in Shakespeare's *Comedy of Errors*), who were first cousins to Soames, rode in it most mornings with other members of the so-called 'Liver Brigade' who needed some kind of a shake-up to put them right after attending some rout the night before. Later, the more leisurely displayed themselves in Rotten Row while, nearby, the Four-in-Hand Coaching Club, founded in 1856, met regularly near the Powder Magazine. (As a safety precaution Bath chairs were banned from the Park between the hours of eleven and two.)

After lunch, however, it was no longer the done thing to drive one's own carriage, and the coachman or groom took over. From tea time onwards, till about seven if it was still light, carriages of all kinds were to be seen proceeding at measured pace between Hyde Park Corner and Albert Gate, or even beyond, and back again. The gay dresses, hats and parasols of the women were prefectly set off by the black body of the carriages and the dark grey or brown liveries of the coachmen. In addition to the family carriage with the 'lozenge' on the panels, and the footman or 'tiger' (a boy in livery and a black-and-yellow striped waistcoat) on the back, you might see the man-about-town being driven in his dog-cart, the fashionable doctor in his brougham, victorias (open carriages without doors), landaus (open carriages with doors and collapsible hoods), barouches and curricles with two horses abreast, and perhaps a phaeton (a kind of abbreviated stagecoach) with a black-and-white Dalmatian dog trained to run beneath it.

The care and maintenance of pedigree dogs was incidentally already one of the spare-time preoccupations of the Victorian upper classes.

The year 1886 in which we were formally introduced to the Forsytes was also the year when *The First Great Terrier Show* was held in London at the Royal Aquarium, Westminster. Its Secretary was Mr Charles Cruft. Cruft was the son of a Bloomsbury jeweller, and his father had intended him to adopt the same livelihood. But it happened that James Spratt, who had been making a good thing out of selling his special dog cake for sporting dogs from a site in Holborn Bars, decided in 1866 to move to more commodious premises at 28 High Holborn, once part of an Elizabethan farmhouse.

Cruft, then fourteen years old, took a job as his assistant. His task was to promote sales and keep the books while Mr Spratt himself attended to the production of dog cake. Cruft

(*opposite above*) 'Hyde Park was the nearest centre of relaxation for the Forsytes'
(*opposite below*) Rotten Row

'It would never have been done to have been seen with it in
Hyde Park' ...

soon saw the best way of increasing sales was to
fraternize with as many dog owners as possible,
and that this could best be accomplished by
promoting dog shows and by multiplying the
number of breeds shown there. He was an
outstandingly successful organizer, gaining
the confidence of dog fanciers both in Britain
and on the Continent. Foreigners dispatched
not only dogs, but some of their best judges, to
the British show ring. Cruft was even put in
charge of the Dog Section at the Paris Exhibition of 1878; he also helped to found the
Schipperke Club of Brussels.

The First Great Terrier Show took place, as
The Times reported, 'in a new and spacious
building over the swimming tank' of the
Aquarium. Five hundred dogs were to be seen
(and heard) – among them Airedales, Bed-
lingtons, Bull Terriers, Dandie Dinmonts,
Fox Terriers, Skye Terriers, Yorkshire
Terriers and a few other breeds besides. It was
not long before the Royal Family became
interested in Mr Cruft's activities. Queen
Victoria, while visiting Florence in 1888, had
been greatly struck by some Pomeranian dogs
she had seen there – miniatures of the original
thirty-pound animals – and she sent three
Pomeranians, Gena, Fluffy and Nino, to the
1891 Cruft show. She also sent a Collie which
won first prize and a cup in the Open Collie
Class.

Edward VII was also a dog enthusiast, and
entered four Basset Hounds in the same show.
He also possessed an Irish Terrier, Jack, and a
black Bulldog which frequented the billiards
room at Sandringham and showed a marked
partiality for the evening trouser-legs of unwary
players. The King's white Fox Terrier, Caesar,
however, was his favourite and walked behind
the coffin at his funeral procession.

Fox Terriers, especially smooth-coated ones,
were by far the most popular breed about the
turn of the century with Irish and Scottish
Terriers not far behind. There was a steady but
limited interest in Dachshunds, Basset Hounds
and Skye Terriers, but the demand for the
larger Landseer-type dogs such as the St
Bernard, the Great Dane, the Newfoundland
and the Deerhound was falling away.

The Forsytes, like the Royal Family and Mr
Cruft, were dog-lovers. Young Jolyon kept a
cynical but friendly mongrel, which was said
to be 'the offspring of a liaison between a
Russian Poodle and a Fox Terrier'. It was
brown and white with a fluffy coat and a tail
curled tightly over its back. It would never have
done to have been seen with it in Hyde Park.

The Prince of Wales and Princess Alexandra

used to appear there about five o'clock. But the populace was by no means absent from the Park. Speakers' Corner near the Marble Arch had already earned a reputation, and flags were hoisted for an hour before 8 a.m. and again at 8 p.m. to warn the fastidious that the public were bathing in the Serpentine.

Hyde Park was only one of many outdoor attractions for men and women of leisure. There were cricket matches to watch at Lord's or to play in at Burton's Court, Chelsea. There were polo and driving contests at Ranelagh, croquet at Wimbledon, pony racing and pigeon shoots at Hurlingham. Badminton and lawn tennis had been played since 1874, and a Ladies' Tennis Championship was organized ten years later. Ladies had been whacking golf balls round the links as early as 1867, when a special course was laid out for them at St Andrews. For the less athletic the Royal

Botanic Gardens in Regents Park proved a big draw – especially when dog shows were held there.

Improved transport encouraged people to go further from home. The hansom cab, greatly ameliorated since Joseph Aloysius Hansom's original design, was a revolution in itself. For who would have thought of seating the passengers in front of the driver in a cab with only two wheels, and the horses remotely controlled by reins passing over the roof? And who would have dreamed of talking to the driver through a trap door in the roof? Yet so it was. And the passengers drew comfort from the large wheels and the better view they got of the road before them. The driver, in his smart top hat, also got a magnificent view. Indeed the whole outfit could look impressive, with its wheels painted bright yellow, its bells a-jingle and a bunch of flowers in water for the passengers to gaze at. The only thing to be said in favour of the four-wheel cab, or 'growler' as it was called, was that it would

'The next-to-least glamorous form of public transport was the horse-bus'; drawing by George du Maurier

carry luggage as well as passengers. It was also less alarming if the horse fell, as it frequently would, especially on the treacherously steep slope of St James's Street.

The next-to-least glamorous form of public transport was the horse-bus. There was plenty of variety in the colours adopted by the various private companies that ran them. Normally, they carried twenty-six passengers, twelve inside with damp straw on the floor, and fourteen in conditions of extreme discomfort on top. Up to 1925 the police refused to sanction roofed tops, and, when the weather was bad, the upstairs passengers had to protect themselves with the help of tarpaulin sheets provided by the bus company. In earlier models

the passengers sat back to back in two rows, with a divider known as a 'knife-board' between them. Even when the weather was fine, ladies felt too modest to mount the outside staircase – which made it all the more unconventional for June Forsyte to have insisted that Philip Bosinney should ride with her on top of the bus on their way to the theatre. Horse trams were also tried out from 1861 onwards, it having been found that horses could pull twice their normal load if the carriage ran on rails. Passengers found the trams spacious and comfortable because the wheels, being small, could be tucked underneath the vehicle, allowing the seats to spread over the top. Horse trams ran only in outer London, rails being banned at that time from the centre of the capital for fear that they might lead to traffic blocks.

The steam trains which had offered suburban services since the 1830s likewise halted at termini which were remote from the hub of the city and from each other, and the expense of moving them further into London would have been prohibitive. It was therefore decided to build an inner rail circuit, part of which would run underground to link the main line stations together, with the Metropolitan Railway constructing the northern half and the Metropolitan and District Railway the southern. The first part of the northern sector was opened in 1863, although for one reason or another the complete inner circle did not run until 1884.

In theory the journey by underground should not have been too unpleasant, for the steam and smoke from the engines passed into condensing tanks, and Sir William Hardman, one of the earliest passengers, claimed that there was 'no disagreeable odour, beyond the smell common to tunnels'. Ventilating shafts were sunk and various blow-holes bored from the tunnels upwards to the street in the hope of freshening the air, but a reporter sent by the *English Illustrated Magazine* (August 1893) found a journey on the footplate something of an ordeal, particularly on the up-hill stretch between Kings Cross and Baker Street where the engine was under stress, and was told by one of the drivers that smoke was sometimes so thick that it obscured the signals.

R. D. Blumenfeld, future editor of the *Daily Express*, who loved to sit on top of a London omnibus watching the black silk hats moving 'like dark poppy fields' below him, also travelled on the Underground, and wrote:

I had my first experience of Hades today, and if the real thing is to be like that I shall never again do anything wrong. I got into the Underground Railway at Baker Street after leaving Archibald Forbes' house. I wanted to go to Moorgate Street in the City. It was very warm – for London, at least. The compartment in which I sat was filled with passengers who were smoking pipes, as is the British habit [R.D.B. was American born], and as the smoke and sulphur from the engine fill the tunnel, all the windows have to be closed. The atmosphere was a mixture of sulphur, coal dust and foul fumes from the oil lamp above, so that by the time we reached Moorgate Street, I was near dead of asphyxiation and heat. I should think these Underground railways must soon be discontinued as they are a menace to health. A few minutes earlier can be no consideration since hansom cabs, and omnibuses carried by the swiftest horses I have seen anywhere, do the work most satisfactorily.

These disadvantages could clearly be overcome if the train, instead of being steam powered, was driven by electricity – a possibility which emerged in the 1860s when the new type of dynamo fitted with electro-magnets, instead of the old permanent sort, came into use. But, even so, various problems had still to be overcome. One was the difficulty of feeding current to a moving motor; and the right sort of 'brush' which could both conduct well and stand up to the friction from the rails, had to be found.

In 1884, while the electric motor was still in the testing stage, the City of London and Southwark Subway Company received permission to bore a tunnel from the Monument to the Elephant and Castle with a view to hauling carriages to and fro by cable. This plan foundered when the cable company went bankrupt. The plan was changed: instead, the first 'tube' would be run by electricity. It was opened by the Prince of Wales on 4 November 1890.

An electric tramway was already operating in 1885 between Portrush and Bushmills in Northern Ireland, but London was slow to follow suit and did not catch up with the provinces until after the turn of the century.

The bicycle, of course, was a blessing to the young and active, for it made it possible for them to take part in a picnic or a game of tennis without being dependent on a horse to get them there and back. The models of the 1870s were constructed on the penny-farthing principle which obliged the rider to climb up from behind on to a precarious perch above a giant 'penny' wheel to which the driving pedals were fixed. But in 1884 'safety' bicycles were introduced with smaller wheels of equal size back and front, so that there was less chance of overbalancing, and less far to fall. The bone-shaking solid tyres were on their way out about the time that *The Forsyte Saga* began, and novel pneumatic ones were to be seen on the streets in 1888. But as yet there was no free-wheeling, and foot-rests had to be provided so that you could take your feet off the revolving pedals when coasting downhill. (Brakes on both front and rear wheels came later too.)

The drop-frames which allowed ladies to mount the machine without throwing a leg over the saddle were not introduced till the early nineties, which may have been unfortunate for Euphemia Forsyte: in April 1890 Swithin Forsyte, having watched her mount and ride away on what might have been one of the old cross-bar models, 'showing her legs' in an unladylike manner, immediately cut her out of his will, a decision which cost her six or seven thousand pounds. One other bicycle rider perhaps deserves mention, though she

'The drop-frames which allowed ladies to mount the machine without throwing a leg over the saddle were not introduced till the nineties'

was not a Forsyte. Mrs MacAnder was the greatest friend of Soames's sister, Winifred, and a modern woman who belonged to a Woman's Club. 'Her own marriage, poor thing, had not been successful, but having had the good sense and ability to force her husband into pronounced error, she herself had passed through the necessary divorce proceedings without incurring censure.' So when, out for a constitutional on her bicycle, she noticed Irene Forsyte and Philip Bosinney walking from the bracken grove of Richmond Park towards Sheen Gate, she was not the woman to mis-understand the circumstances. The bicycling public was large enough to support a journal, *The Bicycle News*, of which, as some will remember, Mr Pooter, the hero of *The Diary of a Nobody*, was a reader.

Private cars had not become sufficiently practical for the Forsytes to consider one until after 1898 when the Prince of Wales made the motor car fashionable by climbing into one. The earlier models had neither windscreens nor hoods, and had to be provided with a wicker guard to protect the clothes of the passengers getting into or out of the vehicle, all of which made motoring an all-male sport for some years to come.

But the general absence of cars in London in 1886 did not mean that there were no traffic blocks. Horse traffic moved comparatively slowly and carriages and carts were less manoeuvrable (since the horse usually showed a marked reluctance to reversing and not infrequently fell down even on the flat and refused or was unable to get up). Apart from this there were complaints of hold-ups in Bond Street as a result of advertisement vans which crawled along obstructing those behind.

Neither drivers nor coachmen showed much consideration for each other. Swithin, indeed, would not have stopped on any account after the incident in which the phaeton he was driving overturned the cart of a coster who had endeavoured to mimic his style.

The pedestrian received least consideration of all, and *The Times* of 14 February 1886 recorded that Mr Dixon Hartland, Member of Parliament, was knocked down while crossing Queen Victoria Street on his way from Blackfriars Station to the House of Commons. Several details of the report call for comment. It was stated that when Mr Hartland 'had reached the middle of the road, the defendant suddenly pulled out of his proper line of traffic and tried to pass a vehicle in front of him. The result was that the witness was struck violently in the chest by the shaft of the defendant's cart and knocked down in the mud.'

From this it is clear that, although the crossing opposite the station was well used, there was no island or refuge in the centre of the road on to which the pedestrian could jump to safety. Secondly, although this was a busy street, there was mud in the centre of it. In other words, the crossing sweepers, who were supposed to clear the mire and horse dung from street crossings so that the pedestrians could get from one side to the other without fouling their shoes, had overlooked this part of the street. (The Court did not condemn them in any way for their negligence.) It was the same in Regent Street where, in November 1900, a Monsieur van Brantegham, a Belgian, lost a bet of £5 that he would not walk from Verrey's Restaurant to Swan & Edgar's, keeping close to the kerb without receiving more than three mud splashes on his collar. He finished up with five on his collar and two on his face.

But the main travel obstacle for pedestrians and drivers alike – at certain times of the year – was the choking pea-soup fog for which London was already world famous. As Soames found one evening on his way home:

The fog was worse than ever at Sloane Square Station. Through the still, thick blur, men groped in and out; women, very few, grasped their reticules to their bosoms and handkerchiefs to their mouths; crowned with the weird excrescence of the driver, haloed by a vague glow of lamplight that seemed to drown in vapour before it reached the pavement, cabs loomed dim-shaped ever and again, and discharged citizens bolting like rabbits to their burrows.

It was in such a fog that Bosinney, 'the Buccaneer', heedless and anguished, was run over and killed.

But when there was no fog, Londoners could choose from a great variety of evening entertainment. There were lectures on every conceivable topic, and ballad-singing at St James's Hall (where the Piccadilly Hotel now stands); and Henry Wood, who had conducted orchestras for the Carl Rosa and D'Oyly Carte Opera Companies, was soon (1895) to launch the Promenade Concerts at Queen's Hall. There was music hall and ballet at the Alhambra Theatre of Varieties, *Aladdin and the Forty Thieves* at Sanger's Grand National Amphitheatre in the Westminster Bridge Road, and a circus at the Covent Garden Theatre. Other attractions were clearly designed for a less exalted public. Thus an advertisement in *The Times* of 18 June 1886 reads: 'Piccadilly Hall: *King Theebaw's Sacred Burmese Hairy Family*. Receptions Daily 2 till 5 & 7 till 10. Greatest Living Curiosities in the World. Piano by Brinsmead.'

Madame Tussaud's waxworks offered a mixture:

Superb Bridal Group, Princess Beatrice and Prince Henry of Battenberg; Prince Alexander of Bulgaria, and King Milan of Servia; Kings and Queens of England; Royal Costumes. Orchestral and other music throughout the day. Upwards of 400 portrait models. The Netherby Hall Burglary; Cumberland Murder; Portrait models of the Condemned Men now added. Admission 1s. Extra rooms 6d. Open 10 till 10.

Before condemning the impresarios who offered such fare it is worth recalling that public executions had been abolished only in

1868, and a taste for the shock-horror spectacle survived among a section of the public. As recently as 1880 the Bearded Lady had been one of the sensations of the metropolis.

But it was the theatre which most attracted the average Forsyte. It had taken a long time for the theatre to become respectable enough for a family audience. In the early days of Queen Victoria's reign the ground floor of the auditorium, generally known as the Pit, was still filled with benches occupied by less refined theatre-goers. These were not only boisterous and rowdy but disrespectful to their betters in the boxes behind them.

It took courage on the part of the Bancrofts to replace the Pit benches in 1886 with orchestra stalls. But this was merely the culmination of some radical redesigning which had taken place over the preceding century. Originally the stage extended out into the auditorium and was flanked on each side by boxes, an arrangement which deprived the actors of much of the mystery they needed if they were to create the illusion of reality. By the end of the eighteenth century, however, the stage had retreated almost entirely behind the proscenium arch, to a position which not only enabled the actors to get on and off the stage more effectively, but permitted changes in scenery and lighting to be made without revealing to the audience the secret of how it was done.

Other reforms were introduced to attract fashionable audiences. The curtain was raised at a later hour. The seating was systematized, classified, numbered, and made bookable. The Dress Circle, reserved exclusively for those who were prepared to wear evening dress, became for a time the most fashionable sector of the theatre. The style of acting was changed. Melodramatic orations and overwrought gestures were discarded in favour of the natural manner first introduced in the mid-1860s by

(*opposite*) 'Irving was playing *Faust* at the Lyceum'

Tom Robertson. More attention was paid not only to who was appearing on the stage but to the words written for them; and, with the passing of the International Copyright Act of 1886, serious and original authors who had something to say, and whose plays could no longer be cribbed, became more important in the theatre.

At the less ponderous end of the scale Gilbert and Sullivan established musical satire in light opera as a form of entertainment, and in the nineties George Edwardes 'invented' respectable musical comedy to replace the more boisterous burlesques.

Above all, there was Henry Irving, who was the first actor to have been knighted and have his ashes buried in Westminster Abbey. In his hands the theatre became a temple of dramatic art offering the mystique and majesty of a religious occasion, and the audience, probably for the first time in their experience, were treated as distinguished patrons and honoured friends. Irving advertised, for instance, that he had retained a considerable number of seats for those who wished to book them, presumably more cheaply, through the theatre, and had

'At the less ponderous end of the scale Gilbert and Sullivan established musical satire in light opera as a form of entertainment'; design by Alice Havers

not parted with all his seats to the 'libraries'. No charge was made for the programme. His company was well managed, and the actors at the Lyceum were provided with no fewer than three separate 'green rooms' in which to relax. Irving's acting was impressive and no one who had watched him ever forgot the experience. (Shakespeare was never quite the same again, either.)

In 1886, the year in which we are introduced to the Forsytes, Irving was playing *Faust* at the Lyceum. Charles Hawtrey was in the play that made a fortune for him, *The Private Secretary*, at the Globe. Lillie Langtry, who relied on the theatre after her affair with the Prince of Wales, was managing the Prince's Theatre for a season, and was appearing in a 'comedy-drama' entitled *Enemies*. The theatre proudly proclaimed the fact that it was lit by electricity and that seats were bookable by telephone.

At the same time Marie Tempest was playing a comic-opera entitled *Erminie* at the Comedy Theatre; Drury Lane, in its tradition of spectaculars, was offering *A Run of Luck* in which Daisy, a mare about to race at Goodwood – and in danger of being seized for debt – appeared in person on the stage. The Adelphi was presenting *The Harbour Lights*, a drama, and *The Man with Three Wives* was running, under Charles Wyndham's management, at the Criterion. The original Royal Court Theatre – not in exactly the same place as the present house – had become famous through Pinero's farces, but was about to close because of the redevelopment of Sloane Square. *The Mikado* was playing at the Savoy. *Trilby* and *Charley's Aunt* were still to come.

The music hall, however, was what most attracted the younger and more raffish members of the Forsyte family. Originally, in the 1850s, artistes were engaged for concerts put on by the landlords of drinking saloons for their customers who sat at the tables, glass in hand. You could smoke in them too – which was not

permitted at most theatres. Eventually a minimum charge entitling the customer to admission and a drink was levied. The idea spread, and by the 1880s music halls blossomed throughout the West End and the surrounding areas. The earlier music hall audiences were drawn from among the artisans and shop assistants who lived over their work – there was great agitation in 1908 when Swan & Edgar abolished the living-in system which their employees had hitherto enjoyed. The music halls had a chairman who sat below the stage and announced the acts, endeavoured to keep order, and downed innumerable drinks provided by those who wished to show others that they were his friends.

The Empire Theatre had opened its doors in 1884, but did not become a Theatre of Varieties until 1887, when it rapidly attained notoriety on account of the spacious promenade immediately behind its Dress Circle, a thoroughfare soon invaded by enterprising ladies who believed that they had as much, if

(*above*) The 'Dress Circle, a thoroughfare soon invaded by enterprising ladies who believed that they had as much, if not more, to offer the male audience'
(*opposite*) 'The Empire Theatre had opened its doors in 1884, but did not become a Theatre of Varieties until 1887'

THE EMPIRE

THEATRE OF VARIETIES

Doors
Open at
7.45.
Commence at
7.50.

EMPIRE ORCHESTRA,
Under the Direction of
LEOPOLD WENZEL.

Maitresse de Ballet,
Madame **KATTI LANNER.**

Manager, Mr. H. J. HITCHINS.

Managing Director,
Mr. **GEORGE EDWARDES.**

The EMPIRE PALACE, Limited

Printed by HENRY GOOD & SON, 12 MOORGATE ST & 39 MOOR LANE, E.C.

not more, to offer the male audience than the ladies on the stage. In 1894 a social reformer, Mrs Ormiston Chant, took the trouble to get herself accosted in the hope (unfulfilled) of preventing the renewal of the theatre's licence, and a head-high barrier was then erected to protect the audience from feminine high-waymen; but the Empire remained nevertheless a rendezvous of opportunity for residents and visitors alike.

The music hall performers were as uninhibited as the audience (which was one of the reasons why the elder Forsytes had no intention of allowing themselves to be seen at such entertainments). There was Marie Lloyd, petite, fair haired, blue eyed, who rose to fame from the Eagle Music Hall, City Road. Her motto was 'To cut it short is best; you can let them guess the rest', and her husky voice and Cockney accent were peculiarly suited to the sentiments she wished to impart. There was also Lottie Collins, who in 1892 was to succeed in expanding her war-cry, 'Ta-ra-ra-Boom-de-Ay', of the year before, into a fifteen minute act – in the same year, incidentally, that Harry Dacre's 'Daisy Bell' ('Give me your answer, Do') hit the music stands.

Then there was Albert Chevalier, an actor turned music hall singer, whose conversational pieces included ''E Ain't Got the Shadder of a Notion', 'The Future Mrs 'Awkins' and 'My Old Dutch'. And there was Dan Leno, the pathetic genius, whose character studies of a shop-walker, a recruiting sergeant, and a railway guard have never been successfully imitated. George Grossmith's 'You Should see me Dance the Polka' bridged the gap between the music hall and the ballroom.

This was the golden age of Variety, before the cinematograph (forerunner of the movies)

(opposite) 'Lottie Collins, who in 1892 was to succeed in expanding her war-cry, "Ta-ra-ra-Boom-de-Ay", of the year before into a fifteen minute act'

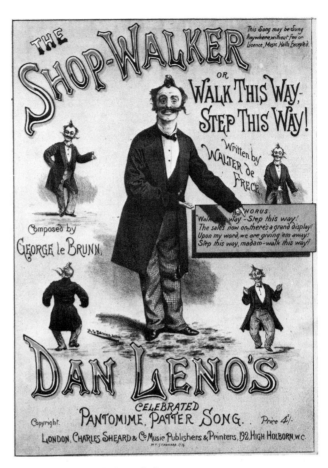

'Dan Leno, the pathetic genius'

first appeared in 1896 as an item on the bill at the Empire.

Restaurants began to keep pace with the theatres. A standard guidebook to London, published in 1889, which informed the traveller that 4 to 8 p.m. was the dinner hour at the best restaurants and that 'some of them are closed after eight', was already becoming outdated. The more fashionable ones like Verreys, the Café Royal in Regent Street, and Scott's were beginning, like the theatres, to keep open later. By the end of the century dinner after the theatre at such places as the Carlton and Prince's was a well-established routine, and customers arriving at 10.30 p.m. would expect to find the tables waiting for them, with glasses and cutlery gleaming against

snow-white cloths and napkins. Those who felt like something less elaborate could patronize an oyster bar or, if they were sufficiently talented, the artists' room at Pagani's. The licensing laws allowed bars to be kept open for twenty and a half hours out of the twenty-four.

Ladies out shopping could refuel themselves at almost any hour of the day, from confectioners selling such dainties as soup, jelly, cherries in brandy, and champagne by the glass. The young drank chocolate at Charbonnel's in Bond Street. Tea in Kensington Gardens was a fashionable affair. Joe Lyons began to flood London with tea shops from 1894 on, but in 1900 a tea shop in Baker Street run by women was still considered a novelty.

The growth of leisure and pleasure industries, however, did not prevent Sunday from being celebrated with due solemnity by the classes to which the Forsytes belonged. There was a soothing absence of street cries: the sweep in search of chimneys was not heard, nor the coalman, nor the man calling for scissors to grind or chairs to mend or clocks to repair. Neither watercress, nor chestnuts, nor ice-cream were hawked, nor was there any old iron to be collected.

The Forsytes, their wives and their children were regular attenders at the more fashionable London churches, and some of them paid for pews, thus expressing in the most practical form their sympathies for the teaching of Christ. They were not even averse to listening to a sermon denouncing the selfishness and wickedness of mankind since they were convinced that it could in no way be applied to them.

No one except invalids took their carriages into Hyde Park on Sunday mornings. Nevertheless an impressive 'church parade' took place there in the interval between the end of

The Café Royal in 1903

morning service and luncheon, which was not normally served until two o'clock since some, if not all, the domestics would themselves have gone to church. The parade was a formal affair, with the older men in frock coats and top hats, and it grew more picturesque with the passing of the years as the custom of raising the hat, once thought to be 'foreign' and therefore in bad taste, became accepted by all classes.

In the afternoon, it was considered fashionable to visit the Zoological Gardens, since on Sunday tickets were restricted to Fellows of the Zoological Society and their friends. Forsyte opinion about the zoo varied. Some of the ladies were distressed because the monkeys who looked so human did not behave at all nicely. Young Jolyon felt that to shut up a lion or tiger in captivity 'was surely a horrible barbarity'. But such an idea never occurred to his father who delighted to take his grandchildren to see the animals:

he belonged to the old school, who considered it at once humanizing and educational to confine baboons and panthers, holding the view, no doubt, that in

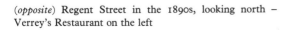
(*opposite*) Regent Street in the 1890s, looking north – Verrey's Restaurant on the left

(*above*) Not so fashionable St James's Park
(*right*) 'Forsyte opinion about zoos varied';
London zoo, 1902
(*below*) 'The growth of leisure and pleasure
industries did not prevent Sunday from being
celebrated with due solemnity'; shopgirls,
1899

course of time they might induce these creatures not so unreasonably to die of misery and heart-sickness against the bars of their cages, and put the society to the expense of getting others!

Soames usually stayed at home on Sunday afternoon to contemplate his paintings before leaving for Sunday tea at Timothy's. For Sunday was not a day on which one went to one's club. Yet during the week, those imposing establishments, to which the rioters on their way to Oxford Street had paid so much attention, constituted a special feature of the Forsyte way of life.

In the days of the earlier Forsytes the clubs had responded to man's desire to get better acquainted with man; and later to his wish to associate with some, but not all men. But in Soames's time many clubs specialized not only in excluding the majority of common and vulgar fellows from their premises, but also in encouraging its members not to make friends with each other, and even at times to avoid each other.

For example, it was a tradition of the Travellers' Club, founded in 1819, that members did not speak to each other. The great Cecil Rhodes was bound to have started talking to other members in his high-pitched voice, so they black-balled him. Soames would have liked that, although it is not clear whether he himself would have qualified for membership of the Travellers' by virtue of having travelled to a city five hundred miles away in a direct line from London.

To Soames, as to many others, a club was something more than a badge of social respectability. It was a retreat, a guarantee of instant solitude to be obtained whenever desired. Inside the club there was an atmosphere of timelessness – except in the pre-dawn hours of the morning when club fines were instituted to persuade the members to return home. The members had no responsibilities to fulfil. Meals could be eaten at almost any hour.

The club waiter did not expect to be tipped and, if the food was not up to snuff, the member was relieved of the burden of saying so openly and had merely to write his comments on the back of the bill. There was a choice of newspapers and magazines to read, and a larger library than was usual at home. And, above all, there was silence of a kind that ensured you that you would not be woken if you chanced to doze off in a chair before the fire after a glass or two of excellent port. Some club members sought refuge there from womenfolk because they were not interested in marriage, or wished actively to avoid it. Captain Gronow in his gossipy memoirs well described the tribe of superannuated bachelor clubmen wedded to the club fender rather than to a wife – and Swithin Forsyte was clearly one of their heirs: 'They swore a good deal, never laughed, had their own particular slang, looked hazy after dinner and had, most of them, been patronized at one time or other by Brummel or the Prince Regent.' Other clubmen, already married, wished to enjoy a respite from the cares of home.

On the whole, the elderly predominated in the club rooms, especially during the day. Most of those who had time to patronize the club were of independent means or had reached the stage in their profession where they did not have to work too hard. Business men were discouraged from joining for fear that they might talk shop. Young men coming from large Victorian families could not be supported in idleness and frequently had to earn their own living in a way which raised obstacles to the day-long use of the club smoking-room.

The importance of a daily routine visit to the club evidently grew with the passage of time until, with some of the older members, it became the high spot of the morning if not of the whole day. If the club possessed a bow window – of the type met with at White's and some other clubs in St James's Street – it would be monopolized by the older members, each having his own special chair. It was considered bad form when sitting in the window to return or acknowledge greetings from passers-by in the street, even if they happened to be close friends. There was an excellent reason for this: it discouraged advances from women who might have hitherto been unknown to members – or, worse still, might have been only too well known to them. It also discouraged attempts by the socially inferior to ingratiate themselves with members, who out of good manners might feel obliged to invite the aggressors into the club.

In the 1880s, when it was still possible to live comparatively cheaply in the heart of London, the clubs, in contrast to the custom today, were used rather more in the evenings than by day. They flourished at a time when many men had time to kill, and there were fewer amusements than today to help them to do so. There was no weekly cinema, little motoring, no mixed cocktail parties, and comparatively few public restaurants which could be depended on to serve better food than could be obtained at home.

Different London clubs would have suited different Forsytes. But Soames would probably have looked askance at some of the very respectable ones founded in his own lifetime. There was, for example, the Arts Club, launched in 1863, of which the avowed object was 'to facilitate the social intercourse of those connected either professionally or as amateurs with art, literature, and science'. To Soames, paintings by acknowledged masters were one thing; 'art' and artists quite a different matter, and it was doubtless to avoid the kind of club that Soames would join that artists established their own.

The Savile, founded five years after the Arts, assumed an interest in letters which soon went far beyond the bounds which Soames would have considered desirable. Its members eventually included not only acceptable eccentrics

like Rudyard Kipling and Robert Louis Stevenson but 'that fellow', H. G. Wells.

Equally eccentric in its raffish way was the Marlborough Club founded by the Prince of Wales; it had a skittle alley. Then there was Hurlingham, with its pigeon shooting and polo, neither of which were much in Soames's line. The Beefsteak, established in 1876, was not his scene either. It had a written rule that members could talk to one another without introduction.

The Reform, the Devonshire, the National Liberal, together with the Carlton and Junior Carlton, were avowedly political. Soames took care not to join 'The Remove', Galsworthy's pseudonym for the Reform, until much later when it had been purged of its predominantly Liberal character. The Naval and Military, the Army and Navy, the United Service (facetiously referred to as the Cripples Home) and the Guards were virtually closed to civilians, and the Victoria Club was addicted to billiards, and cards too, as was the Portland, to which bridge was introduced in 1894. White's was perhaps too rakish – Soames was never a gambler – and Boodle's and Brooks's were loaded with aristocrats for whom Soames would probably have had as much contempt as he later had for Sir Lawrence Mont.

We meet Soames as a clubman about half way through *The Man of Property* at a time when June was still engaged to Bosinney and when Montague Dartie was escaping from a family tea party.

At this moment, glancing out of the bay-window – for he [Dartie] loved this seat whence he could see everybody pass – his eye unfortunately, or perhaps fortunately, chanced to light on the figure of Soames, who was mousing across the road from the Green Park side, with the evident intention of coming in, for he, too, belonged to 'The Iseeum'.

Dartie sprang to his feet; grasping his glass, he muttered something about 'that 4.30 race', and swiftly withdrew to the card-room, where Soames never came. Here, in complete isolation and a dim light, he lived his own life till half past seven, by which hour he knew Soames must certainly have left the club.

The Iseeum was the name given by George Forsyte, the humorist of the family, to this particular club largely on account of its bay window, which enabled those sitting in it to say: 'I see 'em.' From its position and the fact that Montague Dartie belonged to it the Iseeum could well have been the Turf Club. But Soames was hardly a racing man. I am inclined to think that he would have found the Union Club more congenial. It was respectably old, having been founded in 1805, and then had premises in Trafalgar Square on the site of the present Canada House. It also had a fair sprinkling of solicitors, who were by no means always welcome in some other clubs where they might meet clients for whose family affairs they were responsible. Until 1899 it had no telephone. But old Jolyon already belonged to the Disunion, a thinly disguised pseudonym for the Union, and rather despised the club because it had so readily accepted him. So perhaps, after all, it would not have suited Soames.

Apart from the Remove, Soames later joined the Connoisseurs, confirming that no single club could now satisfy all the needs of a Forsyte – a discovery which foretold one of many other changes in the social climate.

'The clubs had responded to man's desire to get better acquainted with man'

9

The Forsytes' Paradise Lost

During the last ten years of Queen Victoria's reign the English were assailed by doubts and self-criticisms which haunt them still. Their mood was due in part to the consequences of the industrial revolution, which left middle-class engineers, shipowners, manufacturers and tradesmen with unwonted affluence and led some of them to question, particularly in the latter half of the century, whether Britannia's land-owning aristocracy had the divine right, or even the ability required to rule the world's greatest empire.

Evidence of the lion's waning strength had already become noticeable in the 1860s when Palmerston at first declared that Britain would fight alongside Denmark in her frontier dispute with Prussia – and then had to back down for lack of allies; and there were several other highly unsatisfactory confrontations in which Britain came out second best.

But few events shook the complacency of Victorian affluent society more than the dramas of the Boer War. From the first there were those who believed that Britain had blundered by going to war at all; and that by doing so she risked losing the whole of southern Africa unless she was prepared to hold it down with a permanent army of occupation.

Next came a nightmarish fear that even winning the war in a military sense could not be taken for granted. During 'Black Week' of December 1899 the British army suffered three defeats in succession: at Stormberg where six hundred men were lost because they were not given the order to retire, at Magersfontein where the Boers inconsiderately surprised the British by entrenching themselves at the base of the hills instead of, as expected, on the summit, and at Colenso, where four hundred men were mown down while attempting to cross the Tugela river on their way to relieve Ladysmith. In London the public took the news so badly that some theatres closed for lack of audiences. Margaret Hobhouse, elder sister of Beatrice Webb, writing to Mary Playne, another sister, declared:

What a blessing it is that our Government is taking these dreadful reverses with courage and decision. I wish I had a son who could go out and fight and help to regain our lost position. It seems that the whole credit of England and her colonies is at stake.

On the other hand, Beatrice Webb, who with her husband Sidney launched the London School of Economics and the *New Statesman*, wrote: 'The Boers are man for man our superiors in dignity, devotion, capacity. Yes, in capacity. That, to a ruling race, is the hardest hit of all.'

Then there was the moral issue of whether the war, even if it could be won, and a permanent settlement secured, would fatally damage Britain's reputation as champion of liberty and

(*opposite*) 'Few events shook the complacency of Victorian society more than the dramas of the Boer War'. Queen Victoria reviewing the families of Life Guards and Reservists at the front, at Victoria Barracks, Windsor

THE ILLUSTRATED LONDON NEWS.

REGISTERED AT THE GENERAL POST OFFICE AS A NEWSPAPER.

No. 3164.—VOL. CXV.   SATURDAY, DECEMBER 9, 1899.   WITH EIGHT-PAGE SUPPLEMENT : SIXPENCE.

THE QUEEN "REVIEWING" THE WIVES AND CHILDREN OF LIFE GUARDS AND RESERVISTS AT THE FRONT, AT THE VICTORIA BARRACKS, WINDSOR.

justice. Inevitably the war became a political issue, with the Liberals on the one hand pursuing their policy of independence for the Transvaal, and the Government and the Queen on the other hand calling for more effective prosecution of the conflict. The dispute became increasingly bitter during the campaign for the General Election of October 1900 during which the opposition and the 'Stop the War' campaigners were categorized as 'Pro-Boers' and shouted down with choruses of 'Rule Britannia' and 'Soldiers of the Queen'.

On top of all this there was the scandal of the concentration camps, which were set up when Kitchener determined to lay waste the farms which the Boers were using as supply points in their guerilla campaigns. After the food stocks and the buildings had been destroyed, the wives, children and other relatives who had lived on the farms had to be moved somewhere else. The army solution was to house and feed them in camps. At first the camps were treated as part of the war operations, and therefore as top secret. But later, news began to leak out that all was not well in them. Emily Hobhouse, the 'do-gooder' who had travelled to South Africa to hand out extra comforts to displaced Boer women and children, found that they were still in need of absolute necessities such as mattresses, soap and clean water. Worse still, women and children in the camps were dying in thousands from epidemics of measles, pneumonia and scarlet fever, partly through lack of medical care.

Lloyd George, then Radical Member for Caernarvon, drew blood with his speeches in which he called for sympathy for the 'poor hunted Boers' and compared the British commanders with Herod. He barely escaped with his life when he tried to speak at a political meeting in Birmingham.

There is little doubt that some Forsytes were anti-Boer. When the Boer War had been in progress for some time and things were going badly, Giles and Jesse Hayman decided to enlist in the Imperial Yeomanry. Thus, in the episode recorded in *On Forsyte 'Change*, we read:

Their decision, a corporate one – for they never acted apart – was made without unnecessary verbal expenditure. Giles, the elder by one year and the stronger built, withdrew his pipe from between his teeth, turned a fox-terrier off his lap, and pointing to the words 'Black Week' in the *Daily Mail* said:
'Those beggarly Boers!'
Jesse, on an armchair on the other side of the hearth took the fox-terrier on his lap, tapped out his pipe, and answered:
'Brutes!'
There was again silence. Then Giles said:
'What price the Yeomanry? Are you on?'
Jesse put his empty pipe between his teeth and nodded. The matter had been concluded.

At Oxford young Val Dartie called old Jolyon's grandson, Jolly, a pro-Boer, and they fought about the incident. They both enlisted, but only Val survived.

Understandably it did not occur to Soames, who was then forty-five, to take the same course. But he discussed the Boer War one Sunday afternoon with Madame Lamotte and her daughter Annette whom he had invited down to his house at Mapledurham with a view, later on, to marrying her. Soames argued in favour of upholding British suzerainty over the 'half-civilized' Boers. There was another memorable confrontation between Soames and June one afternoon at Timothy's, with June hotly defending the Boers' right to be left to themselves.

But the misgivings of the British were not confined only to matters of foreign policy or military strategy. Darwin had raised serious doubts as to whether man had in fact been created in God's image. Samuel Butler in *The Fair Haven* had written a highly ironical defence of Christian tenets, and Charles Bradlaugh, the atheist, had been allowed to take his seat in the House of Commons despite his refusal to swear the required oath of allegiance on the Bible.

Writers and artists in their various ways were attacking the foundations of society as the Forsytes knew it. Thomas Hardy, who like the Forsytes came from Dorset stock, was accused in the 1890s of advocating 'free love' in his novel *Jude the Obscure*, the story of two women who, in their different fashions, fascinate, subjugate and help bring shamelessly to ruin a hero who is trying to better himself. The Bishop of Wakefield in an open letter to the *Yorkshire Post* said he was so disgusted with the book that he threw it on the fire.

George Moore, the novelist, shocked the Mudie-library-reading public with his *Confessions of a Young Man*, in which he admitted that Shelley had helped him to shake off all belief in Christianity, that he enjoyed feeding guinea-pigs to his pet python, and that his 'university' was the Nouvelle Athènes, a café on the Place Pigalle. (But if only Soames had listened to what he had to say about Manet, Degas, Monet and Pissarro, how much higher his reputation as a connoisseur could have been.)

Then there was Havelock Ellis, who chose to make a serious study of sexual perversion or inversion as he called it. The man himself was clearly not normal in Forsyte eyes. He was, for instance, a friend of Miss Caroline Haddon, the tireless advocate of polygamy; he was friendly, too, with Eleanor Marx, Karl Marx's daughter; and his wife Edith, unable to obtain the physical satisfaction she might have expected from her husband, entered into a number of Lesbian liaisons which, so far from leading to a separation, provided Havelock Ellis with fresh research material.

He had indeed studied sexual abnormality for at least six years before his marriage in 1891, and he continued to do so for another six before his work *Sexual Inversion* appeared. It raised questions that many of his contemporaries felt should not have been asked, and

left them wondering, perhaps for the first time, whether homosexuality could really be accounted for by individual freakishness, or arrested development or even mental disorder. Ellis put into their minds the thought that, on the contrary, many normal people might have abnormal tendencies which they controlled only by suppressing them. He also supported the theory that affairs between men and men or between women and women should be regarded as no less (or no more) decent than intercourse between men and women, and that all sexual practices should be regulated by private conscience alone.

Other writers were always stirring up political trouble and social unrest. Arthur Morrison's *Tales of Mean Streets* had appeared in 1895 and introduced its readers to a world which the Forsytes, at any rate, would have preferred to ignore, since apparently it was peopled mainly by men and women who lived on penn'orths of gin and seldom washed. And George Gissing with his melo-saga *Workers in the Dawn* was just as bad. Then there was H. G. Wells turning the world upside down with *The Time Machine* and other science fiction.

George Bernard Shaw was in many ways more dangerous, since he had various proposals for changing the social order. Shaw declared in March 1898 that he was ill equipped to write plays which would please the London public.

I had no taste for what is called popular art, no respect for popular morality, no belief in popular religion, no admiration for popular heroics. As an Irishman I could pretend to patriotism neither for the country I had abandoned nor for the country that had ruined it. As a human person I detested violence and slaughter, whether in war, sport, or the butcher's yard. [He had become a vegetarian in 1881.]

Nor would Shaw's *Maxims for Revolutionists*, in which he set out his creed to be applied to the more controversial issues of the day, have proved more acceptable to the average Forsyte. His views on property were summed up in two

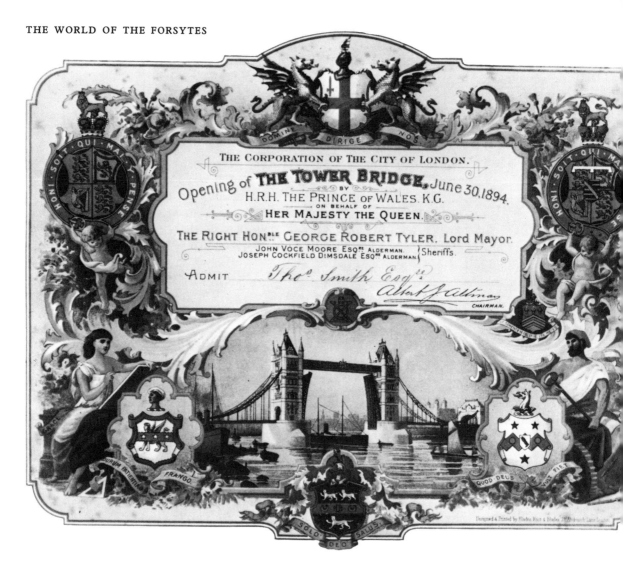

Tower Bridge was opened in 1894

sentences: '"Property", said Proudhon, "is theft." This is the only perfect truism that has been uttered on the subject.' On the social question he wrote: 'Do not waste your time on Social Questions. What is the matter with the poor is Poverty: what is the matter with the rich is Uselessness.' And on the empire: 'When we learn to sing that Britons never will be masters we shall make an end of slavery.'

His play *Mrs Warren's Profession*, in which a nicely brought-up undergraduate discovers that the money her mother provided for university fees came from a chain of brothels, was considered so shocking that permission to perform it was not granted until 1923, thirty years after it was written.

Conditions were such as to stimulate rather than abate the ferment. The Education Act of 1870, which set up state schools in many parts of the country, thereby breaking the monopoly of private and church schools, led to inquiries into activities and practices which had hitherto been taken for granted. Popular newspapers, such as the *Daily Mail* and after 1900 the *Daily Express*, were publicly airing problems which had hitherto received little attention in Parliament, the pulpit or *The Times*.

People, as well as ideas, circulated more. Tower Bridge was opened in 1894; the first petrol-driven motor bus in London ran in 1899 between Victoria and Kennington; the Royal Aero Club was founded in 1901.

One new discovery seemed to lead to another. Only a few years after electricity came into general use, Sir Joseph Thomson was explaining the workings of x-rays and the nature of cathode rays; later (1897) he unearthed, so to speak, the electron, a discovery which led Sir Joseph Larmor to put forward his theory that all matter was composed of electrons moving about the ether according to electro-magnetic laws. It was the year when Marconi sent the first wireless signal across the Bristol Channel – a distance of three and a half miles.

On a less elevated plane there was Charles Cross's discovery in 1892 of viscose, the fore-runner of rayon, which enabled shop girls to dress like duchesses. And in 1901 a patent was taken out for a device which would make a duchess independent – if she wished to be – of all housemaids: the vacuum cleaner.

Meanwhile the artist's general standing in the turbulent waters of the 1890s showed little change. It was carefully delineated by Lady Greville in *The Gentlewoman in Society*. Her view was that:

People can be asked to luncheon who could not so well be invited to dinner; in fact it is often a criterion of the exact degree of intimacy which prevails whether a man is asked to dinner or luncheon. Poor relations, country cousins, men of business, artists or professional men may be asked to luncheon, who neither could nor would care to come to dinner, though it is seldom now that a literary man is sufficiently Bohemian not to possess a dress suit; still, his business and his preferences point towards luncheon.

Guglielmo Marconi with his assistant Mr Kemp

Obviously, painters *could* be respectable and

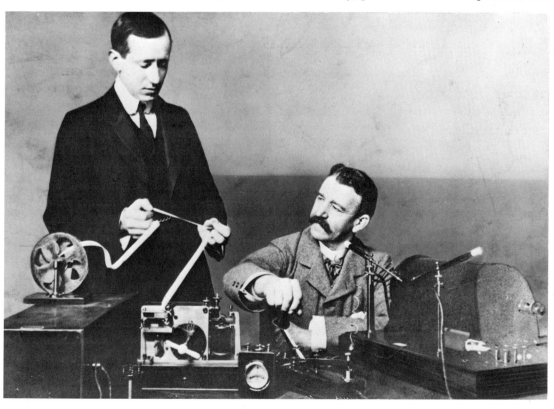

'Sir Lawrence Alma-Tadema's paintings of life in ancient Greece and Rome had procured him a knighthood'; 'A Priestess of Apollo', about 1888

been named a Companion of the Victorian Order, a decoration awarded for special services to the Queen. Sir Lawrence Alma-Tadema's paintings of life in ancient Greece and Rome had procured him a knighthood, and John Tenniel, illustrator of *Alice in Wonderland*, and progenitor of many *Punch* cartoons, had been equally fortunate. But the trouble was that one never knew who was going to be successful and who not. (Lord Leighton had received his Letters of Patent only on the day before he died.)

And on the other hand there were a lot of dubious characters – some very dubious:

Sir John Millais had been awarded a baronetcy after pleasing the Queen with his portrait of Disraeli

might even care to come to dinner if asked. Edwin (*Monarch of the Glen*) Landseer had been knighted; Millais had been awarded a baronetcy after pleasing the Queen with his portrait of Disraeli; Frederick Leighton, that tireless worker for the Royal Academy, had become a lord. William (*Derby Day*) Frith had

Augustus John, Walter Sickert who spent so much time with Degas in Dieppe but who redeemed himself only many years later by teaching Winston Churchill to paint, and Whistler and that Chelsea Set. And of course Oscar Wilde, who was tried in 1895 and condemned for homosexuality.

So it must be confessed that artists, as distinct from their work, did not rate very highly in the Forsyte household. Almost wherever we turn, they are derided and disapproved of. Men to be beaten down if possible in any and every transaction. Thus Swithin relates with pride the circumstances in which he bought the piece of Italian marble statuary which decorated his rooms:

James McNeill
Whistler

'The poor foreign dey-vil that made it . . . asked me five hundred – I gave him four. It's worth eight. Looked half-starved, poor dey-vil!'

'Ah!' chimed in Nicholas suddenly, 'poor, seedy-lookin' chaps, these artists; it's a wonder to me how they live. Now, there's young Flageoletti, that Fanny and the girls are always havin' in, to play the fiddle; if he makes a hundred a year it's as much as he ever does!'

James shook his head. 'Ah!' he said, '*I* don't know how they live!'

Walter Sickert

Soames, of course, came to have a better idea of how artists lived when he commissioned Philip Bosinney to design and supervise the building of his country house.

Augustus John

A House in the Country

Until the 1890s the term 'country house' had only one generally accepted meaning. It was a residence set in the middle of a park, the centre of a country estate, providing an income not only for its owner but for a large staff of servants, gamekeepers, gardeners – Eaton Hall, the Duke of Westminster's place, had forty – and perhaps tenant farmers in the surrounding area.

But even before the last years of the century the scenery was being shifted. The agricultural depression which led to the riots of 1886 threatened the future of farming in Britain, and thus the prosperity of the landed aristocracy. Those who could now afford to build 'country houses' were factory owners – the industrial peers created by Gladstone in 1885–6 and by his successor in office, Lord Salisbury. Tea, biscuits, carpets, as well as shipping and banking provided the wherewithal for mansions so big that today they are ruins or museums, or inhabited by civil servants, schoolgirls (as at Benenden and Alton Towers), police, or even Borstal boys.

Many houses were built without regard to their surroundings. Rendcomb House, the mansion erected near Cirencester by Sir Francis Goldsmid, the bullion broker, possessed an Italianate tower, stables in the French Renaissance style, and a massive marble statue of King David in the hall.

Kent, Surrey, Oxfordshire and Berkshire were sites favoured both by manufacturers who wanted to get away from the smoke and grime of the north, and by those business men who did not wish to be too remote from the metropolis.

Improved transport made it possible for some to lead a dual existence. Sleeping-cars had been introduced on the west coast route to Scotland in 1873; dining-cars came in 1880 and the Great Western Railway introduced their corridor train in 1892. No longer was it necessary to spend the autumn, winter and spring in the country, as so many well-bred families did, beguiling the days with hunting, shooting, fishing and skating parties, and spending only 'the Season' in London. One could spend every week in London attending to business and yet enjoy 'the country' at weekends.

Hostesses invited influential politicians to meet one another at country houses in an atmosphere of luxurious relaxation. Financiers planned their deals in the water-garden or the smoking-room. In short the larger country houses, so far as they survived, were invaded by a new type of occupant, a supplanter with new interests, who was eager to enjoy the amenities of the country, but not so eager to undertake the responsibility for its welfare or its way of life.

Naturally, the ambitions of professional men such as Soames were not set so high, but it is worth recording, as Mark Girouard did in his invaluable work *The Victorian Country House*, that one of the notable residences built towards the close of the century, namely Standen, near East Grinstead, Sussex, was erected for a solicitor, J. S. Beale, who lived in London, had friends in the Holland Park and Campden Hill area (which Galsworthy himself frequented), and who wanted a house in the country for weekends and holidays. Beale himself was not particularly rich and, since Standen was to be a secondary residence, he curbed the original plans of the architect Philip Webb. It was a decision that many others, including Soames, had to emulate.

Indeed for the new breed of owner a new type of architect was needed – someone who realized, for instance, that the problems of securing privacy and seclusion, so easily attainable in a large house which was already blessed with spacious grounds, called for special treatment on a site of perhaps only one or two acres, which might have no unspoiled view of the horizon across its own fields.

And if the building was not going to be a palatial edifice imposing its own character on the landscape, it was all the more important that it should merge with its surroundings and harmonize not only with the contours of the site but with other houses in the area. It needed a man who was familiar not only with the techniques and practices of the local builders but also with the advantages and limitations of the materials they used, in other words with what is known as vernacular architecture as opposed to classic or gothic style.

Webb was one of the first architects to recognize this need, and at Standen he endeavoured, though not with complete success, to marry the existing farmhouse with his new building. George Devey was another Victorian architect who specialized in the vernacular style – in Kent. But, strange to say, it was Edwin Lutyens, the architect who afterwards designed the gigantic and grandiose vice-regal buildings in New Delhi (as well as the Cenotaph in Whitehall), who proved to be one of the most successful practitioners of this unassuming branch of architecture.

As a young man of twenty-two at the outset of his career, Lutyens, a man of high spirits and great charm, was taken in hand by Miss Gertrude Jekyll, a formidable lady endowed with great erudition and enterprise, who lived at Munstead, a few miles south of Guildford in Surrey. Miss Jekyll designed gardens and also wrote about them in *Country Life*. It was a valuable association for them both. Miss Jekyll perceived that young Lutyens had the technical knowledge she needed for the construction of the gardens that she designed, and surmised that in return she might be able to secure commissions for him from clients of hers who might want to build stables, terraces, outhouses and the like, as well as garden walls.

Often old buildings needed to be adapted to new uses; cottages and farmhouses needed modernizing, and old barns required to be converted into dining halls, or even transformed into houses that could be lived in. Soon the unlikely duo travelled out together on expeditions during which they noted the construction and style of farmhouses, manor houses and cottages, and learned the secrets of comfort from the people who lived in them. Their travels took them as far afield as 'Bessie' would pull the pony cart, and afterwards they would discuss their discoveries in Miss Jekyll's chimney corner before a blazing log fire, consuming hot glasses of her elderberry wine. Lutyens became aware of the attractions of tile-hung gables, oak timbers, roofs of Horsham tiles, and walls of local sandstone, as assets which could add a romantic touch to the English tradition. His early work, still to be seen in profusion in the western part of Surrey, was quickly noticed, and attracted publicity in *The Builder* magazine as well as at the Royal Academy. In short, he was as well known as Bosinney was little known.

It is against this background that we should assess the country house that was being built for Soames at Robin Hill in the year 1886. Soames had two reasons for moving to the

Standen, East Grinstead, Sussex; designed by Philip Webb

country. He saw the chance of a profitable investment, and he wanted to isolate his wife, Irene, from June Forsyte, who appeared to have a disturbing influence on her. It was, of course, absurd flattery to describe Robin Hill as a 'country house', for it formed part of a development, though admittedly a superior one, and, since a ground rent was payable, it was not even an unrestricted freehold. Nor was

it really in the country, although its twenty acres eventually included a model farm.

'It's an odd sort of house!' said Soames when he first saw the plans. It was 'a rectangular house of two storeys . . . designed in a quadrangle round a covered-in court', we are told. 'This court, encircled by a gallery on the upper floor, was roofed with a glass roof, supported by eight columns running up from the ground.' It was indeed, to Forsyte eyes, a peculiar house. But, as Bosinney explained acidly:

I've tried to plan a house here with some self-respect of its own. If you don't like it, you'd better say so. It's certainly the last thing to be considered – who wants self-respect in a house, when you can squeeze in an extra lavatory? . . .

I can see what it is . . . you want one of Littlemaster's houses – one of the pretty and commodious sort, where the servants will live in garrets, and the front door be sunk so that you may come up again. By all means try Littlemaster, you'll find him a capital fellow, I've known him all my life! . . .

Space, air, light . . . you can't live like a gentleman in one of Littlemaster's – he builds for manufacturers.

The architect could also have pointed out that Mentmore, the mansion built in the 1850s for Baron Meyer Amschel de Rothschild, Thoresby Hall, built for Earl Manvers, and many other grand houses of the period had been built round either a central courtyard or a glass-roofed Grand Hall, as used by the barons of an early vintage for the entertainment of their tenants.

In his relations with the architect Soames showed himself in his true Forsyte colours. He wanted new ideas on the cheap, and believed he could get them for a cut price from Bosinney, who was young and unknown, with his way to make, and, since Bosinney was engaged to be married to a member of the family, he should therefore be to some degree respectful, if not obsequious, towards his client. In this Soames was mistaken.

Indeed, not only the building of a country house but the countryside in which it stood faced Soames with the most painfully unfamiliar problems.

John Bennett as Philip Bosinney

The Desire to Escape

As professional men and property dealers, whose interests lay mainly in London, the Forsytes knew little of the Great Outdoors. We see this when Soames arrives to choose the site for his house in the country: 'Soames, the pioneer leader of the great Forsyte army advancing to the civilization of this wilderness, felt his spirit daunted by the loneliness, by the invisible singing, and the hot sweet air.' Larks spring up at his feet and the air is full of butterflies and there is a sweet fragrance from the wild grasses. But Soames pays no attention to them, or to the scent of the bracken, or to the pigeons cooing nearby. He walks with his eyes on the ground, congratulating himself on the bargain that he is about to make with the house agent.

Yet in contrast to Soames, many upper-middle-class families were showing during the second half of the nineteenth century an increasing interest in 'Nature': not merely in the Nature of the tropics, the arctic or the great plains, but of their own fields and woods. The Commons, Open Spaces and Footpaths Preservation Society had been founded in 1865 and the National Trust followed in 1895.

The inhabitants of large cities such as London or Manchester, who found it increasingly difficult to reach real country even on Sunday, soon learned that a stroll on the asphalt of a municipal park was no substitute for swinging down the lane. A kind of nostalgia afflicted both those who, as they grew up, had been forced to renounce the pleasures of the countryside, and those who had heard about the outdoor world only from their parents; and, with improved education, there came a desire to be able to recognize the birds, insects, fishes, plants and trees seen in schoolbooks, and to know more of their behaviour.

The writings of Richard Jefferies helped to some extent to bridge the gap between town and country. Jefferies, the son of a Wiltshire yeoman farmer, was born in 1848 at Coate Farm near Swindon. He was a withdrawn romantic, who, during his walks on the downs around Marlborough, dreamed of something better than the life of a farm labourer. Understandably so. For the goods which Britain exported to the world in the nineteenth century were being paid for with cheap imported food – wheat from Canada and the United States, corned and frozen beef and lamb from Australia and New Zealand – and furthermore the newly discovered margarine was becoming a threat to the livelihood of the dairy herdsman. Many English farms had been allowed to run down, their drainage choked and their soil overworked.

Jefferies, indeed, thought of escaping to Moscow with a friend, but they turned back soon after landing in France. He ran away to America but got no further than Liverpool. He became a reporter on the *North Wilts Herald*, and wrote novels about fashionable folk, about whom he knew practically nothing. But a letter of his, several thousand words long, about the plight of the farmworkers in Wiltshire, was published in *The Times* and the realism and authority with which it was written attracted immediate attention. Soon his articles on countrymen and the countryside began appearing regularly in magazines. My own copy of *The Life of the Fields*, published by Chatto and Windus in 1889, includes pieces which had previously appeared in *Longman's Maga-* zine, *The Graphic*, *The Standard*, *The Magazine of Art*, *The Gentleman's Magazine*, *The St James's Gazette*, the *National Review*, the *Manchester Guardian* and the *Pall Mall Gazette* and so would very likely have met the eye of more than one club-haunting Forsyte and almost certainly of the 'Dromios'.

Part of Jefferies' appeal was his knowledge of the inner workings of the countryside as seen through the eyes of the gamekeeper, the poacher, the shepherd or the woodcutter. He

The National Trust was founded in 1895. The Old Clergy House, Alfriston, Sussex the first building to be taken into their care

turned an outing into an adventure as he described the ways of animals – rabbits, pheasants, pigeons, hawks and foxes. His books were not manuals of instruction but invitations to see, hear, feel and smell all the treasures he had discovered.

Jefferies suffered in sympathy with the farm labourers and the workhouse inmates – about whose hardships he wrote with passion – and perhaps with damage to his own credit with his leisured readers. Some even regarded his nature-worship as a form of atheism.

But when portraying the countryside he romanticized only what he saw and was impatient of those who discerned a Merrie England without trees that drip on the wayfarer, wet grass that clings round his ankles, chalk that sticks to the boots like mortar, or damp mist that chills the soul.

After pointing out in one of his articles that the threshing machine which works out in the open air is not less interesting than the old-fashioned flail which could only be wielded in a barn, that the mowing machine is no more ugly than the scythe it replaced, and that the reaping machine has as much colour as men with reaping hooks, Jefferies went on to say:

It is, I venture to think, a mistake on the part of some who depict the country scenes on canvas that they omit these modern aspects, doubtless under the impression that to admit them would impare the pastoral scene intended to be conveyed. So many pictures and so many illustrations proceed on the assumption that the steam plough and the reaping machine do not exist, that the landscape contains nothing but what it did a hundred years ago. These sketches are often beautiful, but they lack the force of truth and reality. Everyone who has been fifty miles into the country, if only by rail, knows while looking at them that they are not real. You feel that there is something wanting, you do not know what. That something is the hard angular fact which at once makes the sky above it appear likewise a fact. Why omit fifty years from the picture?

Jefferies became seriously ill in 1881 and spent the last few years of his life at the village of Goring, near Worthing, in Sussex, where doctors hoped that he might benefit from the mild climate. And it was there, as a tribute to Jefferies, that another great Victorian naturalist W. H. Hudson asked to be buried.

Like Jefferies, Hudson suffered from ill health and was brought home to England from Argentina after suffering from bouts of typhus and rheumatic fever. Like Jefferies, he lived all his life close to the poverty line. Years of his life were passed in London for he married a woman, Emily Wingate, fifteen years older than himself who established a boarding house at 11 Leinster Square. It failed. She set up another in Southwick Crescent and it, too, had to be abandoned. Finally in 1901, Hudson, at the age of sixty, was granted a civil pension of £150 a year which allowed him to wander and write, as he had always wanted to do, about the British countryside. In the world of letters he was greatly helped by Edward Garnett the literary critic who also assisted Galsworthy.

People went to the countryside for other reasons than to study nature and build homes. Some were holidaymakers. The first holiday meeting-places were spas such as Harrogate or Bath, described by Jane Austen. These rendezvous were so well patronized that Marshall and Snelgrove and other London stores set up branches there. But resorts that possessed no healing springs soon claimed that the sea was just as good for the constitution and much more fun. Thackeray and the Prince Regent had popularized Brighton and Dickens did as much for Broadstairs – the place to which old Jolyon was to take June after her disappointment with Bosinney.

Margate pier, originally a jetty for fishing boats and grain hoys bound for London, was rebuilt in 1810 and rebuilt again after the great storm of 1877. But by 1873 the beach there already had its kites, its goat-carts, its telescopes for hire and relatives buried up to their necks in sand to make a children's holiday. At that

'There were fewer than fifty self-declared seaside resorts'
(*above*) Punch and Judy Show on the beach at Ilfracombe, 1894; photograph by Paul Martin
(*right*) Aldeburgh, August, 1903

time there were fewer than fifty self-declared seaside resorts on the coast; but within twenty years there were four times as many, including fifty-seven in the south-west of England alone. Factory owners who arranged trips to the seaside for their staffs found that production, instead of falling as a result of the day off, actually increased. Employers encouraged workers to join holiday saving schemes, and social workers felt confident enough to start campaigning for holidays with pay. *The Queen* magazine could be depended on to advise on the relative social standing and merits of Scarborough and St Leonards, Teignmouth and Whitby.

Thomas Cook, the Baptist wood-turner, was already in business as a travel agent in the

Midlands in the early 1840s, and in 1855 had branched out into packaged tours abroad, though British shipping companies, as long as they were prosperous, did not have the surplus vessels for cruises.

Gradually, holidays which had once been regarded purely as a kind of restorative or period of convalescence, were spent with a more definite object in view: sketching perhaps, or sailing or mountaineering.

The holiday spirit had its effect on clothes after the turn of the century. Men threw off their waistcoats and braces at the seaside and wore a belt or a cummerbund instead. On the beach they wore a Panama hat, or a 'boater', or even one of those almost peakless cricket caps close to the skull. Women's bathing costumes,

'The river Thames was a favoured resort for those who had time enough to get there'; photograph by Paul Martin

as drawn by Du Maurier in the 1890s, featured a high bodice, short puff sleeves and knickerbockers. Men's bathing dresses were often fitted with half-sleeves. There was no 'kippering' or sun-bathing; in fact women wore floppy hats partly to protect their complexion from the sun.

London itself was becoming something of a tourist centre and a point of departure for excursions. In 1898 the London, Brighton and South Coast Railway introduced a Sunday Pullman Car service from London which reached Brighton in sixty minutes (roughly the same time it takes today). By 1902 char-a-banc trips were offered from Trafalgar Square to Kew Gardens, and Hampton Court, Sundays included.

The river Thames was a favoured resort for those who had time enough to get there, and Jerome K. Jerome's *Three Men in a Boat* which appeared in 1889 must have launched a thousand skiffs. Soames eventually had a punt of his own, though he would never have slept on it. A day on the river was more in his line and he would probably have worn boating flannels for the occasion. For day-trippers a very convenient train left Paddington for Maidenhead every Sunday morning at 10.30 and R. D. Blumenfeld who used it in 1887 noticed about five thousand people waiting for trains with men and women all in white and wearing 'boater' straw hats.

Naturally the tourists who visited London (and George Sims, the well-informed editor of *Living London*, reckoned that in 1902 the capital was host to 120,000 visitors every day) expected to be well lodged. Some hotels, still surviving today were already established – among them Claridges and Brown's Hotel in Dover Street and the Savoy which at first had only a river entrance. The Langham Hotel, now used by the BBC, had already been opened by the Prince of Wales, and the Carlton Hotel (now New Zealand House) was equally famous for the cuisine of its chef Georges Escoffier, who, while previously at the Savoy, had created Pêche Melba in honour of the world-famed singer. The Ritz Hotel made its début in 1906, replacing the Bath Hotel which up till the turn of the century still used candles and tin baths filled by hand.

Holidays and tourism also meant family photographs, albums of which, like Aunt Juley's album of seaweed, could be seen in most upper-class late-Victorian drawing-rooms. Pioneers had been experimenting for at least fifty years with various chemical compounds which, they had discovered, were sensitive to light; and in 1826 Joseph Niepce had produced an image on a metal plate coated with light-sensitive asphaltium. Louis-Jacques-Mandé Daguerre, a French artist, had succeeded around 1839 in producing Daguerreotypes by a process in which the image was recorded on a silver-coated plate sensitized with iodine vapour and then developed with mercury vapour. The main disadvantage of this was that it was a 'one-off' affair; that is, you could not produce copies without taking a fresh picture of the original.

An English country gentleman, William Fox Talbot, solved the problem. Talbot, who was fond of painting, had decided while on holiday in Como in 1833 to try out a new device for making 'sketches' of the scenery which could be worked up into finished pictures later. His first idea was to use a 'pin-hole' camera, a box with a small hole or, better still, a lens through which rays of light passed, reproducing, as scientists had long been aware, an image of the scene in front of it. Talbot arranged for the image to be projected on to a sheet of paper, waxed to make it transparent so that he could see it for himself; he hoped that it would be possible to preserve the picture he saw by pencilling in the lines on 'his' side of the transparent sheet.

When this proved to be only partially successful he decided to improve on it by recording a negative image (i.e. white represented as black and vice versa) on paper coated with silver iodide to make it light-sensitive. By 1835 he had realized that by repeating the

'Soames would probably have worn boating flannels for the occasion'. Advertisement from *The Graphic*, 10 April 1886

same process he could turn the negative back into a positive. Later, by developing the negative, with gallic acid, fixing it with 'hypo' (sodium thiosulphate) and using silver chloride paper, he was able to produce almost any number of positive contact prints about one inch square (which he called calotypes) from a single negative. His process, which amounted to the foundation of modern photography was patented in 1841. In 1844 Talbot produced the world's first book with photographic illustrations – *The Pencil of Nature*. An exposure lasting five minutes in bright sunshine at a stop of f.8 was required for these early photographs.

As new and more effective chemicals were discovered for developing the picture, glass plates replaced paper. At first these plates had to be coated with a light-sensitive solution of gun cotton dissolved in ether. But collodion, as it was called, dried very rapidly and had to be applied to each plate separately shortly before exposure. It was therefore useless for the so-called 'instantaneous' pictures which the researchers hoped would soon be possible. It was 1879 before an effective dry plate came into general use. The camera itself was at first a bulky object, depending on a tripod for support, and Roger Fenton, founder of the Photographic Society of London (now the Royal Photographic Society of Great Britain), deemed it necessary to travel with thirty-six

large chests of equipment when he set out to take his historic photographs of the Crimean War. Despite these handicaps, photography thrived, and one of the most successful practitioners was Mrs Julia Margaret Cameron who set up her studio in the chicken shed and her dark room in the cellar of her house on the Isle of Wight. To her we owe portraits of Tennyson, Browning, Darwin, Carlyle and others. Lewis (*Alice in Wonderland*) Carroll was also one of the earlier cameramen and took photographs of Dante Gabriel Rossetti as well as of his favourite, Beatrice Henley, daughter of the Vicar of Putney. Lord Walter Campbell added a touch of class to the hobby with his 'Portrait of Mrs Finney lying on a Couch', the public display of which led no doubt to a good deal of talk about Mrs Finney.

For the general public, including the Forsytes, the real turning point came around 1889 with the arrival of the first hand camera for use with roll film; it was not only compact and light, but would yield a comparatively large number of exposures without reloading. With it, the word snapshot, originally used to describe a hurried gun or rifle shot taken without considered aim, acquired an added and equally appropriate meaning. There would now be photographs rather than new miniatures of the latest Forsyte generation displayed for visitors to see in Forsyte drawing-rooms.

'Holidays and tourism also meant family photographs'

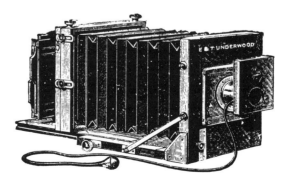

Pre-War Childhood

One of the youngest of the fifth generation of Forsytes was Jon, son of young Jolyon, whom we meet in the day nursery at Robin Hill in 1909. The boy, eight years old, is awaiting the return from Ireland of his mother, Irene, and father.

Jon, an only child, was born of a mother thirty-eight years old and a father fifty-four years old (Galsworthy apparently slipped up here in making young Jolyon a father at fifty-two in contradiction to the clear evidence of the family tree), and one might therefore have expected the young boy to be rather serious for his age and perhaps introspective. But this does not appear to have been the case, as his most immediate worry, we are told, was how best to slide down the banisters from the nursery to the hall.

He is dressed in a blue linen suit, and Bella, the maid, looks critically at his bare knees, suspecting, wrongly for once, that they might have been green from tree-climbing, or muddy. He seems, therefore, to have escaped from the tyranny of the sailor suit and the velvet or velveteen knickerbockers which he might have been expected to wear, on this particular day, to welcome the return of his parents.

The day nursery from which young Jon was descending is not described in detail, but, formerly, if not now, it would have been isolated from the banisters by a wicket gate. Inside there would have been a solid deal table, sometimes covered with a cloth stained with ink and paint-water, a wire fireguard

three feet high round the fireplace probably with some clothes hung on it to dry, a book case, and a large chest filled with toys; and on the floor, linoleum or the oldest carpet in the house. There might also have been a rocking-chair for 'Da' who had been Jon's nanny, but perhaps not a rocking-horse for Jon as he had his own pony.

As to books, we are given a fairly full account of what young Jon had been reading. He first took to print during an attack of what sounded like measles, when June came down to help nurse him, bringing with her some books that had helped to feed her Berserker spirit some twenty years earlier. They led him to dream of 'midshipmen and dhows, pirates, rafts, sandal-wood traders, iron horses, sharks, battles, Tartars, Red Indians, balloons, North Poles and other extravagant delights'. June would probably have been too old to have appreciated Beatrix Potter's *Peter Rabbit* when it appeared in 1900 but may have assumed that young Jon already knew Squirrel Nutkin and Mrs Tiggy Winkle. The same might have been said of Kenneth Grahame's *The Wind in the Willows* which first appeared in 1908. It is also clear that the older Victorian stories with a moral, such as Dean Farrar's *Eric or Little by Little* or *Katie Brightside and How She Made the Best of Everything* were not to be found in June's personal lending library. Bitter experience had taught children, and some parents too, including perhaps old Jolyon, June's grandfather who had brought her up,

that Moral Instruction and Education were one thing and Entertainment another.

Almost certainly, however, G. A. Henty would have been on June's book-list. He had seen death and glory at first hand, having been a war correspondent in the Austro-Italian war of 1866, the Ethiopian war of 1867, the Franco-Prussian war of 1870 and the Ashanti campaign of 1873. He was also prepared to range further afield in such works as *Out in the Pampas* and *The Tiger of Mysore*. R. M. Ballantyne who had been a clerk in the service of the Hudson's Bay Company, and had actually traded with the Indians, was another writer with the necessary background, and willing, as in the case of his bestseller *The Coral Island*, to be as global as Henty.

Jon's father, in an attempt to 'steady his imagination', next brought him *Ivanhoe*, *Bevis*, *Tom Brown's Schooldays* and a book about King Arthur. Clearly Frances Burnett's *Little Lord Fauntleroy*, first published as a book in 1886, stood little chance, if only because young Jolyon

(opposite) 'The sailor suit'
(above) 'As to books, we are given a fairly full account of what young Jon had been reading'

would not have been in sympathy with its Forsytean philosophy. It was crowded out by Tom Sawyer and Huckleberry Finn. Kipling and Stevenson were absentees, too, apparently, and likewise the famous *Boys' Own Paper*, founded by James Macaulay in 1879, not to speak of the highly popular *Children's Encyclopaedia* which Arthur Mee had begun in 1908.

At the time we first meet Jon, he was marshalling armies of tin soldiers with which to re-fight the great campaigns of history on the floor of the day-nursery; outdoors, he lay in wait with a deadly pea-shooter for whatever targets he could ambush. Marbles are also mentioned but not conkers (it was still July), and tops and hoops were toys more suitable for the pavements of London than for the terrain of Robin Hill.

We know that young Jolyon 'thanked Heaven' that his son had no turn for wheels or engines, which accounts for the fact that there is no mention either of the toy construction system christened Meccano in 1907, or of the quality toy steam engines which Mr W. J. Bassett-Lowke of Northampton had been producing since 1901. Collecting birds' eggs or butterflies would have been contrary to young Jolyon's ideas on conservation, and there was no one with whom Jon would have been able to swap cigarette cards or stamps.

A child of 1901, he [Jon] had come to consciousness when his country, just over that bad attack of scarlet fever, the Boer War, was preparing for the Liberal revival of 1906. Coercion was unpopular, parents had exalted notions of giving their offspring a good time. They spoiled their rods, spared their children, and anticipated the results with enthusiasm.

Galsworthy was right in his analysis of the

'Terrible encounter with a shark'; illustration in *The Coral Island*

spirit of the age. It was, indeed, more than ten years since the Lincolnshire Board of Guardians had been cross-examined by the Local Government Board as to the number of currants put into children's puddings. And had not Mr G. Archibald, a child specialist in Montreal, declared in 1904: 'Whenever you say "Don't" to a child you crush the creative instinct within him, which is the richest and most precious thing he has'? The wind of change was indeed blowing aside the nursery curtains.

Already, in 1892, a well-thought-out plan had been set in motion to improve the standards of child nursing. The Norland Nursing Institute, which advocated some revolutionary theories of child management, had been established in Bayswater by Mrs Walter Ward. It propagated the undreamed-of-idea that child-nurses must be trained, and that it was not enough for them to rely on the experience of the mother or of her aged household retainers. By 1903 it had been laid down that the training programme for children's nurses should include three months of domestic and theoretical instruction at the Norland Institute, followed by three months' practical service in a Children's Hospital or Babies' Home. Another three months' instruction in Domestic Science and Teaching followed at the Norland Institute, and then a year's work as under-nurse to a trained Norland nurse or some-one of equal ability. Probationers who stayed the course qualified for a certificate of proficiency.

But this was not the end of the story. Norland nurses who took jobs were paid, not by the employer, but by the Institute. The employers paid the Institute and, in practice, developed a special relationship with it. The child's mother, for example, regularly signed a Testimonial Book which was forwarded to the Institute for inspection, and mothers were invited to contribute to the Institute's *Quarterly Magazine* and to say what, in their opinion, counted most in the relationship between nurse and child and mother and nurse. Young girls, one mother pointed out, were apt to forget to turn down their beds, air the bedroom, to ventilate the schoolroom, and to tidy up the nursery hearth. Sometimes they came in late from walks, on which they had set out without taking an umbrella or making sure that their charges were well wrapped up. Sometimes they brought mud into the house. (No doubt these ancillary points were thereafter re-emphasized in the training schedule.)

The *Quarterly Magazine* also proclaimed some doctrines, particularly on the question of punishment, which must have been anathema to the more old-fashioned brand of nanny. The old nursery tyrants would also have disagreed violently with the advice, reprinted from the magazine *Childlife*, given in the Norland *Quarterly* of June 1902, that the nurse should not strive for victory over the child but rather get the child to see its own interests by winning victory over itself.

And there are other notions equally disturbing to the peace of the old-time nursery: the suggestion that the beloved carpets might be a germ and death trap, that every ray of sunshine should be admitted to the nursery since it was better to have faded cretonnes than a faded child, that nurses should interest the child in silkworms or an aquarium, as well as in paper folding, cane and rush weaving and clay or (cleaner) plasticine modelling.

'Nurse'; Harrods Catalogue, 1895

Well, whatever might be thought or not thought in England about such doctrines, they soon caught on abroad, and by 1906 Norland nurses were writing back to the *Quarterly* from Sweden, Hong Kong, Ceylon, Naples, Philadelphia and the Sultan of Turkey's Yildiz Palace, in which Miss Kate Fox had stayed while nanny in the household of H.R.H. Prince Nicholas of Greece.

But there were no signs of such modernity having penetrated to Robin Hill. On the contrary Jon's nurse, to whom Galsworthy had attached the faintly ridiculous name of Spraggins, was clearly an old-type family servant. Jon knew her as 'Da' which suggests that she had been with him since before he could talk. 'Da' would have been paid around £30 a year with all found, including the violet uniform she wore on Sundays.

Her prospects and influence, however, would have been on the decline since the beginning of the century. The perfect inflorescence of the British nanny occurred towards the end of the nineteenth century at a time when families were too improbably large for parents to manage by themselves while the imperial opulence of the day made it unnecessary for them to do so. By 1909, however, the conditions which were essential for the pervasive power of nannydom were slowly vanishing. Families were becoming smaller and taxation began to affect the upper classes and even to some extent the very rich, limiting the number of servants that could be kept. There was evidence of a do-it-yourself trend in the first school for mothers established as a child welfare centre in St Pancras in 1907.

Jon's nanny would have had to keep on good terms with Jane, the cook, who would have to provide separate dishes for her and Jon in addition to what was served in the main dining-room. Indeed in some ways the cook was a rival for the friendship and affection of young Jon, who, we are told, visited the kitchen each morning after lessons for a thin

(*left*) and (*below*) 'Nannies saw children as dwarf adults'

enclosure at the time the young raspberries were ripening. Bob, the Forsytes' groom, could be a disturbing influence with the songs that he used to play on his concertina and with his horsey talk. 'Mamselle', the French governess, was less of a problem, since she came for only two hours a day and, being foreign, could not command the respect which would have been due to an English governess.

Finally, there was the relationship between 'Da', the parents and Jon. Young Jolyon, of course, who was sixteen years older than Irene, had the *laissez-faire* tolerance of a man who had already brought up two families with two different wives and, having broken away from his father to take up first insurance and then painting, had tested through his own experience the limited effectiveness of parental advice. In other respects the relationship seems to have been the one normally prevailing in upper-middle-class houses. The mother appears as a relatively distant, fragrant-smelling angel of sweetness and light, who dispenses grace and favour in addition to more substantial treats at all too infrequent intervals. Irene was prepared to offer counsel to her small son on such matters as what constituted beauty and why people did or did not go to church and to give music lessons, but she stopped short of giving up too much of her time.

Edwardian mothers when they visited the nursery, which was seldom enough, liked to pretend that they were all-knowing. But in fact they hesitated to make a confidante of the nanny for fear of causing resentment among the rest of the staff and so learned comparatively little about nursery life.

And so it was from nanny that Jon sought affection day by day and hers was the responsibility of seeing that he did not become spoilt. Even in Edwardian days, nannies saw children as dwarf adults, possessing a capacity for evil which it was the nurse's mission to eradicate before the child grew up – or died, as so many must have done, unshriven. In an

slice of cheese, a biscuit and two French plums. 'Da' would have to establish a close relationship with Bella, the maid, who would carry the dishes from the kitchen to the table and fetch them away afterwards. Garratt, the gardener, had also to be placated especially if young Jon ran across the flower beds or invaded the fruit effort to comply, the more severe guardians invented new rules which had to be observed, treating constipation as obstinacy and loss of appetite as disobedience. They doled out discouragement rather than praise to prevent the child from 'showing off', thus making their charges even more anxious to win praise through exhibitionism.

ROYAL WORCESTER CORSET WAISTS
Don't forget, in overhauling your children's wardrobes, that the corsets want very careful attention. We don't mean only because they may be worn. The same size does not do from one term to another, and besides, the figure alters.

(*above*) and (*above right*) 'Little girls were wearing the same kind of "grown-up" dresses with puffed sleeves'

There is no evidence that 'Da' regularly went to extreme lengths to enforce obedience from Jon; but cold baths and bare knees are mentioned as part of the hardening process to which young Jon was subjected, and there was one occasion, shortly before Jon was seven, when 'Da' held him down on his back while he screamed impotently for nearly a minute.

Little girls, like little boys, were dressed as midget adults as we see from an advertisement in the February 1909 issue of *Baby*:

We also notice that little girls in the days of Edward VII were wearing the same kind of 'grown-up' dresses with puffed sleeves and lace trimming that they had worn in the nineties. The bonnets that they were supposed to wear when out walking were still elaborate pieces of nonsense. Gloves which could be of Cape kid or doeskin, lisle thread, taffeta or silk, were worn on various occasions with up to six buttons.

So when Fleur appears in person for the first time in the Saga at the age of eighteen and a half, some people at least might not have noticed how much she had altered since childhood.

Forsytes at Oxford

The sons of the Forsyte class had no difficulty in obtaining places at university. Val Dartie, Soames's nephew, and Jolly Forsyte, the older son of young Jolyon, were undergraduates together at Oxford during the early months of the Boer War. They found there an atmosphere quite different from that of their public schools and even more different from the polytechnic sweat-shop atmosphere that they would meet at Oxbridge today.

Bernard Shaw once wrote: 'When a man teaches something he does not know to somebody else who has no aptitude for it, and gives him a certificate of proficiency, the latter has completed the education of a gentleman.' And in the case of the Forsyte undergraduates if not also of the dons, he came perilously close to the truth. At any rate the Warden of St Mary's, that mythical foundation attended, most probably in the 1890s, by Michael Fane, the hero of Compton Mackenzie's *Sinister Street*, concluded his address to newly arrived Freshmen with the following exhortation:

You have come to Oxford, some of you to hunt foxes, some of you to wear very large and very unusual overcoats, some of you to row for your college and a few of you to work. But all of you have come to Oxford to remain English gentlemen. In after life when you are ambassadors and proconsuls and Members of Parliament you will never remember this little address which I have the honour of delivering to you. That will not matter, so long as you always remember that you are St Mary's men and the heirs of an honourable and ancient foundation.

It was said by irreverent undergraduates to have been the very same speech that the 'Wagger' had made for the past twenty years, but it would surely have gladdened the Forsyte family, who would have felt that they were really getting their money's worth for the not very exorbitant fees then charged for residence and tuition.

At any rate, though neither Jolly nor Val belonged to St Mary's – Jolly was at 'the House' (Christ Church) and Val at B.N.C. (Brasenose) – they had been profiting from the Wagger's advice when they met on a November afternoon in 1899:

Jolly Forsyte was strolling down High Street, Oxford ... Val Dartie was strolling up. Jolly had just changed out of boating flannels and was on his way to the 'Frying-pan', to which he had recently been elected. Val had just changed out of riding clothes and was on his way to the fire – a bookmaker's in Cornmarket.

They had met the evening before at a roulette party, though they disagreed over whether it was right or not to play. All good gentlemanly stuff.

But of course Oxford was not given over entirely to dissipation. In those days it was relatively isolated from London, and therefore better adapted to scholarly pursuits. There were fewer undergraduates than today and no cars to take them out of Oxford most evenings and at weekends. There were no tourists, no punts on the Cherwell carrying transistor sets

'But all of you have come to Oxford to remain English gentlemen'

or even portable gramophones. The undergraduates took most of their meals, except dinner and Sunday breakfast, in their own rooms. Dinner in college was early – often at half past six – and there was little need, therefore, for afternoon tea. Nor had the time-consuming custom of mid-morning coffee been introduced. Eights Week and Commemoration Week, both celebrated towards the end of the summer term, were the occasions on which parents and girlfriends were most likely to visit the university.

The freshman arriving for his first day in college would bring with him a kettle, a coal scuttle and a tin bath, to be filled with cold water, which stood permanently in his bedroom. Sometimes he brought some decanters too.

Top hats and morning coats were still worn on Sundays, when country walks if not study in solitude were the chief occupation. Women undergraduates, when they attended lectures, were accompanied by chaperons. The idea of married undergraduates was unthinkable.

Talking shop, making puns or quoting from the classics were forbidden at Hall meals on pain of being 'sconced', that is, being called on to pay for (or drink at a single draught) a formidable measure of beer. Discussions on general topics – the world, women and sport – were often carried on in the Junior Common Room, where magazines and newspapers were also to be found; and more serious topics were dealt with in the political and literary clubs which existed in many colleges.

On the whole, there were fewer ex-grammar school boys with their way to make, and fewer older undergraduates than we find today. And life was probably less earnest.

But the gambling party which Val and Jolly had attended was probably exceptional; and entertainment among the less affluent might amount to little more than a glass or two of mulled claret after dinner – or even hot cocoa. Rowing, Rugby football or tennis were the

popular sports; little golf was played, and the unathletic went for walks by the upper river to Godstow or perhaps to Cumnor or Boar's Hill, or by the river to Eynsham.

Oxford dons were also rather different from their successors today. The early-Victorian understanding was that once a man had been elected a Fellow of the College, he retained his position until he died or married. Many of the Fellows of All Souls had secured the honour by virtue of kinship with the family of the founder. One of them, Charles Wrottesley, was a fox-hunting squire. Another, Dr Henry Bertie, had held a living in Essex for forty years and had then retired, half paralysed in the legs, to All Souls, bringing with him an aged drunkard of a butler, on whom he was almost entirely dependent. It was not until 1856 that the Universities Act, requiring candidates for Fellowships to have obtained either a First Class Honours degree or a University Prize, came into effect.

Dr James Sewell, who retained his post as Warden of New College till 1903, long after he had passed the age of ninety, had never taken an Honour School and knew very little indeed about the newer Faculties of Science and History. He once showed friends a pair of spectacles which his father and aunt had induced him to buy more than fifty years earlier on the grounds that he might be endangering his sight by travelling in trains moving at thirty or forty miles an hour.

Val Dartie told Holly Forsyte, Jolly's younger sister, whom he was eventually to marry, that the lectures he was supposed to attend were 'nothing', and he may well have been right. Dr Ernest Barker who was at Oxford in the 1890s recalled that he was regularly the only man attending the course of lectures on the

Odes of Pindar given by Professor D. S. Margoliouth. Some dons were noticeably cavalier in their ways, and Professor Yorke Powell, a specialist in Icelandic and Scandinavian history, used to disappear for long periods during term time without leaving an address. During the hard winter of 1895 when most of the Thames was frozen solid, many dons suspended their tutorials altogether in order to go skating on Port Meadow.

The arch-don William Archibald Spooner would have been in residence in New College at the time when Val and Jolly were undergraduates. Spooner was an albino, and extremely short-sighted, and there is a well-authenticated story that he once mistook a black hen for his top hat (which the wind had blown off) and chased it over a garden wall. His 'spoonerisms' have been so widely circulated that it is difficult to be sure which of them are genuine and which have been concocted by others. The transpositions which occurred when Spooner had to 'rusticate' (temporarily send down) an erring undergraduate do, however, have a genuine ring: 'Mr -----,' he said, 'You have tasted a whole worm up here. You have hissed your mystery lectures and you have been caught fighting a liar in the quad. You will leave this university by the next town drain.' (It should be explained that lighting bonfires, or 'bonners', in the college quadrangle was one of the traditional occupations to which 'hearties' devoted their energies even as late as the 1920s.)

In the Forsyte context, the meetings between Val and Jolly, personifying the enmity between the two rival branches of the family, constituted the main interest to be found in the university. There was already the hint of a match between Val and Holly, taking place under Jolyon's nose and this was followed by Jolly's challenge to Val, a 'dare' which led them both to enlist as Soldiers of the Queen in the Boer War. It was as much as could be expected from two Forsytes in *statu pupillari*.

(*opposite above*) The Oxford crew 1896
(*opposite below*) 'Eights Week and Commemoration Week were the occasions on which parents and girlfriends were most likely to visit the university'

Family Scandals

One of the worries that most preoccupied Val Dartie during his time at Oxford was the fear that the details of the proposed divorce between his parents would be revealed by the newspapers to his friends.

The day before he was to go up to the university for the first time, he had ridden in Richmond Park with Holly Forsyte, and then after a hot bath at home came downstairs and found his mother, scrupulous in a low-necked evening dress, and, to his annoyance, his Uncle Soames.

They stopped talking when he came in; then his uncle said:

'He'd better be told.'

At those words, which meant something about his father, of course, Val's first thought was of Holly. Was it anything beastly? His mother began speaking.

'Your father,' she said in her fashionably appointed voice, while her fingers plucked rather pitifully at sea-green brocade, 'your father, my dear boy, has – is not at Newmarket; he's on his way to South America. He – he's left us.' . . .

Val took out a cigarette. His father had bought him that thin curved case. Oh! it was unbearable – just as he was going up to Oxford!

In 1899 a divorce in the Forsyte family signified something more than a conflict of loyalties. It involved also a loss of social status, and Val's concern about this was expressed even before he knew the details of his father's escapade, details which rendered the affair ludicrous as well as distressing.

The divorce courts, of course, were already two generations old when Winifred decided to make use of them. Up until the middle of the nineteenth century the outlook for a girl who had made a mistake in her marriage was unpromising. She had no remedy even if her husband committed adultery. Marriage questions were dealt with by the ecclesiastical courts and although the church could agree to sponsor a separation, it could not, without being false to its beliefs, annul a marriage. For this a special Act of Parliament was required, an operation far too expensive for the average wife.

However in 1850 a Royal Commission was set up to examine 'the law relating to matrimonial offences', and in 1857 some changes were introduced. Marriage disputes were taken out of the hands of the Ecclesiastical Court and transferred to a Statutory Court set up for the purpose of dealing with divorce petitions. It was competent to grant both legal separation and, for the first time, a complete divorce from the bond of marriage.

An aggrieved husband could petition for a divorce on the ground of a wife's adultery provided that he renounced his right to sue the co-respondent. Wives were still at some disadvantage. If a wife wished to divorce a husband she must prove not only that he had committed adultery but had also in addition been guilty of either incest, bigamy, cruelty, or some other equally heinous offence or of desertion lasting two years. This period, however, might be reduced if the respondent failed within six months to obey a Court order for the restitution of conjugal rights – for which Winifred Dartie successfully applied. These limitations remained in force until 1923 and a total of 7321 actions for divorce were brought during the first thirty years after they came into force.

But, if women were to be allowed not only to earn worthwhile salaries but also to marry again, it was vital in their interests to make certain that a woman's worldly goods were not committed for life to her original husband. Up until 1857 husband and wife were legally one person, represented by the husband.

Margaret Tyzack as Winifred

Consequently a woman, once married, was incapable of acquiring, enjoying or parting with any property or personal possessions. The husband might sell off her leaseholds and keep the proceeds. He could control and manage her estates and, if she died before he did, he became entitled to any personal property which she possessed at the time of her death, and also to a life interest in her freehold estates if a child had been born.

A man could not even make a grant to his wife, or enter into a covenant with her, as this would have amounted to admitting that she was legally a person. Exceptions to this occurred where a husband had agreed to sign a special contract with his bride-to-be before they married or where property had been bestowed on her with the express provision that it should be for her separate use. But her only other remedy was to apply to the courts for a special arrangement on the grounds of equity – a procedure which involved an expensive and possibly distressing legal wrangle.

From 1857 onwards, however, the law provided that if a woman was deserted by her husband, or lived apart from him under a decree of judicial separation, she could exercise her rights as if she had been single in respect of property acquired by her after the desertion had taken place or the decree of separation awarded. Moreover, if either of them re-married these assets still remained in the wife's possession. And such rights, limited though they were, did not depend on a Court of Equity but were explicit statutory rights.

Next, an Act passed in 1870 handed out further privileges. Permission was given to a married woman to retain her earnings, and some forms of deposit, even if no desertion or separation had taken place. Moreover, any woman married after 9 August 1870 might also claim the rents and profits of property inherited by her as next-of-kin or as heiress through an intestacy; she might also retain any amount up to £200 which might be devised to her by deed or in a will.

The really vital change came, however, not, as Galsworthy appeared to believe, in 1870 but in 1882 under a new Act which allowed any woman marrying after that date to retain all property owned by her at the time of her marriage and to use it without the intervention of a trustee. Those women who were already married in 1882 could retain any property acquired after that date.

It took some time, however, for the ladies of Britain to establish their rights over their own bodies. As recently as 1891 a Mr Jackson, who detained his wife, albeit with every consideration for her welfare, at home to prevent her from returning to her relations, was supported in the Lower Court though he lost out on appeal; and in 1932, years after World War I, Mr Justice McCardie, 'the bachelor judge', was telling the jury in the 'Helen of Troy' enticement case to consider the almost revolutionary proposition that, since Mrs Place was a free agent responsible for her own decisions, she had not been enticed away from her husband by a Dr Searle but had gone of her own free will. 'A woman's body does not belong to the husband,' he said;

It is her own property. A woman can leave her husband by her own will. She may choose her own occupation. She may take her own political party. She may profess her own separate religious creed. She may decide whether she will bear children or not and she may decide when each child shall be born. No man today can make himself the owner of a woman under the guise of a marriage service. The married woman in this country has gained her freedom. She is a citizen and not a serf. She can exercise her own judgment. She can choose her own path. She can decide her own future.

It was significant, however, that when the judge, following this line of reasoning, ruled that there was no evidence on which the jury could find in favour of the aggrieved husband, the Court of Appeal reversed the decision and called for a new trial, as a result of which Mr Place was awarded £500 in damages.

Moreover, the implicit recognition of the legal propriety of divorce by the Divorce Act and Women's Property Acts did not altogether remove the social stigma which it involved. Galsworthy might write later: 'The legend that the good citizen is visited but once by Aphrodite . . . disguised as a good citizenness in a shower of rice and old shoes . . . is the cherished fairy tale of most British and American readers.' But the Victorians continued to set themselves – or allowed their clergy to set for them – an almost unattainable standard of sexual morality, and felt correspondingly guilty when they failed to achieve it. Moreover their sense of sin was especially sharpened where other people were concerned.

For a Forsyte woman, the disadvantage of being involved in a divorce suit lay in the fact that she could not appear at Court, a handicap suffered until the Golden Jubilee by even the so-called innocent party. And appearing at Queen Victoria's drawing-rooms was important even to a Forsyte.

'Thirty years ago,' said Lady Greville in 1892,

none thought of going to Court unless they were great personages for whom it was a duty, or else people connected in some way with the Court through their offices, or, again, country gentlemen and their families wishing to travel abroad, to whom a presentation at Court served as a kind of passport of admittance into good Society, and enabled them to see pageants or objects of interest from which they would otherwise have been debarred. Now, there is no rule or reason for attendance at Court. Rich merchants; people in business; country squires; American cousins; people of no estimation except in their own; people who are never under any possible circumstances likely to be invited to State balls or parties – all these crowd and press and gather together, and think their season in London utterly wasted unless they have made their bow to the Sovereign.

(*opposite*) 'A woman can leave her husband by her own will'; painting, 'Trouble', 1896, by Sir William Orchardson

(*overleaf*) 'A new Act allowed that any woman marrying after 1882 to retain all property owned by her at the time of her marriage and to use it without the intervention of a trustee'. 'Defendant and Counsel', 1895; painting by William Frederick Yeames, R.A.

For mother and daughter alike to be deprived of this solace was indeed a cruel hardship.

'Society', which was normally privy to any divorce proceedings long before they became public knowledge, was rather more tolerant in other directions. Rouge, for instance, had long become as usual in society as on the stage, though the wearer, if asked, would explain that it was the cold wind or the heat of the room that had given her such a good colour. Often scarlet cheeks, combined with black eyebrows and white skin, turned women into Indian idols. Smoking which had already invaded the dining-room, in some cases even between courses, was not confined to men. Women were becoming accustomed to moving about alone – in trains, omnibuses, and cabs – and going for long country walks. Flirtations in which married women took part were more frequent and less subject to reproof. 'Look, dear,' says one woman to another in *Punch* under a caption headed 'Feline Amenities', 'There's your husband going in to supper with Mrs Scudamore – a dangerously attractive woman, let me warn you.' 'How good of you,' replies the other, 'how I wish he were going in to supper with you, dear, instead.' Chaperons in high society had become less vigilant and, at large receptions, it was often impossible, because of the large crowds and the difficulty of moving through them, for a mother to know exactly where her daughter had got to or even, in a large ballroom, with whom she might have been dancing for the past hour.

'At Ascot or Sandown,' as Lady Greville pointed out, perhaps with some exasperation, there is the rambling about in the paddock, nominally to look at the horses, in reality the better to carry on a flirtation; there is the long drawn-out luncheon in the Guards' tent, where, between the strawberries and champagne much nonsense can be talked, and many loving glances given. In country houses there is the intimacy of billiards or lawn-tennis, the rides in country lanes, or the gentle trot home from hunting.

But be that as it may in the country, the mantle of wickedness had not yet been lifted from the Soho district of London where Soames sought a second wife near the turn of the century.

Soho had been something special ever since 1685 when Louis XIV put an end to the religious freedom previously granted to Protestants by the Edict of Nantes. From then onwards, French Protestant Huguenots, whose livelihood and religious practices were threatened by the counter-Reformation, flocked as refugees to Britain, and chose Soho, hitherto undeveloped, as their sanctuary. They were joined by Swiss and later by Italians and other foreigners. In fact, by the time Soames began to frequent the neighbourhood you could find Andalusian castanet clickers, Bulgarian tightrope walkers, Hungarian horsemen, Tyrolese yodellers and Romany violinists as well as ordinary out-of-work actors.

As today, Soho was studded with none too respectable drinking clubs, and also with houses of assignation, dance salons and gambling dens from which in the event of a raid, the clients could escape through a trap door leading to the roof, up a ladder which could be pulled up after them.

In 1907 you could also eat a good three-course dinner of say, Pot-au-Feu, Beefsteak and divinely flavoured foreign cheese or coffee for eight pence, or impress a good-time girl at Kettners, which already had a reputation for its fine wines, food and private rooms.

Soames's more direct connection with Soho began one evening in April when he dropped in to have a look at a house, owned by his father, which had been turned into a restaurant, a transformation which could have reduced the value of the property, and was not, strictly

(opposite) 'It took some time for the ladies of Britain to establish their rights over their own bodies'; 'Diana of the Uplands', 1903, by Charles Wellington Furse

speaking, permitted by the terms of the lease.

He was pleasantly surprised, however, when he saw the outside of the restaurant 'painted a good cream colour, with two peacock-blue tubs containing little bay trees in a recessed doorway' with the words 'Restaurant Bretagne' above in gold letters. Inside, he noted that several people were already seated at little round green tables with pots of fresh flowers on them and Brittany-ware plates. He asked a neatly dressed waitress if he could see the proprietor and was shown into a back room, where a girl was sitting at a bureau covered with papers, and a small round table was laid for two.

While Soames waited for Madame Lamotte to appear, he suddenly noticed that her daughter, Annette, with her cornflower-blue eyes and creamy complexion was so remarkably pretty that he could not take his eyes off her face. 'When she moved to put a chair for him, she swayed in a curious subtle way, as if she had been put together by someone with a special secret skill; and her face and neck looked as fresh as if they had been sprayed with dew.'

In short, Soames was hooked, and began paying visits to Soho more and more often, even though he realized that, if he were ever to marry the girl he would have first to buy out her mother (who was clearly a good business woman) at a fancy price. Nevertheless he asked Madame Lamotte and Annette to spend Sunday with him in the country and Madame was obviously pleased at the development. As soon as he was free to do so he wrote to Madame Lamotte asking for her daughter's hand and inviting them both to stay at his river house. He and Annette were married in Paris six months later, after Soames had settled £15,000 on his new bride.

Soames was proud to present Annette in her Paris frocks to his family; but when Aunt Juley asked her which part of London she knew best and she answered 'Soho', Soames was disconcerted. That reply would go round the family, he thought to himself, and he warned her afterwards how snobbish people in England could be. But Annette, whose judgment he was coming to respect, comforted him by telling him that things were the same in France.

(*opposite*) 'Appearing at
Queen Victoria's drawing-rooms
was important even to a Forsyte';
illustration in *The Graphic*, 1893

(*left*) Soames (Eric Porter) and
Annette (Dallia Penn)

Family Funerals

For the Forsytes and for many others, the death of Queen Victoria was a personal loss, so closely did she conform to middle-class family standards of respectability. Yet the manner of her departure would have deeply shocked the more conventional of her subjects. At her own expressed wish Queen Victoria had a white funeral. She was laid to rest in her coffin, wearing a white dress, her face covered by her white wedding veil, her head by her white widow's cap. The coffin in which she was borne from Osborne to Gosport, to Victoria Station and to Paddington, en route for Windsor, was covered with a white and golden pall. In London the original black hangings were taken down from the lamp-posts and replaced by purple drapes set off with white bows.

Thus the Queen's style of entry into the life to come was sharply at variance with the usage of most of her subjects. Queen Victoria had made a distinction between funerals on the one hand, and private mourning on the other. But to her subjects, rich and poor alike, death meant a profusion of unrelieved black in surroundings as macabre for the corpse as for the mourners. The funeral of the Duke of Wellington in 1852 had set an almost unattainable standard of perfection in military ceremonial, but even private funerals throughout the century displayed a sombre magnificence hardly credible today.

A death in the family, though already foreseen in many cases by the family and neighbours – through the visits of the doctor in his discreet black brougham – was nevertheless formally announced to all friends and acquaintances who might be interested, by mourning cards, recording not only the death but the date, place and time of the funeral. In the meantime hired mourners, dressed in black with long bands of black crape, known as weepers, round their top hats, were stationed before the front door of the afflicted house. Straw was laid outside in the street so that the family's grief should not be disturbed by the noise of passing carts. The door-knocker would also be draped in black crape.

There was deep respect for the body inside, which represented not only the earthly remains of someone loved or respected by contemporaries, but a work created by God, and there was no inclination to hustle it out of the house as quickly as possible. On the contrary, it would remain there to be viewed by relatives.

There might even be mutes hired to watch over the body inside the house – partly as a token of respect, and partly as the traditional expression of a last hope that the deceased's soul might not, after all, have permanently left his body.

On the day of the funeral the family would gather at the dead person's house in preparation for the funeral procession, which would, of course, be a horse-drawn affair. In front of the procession there might be an outrider or two to lead the cortège on the right route and to prepare the bystanders for its passing. Or the conductors might start out on foot carrying wands or batons draped in black. Behind them would come the almsfolk whose function was to entreat not for money but for prayers on behalf of the dead. Then came the relatives in strict order of precedence, the men, like the professional mourners, wearing crape bands round their hats, the ladies in deepest black, veiled, with black gloves and black-edged handkerchiefs held to their eyes. The coaches with the blinds down would be drawn by black horses with magnificently long tails, each animal carrying on its head a plume of black ostrich feathers. The harness and blinkers would be black, and the animal, even in the warmest weather, would be covered in a cloth of black edged with silver.

Next in the procession came the hearse – black, of course – with clear glass sides dis-

'At her own expressed wish Queen Victoria had a white funeral'

closing the coffin, covered with a black pall with wreaths and flowers around it, and perhaps black ostrich feathers above.

Just as in military funerals the warrior's sword would be publicly displayed on a gun carriage, so, in civil funerals, it was not unusual for some treasured possession of the deceased to accompany him at least to the cemetery – a reminder of the days when it was believed that the dead would have to take a thing or two with them if they were to survive in the world to come. Lord Leighton, the Royal Academician, was buried in 1896 with his palette, laid out with colours, brushes and his maulstick – the stick with a soft leather ball at one end, which painters hold in one hand to support the other arm. When Elizabeth, wife of Dante Gabriel Rossetti, the painter and poet, died in 1862, the widower buried the manuscripts of his poems with her, though he later had the body exhumed so that he could recover the precious documents. Sometimes the body itself was decorated with jewellery or even with a special mortuary ring.

As the procession travelled slowly onwards, the men who saw it would doff their hats as a mark of respect for the dead. The slow pace of a funeral march would probably be maintained throughout those prosperous areas of the city where the display could properly be appreciated. But on longer journeys to the more remote cemeteries, the hired retainers, if they had hitherto been on foot, would find a place in the rear carriages with the other mourners and the horses would then proceed at a brisk trot towards the church or chapel where the funeral service was to take place. Anglicans were buried in consecrated ground, Dissenters in unconsecrated and Jews and Roman Catholics usually had their own separate burial grounds. The women of the party would, if they felt strong enough, leave the carriages to attend the funeral service but might or might not care to be present at the interment itself. Then the relatives and close friends would return home for the 'wake' or feast given to friends and loved ones out of the estate of the deceased. The feeling was that death was the culmination of man's life on earth and that his entry into the life hereafter was surely as important an occasion as his birth. The will might then be read.

All the older generation of Forsytes would remember funerals of this order, which not only honoured the dead but afforded a demonstration of the resources and social standing of the living.

The period during which mourning was to be observed varied with the relationship between the mourner and the mourned. 'A widow's mourning is, of course, the deepest, and continued for the longest period', *The Queen* magazine's expert on etiquette advised in 1880.

For the first twelve months the dress and mantle must be of paramatta, the skirt covered with crape, put on in one piece, to within an inch of the waist; sleeves tight to the arm, body entirely covered with crape, tight-fitting lawn cuffs, and deep lawn collar; the mantle or jacket is of the same material as the dress, and very heavily trimmed with crape.

Velvet, satin, lace, bright or glacé silks, embroidery or any fringe excepting a special crape fringe were unsuitable. In short, a kind of sooty texture, matt as opposed to glossy, was aimed at, and this included stockings, and even petticoats, which were occasionally shown, even by a lady of quality when she lifted her skirt out of the mud, or stepped into her carriage.

After the first twelve months 'widow's silk' may be substituted for paramatta; but it must be heavily trimmed with crape. This is worn for six months, when the crape may be very sensibly lightened, and jet, passementerie, or fringe may be used. After three months more, crape may be left off, and plain black worn for three months; and after the end of the second year half mourning may be worn for five or six months, the change to light grey and lavender being made only gradually. For the first year, while a widow wears her weeds, she of course accepts no invitations; and it is in the worst of taste for her to be seen in places of public resort.

As the century wore on, some slight relaxations of the rules slipped through. Sometimes, the mourning veils did not completely cover the face, but were short token ones, or were allowed, in some cases, to hang over the shoulders. Spotted crape or flounces of crape mounted on a cotton foundation were accepted, and dark red as an alternative to black was also permitted if the wearer was obliged to attend a wedding during her period of deep mourning. Widows who eventually felt themselves free to marry were enjoined to wear a coloured – as distinct from white – dress and bonnet, and to dispense with the veils and orange blossom appropriate to the first-time blushing bride.

Jewellery for those in deep mourning was limited to jet. But later gold and silver ornaments could be worn, and stones, provided that they were not coloured. Opals and pearls, which were considered to symbolize tears, were acceptable.

In addition to the funeral cards, there would be black-edged mourning notepaper and envelopes to be used by the family during the months following the death. Missives would be written with black ink and sealed with black sealing wax, melted in all probability with black candles. The black edging known as 'Broad' was recommended for widows rather than 'Extra Broad' or the still wider 'Double Broad', both of which were thought to be ostentatious. 'Middle' was the right width for a parent or child, 'Narrow' for brothers and sisters, and 'Italian' for all other relatives.

Naturally every effort was made to cater for the needs of the bereaved. Jay's London General Mourning Warehouse had been estab-lished in 1841 especially for this purpose near the Oxford Circus end of Regent Street, as well as Pugh's Mourning Warehouse, which was also in Regent Street, but nearer the Piccadilly end, in 1849. Derry and Toms, John Barker's and the Army and Navy Stores paid marked attention to the funeral business.

At Peter Robinson's Court and General Mourning Warehouse, a brougham stood harnessed and ready to dash off on receipt of a call from a house in mourning. Two coachmen, dressed in black from head to foot with crape hatbands and whips decked with black crape bows, were also at the ready. Two lady fitters, clad also in black, sat inside the brougham, fully equipped with patterns and designs of dresses, which could be run up in a matter of hours.

Harrods' catalogue of 1895 devoted a lengthy section to funeral desirabilia. Lead, oak and elm coffins were available and open or closed funeral cars and mourning carriages. The needs of those participating in the funeral procession were carefully considered. They might need to wear clothes made of French merino, Bradford cashmere, Estamene or Cheviot serge, hop-sack, whip cord, French foule, Vienna cloth, Balmoral crape, 'nuns' cloth, Norwich paramatta, broche satin, pure alpaca or Courtauld's crape.

Strenuous efforts were made from time to time to reduce the costs of dying. Charles Booth, ship owner and social reformer whose *Life and Labour of the People of London*, completed in 1903, is still consulted by historians, bemoaned the amount of money that the poorest families spent on funeral rites, and as far back as 1883 the Revd W. H. Sewell had published his *Practical Papers on Funeral Reform* and was supported by the 'Church of England Burial, Funeral and Mourning Reform Association', founded about that time to encourage 'moderation and simplicity instead of unnecessary show'. Oscar Wilde, writing in February 1885 to the organizers of a meeting on funeral reform, deplored formal wreaths and suggested that coffins should be conveyed to the place of burial by night and that mourners should gather there the next day since it was the publicity associated with a funeral procession that occasioned its extravagance. He urged that white and violet should be recognized as mourning.

Pending the introduction of such reforms, the poor made do, as far as they could, by preparing their own mourning clothes in advance, and by joining Burial Clubs which collected and banked small sums each week towards the cost of family funerals.

There were, of course, cynics, particularly towards the end of the nineteenth century, who questioned whether all those who put on mourning were completely sincere, and Mrs F. Douglas in *The Gentlewoman's Book of Dress* published around 1890 put it this way:

The widow who considers with seriousness whether she will best express her sense of loss by a Marie Stuart cap or an Alsatian Bow of tarlatan, is already half consoled, and will return in a month for another which will express 'mitigated' grief by various lightsome pleatings.... She will ... express her appreciation of the solace a good dinner affords by donning a cap of tulle to eat in. The black dress will soon ... require a dainty frilled fichu of tulle to make it endurable. She will ere long, bestring herself with jet beads that will take the place of the tears that have ceased to flow ... and the day when grey, and violet, are permissible, is one characterized by a sober but genuine joy.

Nevertheless the balance of evidence shows that, among rich and poor alike, there were strongly held convictions that the dead were worthy of honour. This reverence for the departed arose partly from the fact that in Victorian times death was regarded largely as an Act of God. Doctors, it seemed, were powerless to intervene when the Angel of Death beckoned. Reverence for the dead was also the natural continuation of the respect in which the elderly were then held. There were fewer of them, of course, in those days when sanitation was poor and doctors relatively ill-informed, and so they did not yet constitute much of a problem. Their opinions, the fruit of experience, were probably worth more in the days before popular education, newspapers, and television had made it possible for the rising generation to absorb the experience of the centuries from other sources than the family chimney corner.

It was not entirely tribal snobbism that led the Forsytes to have a family tomb of their own. There had long been a general realization dating from the early days of Queen Victoria's reign that the arrangements for interring bodies in London and other large cities were repulsive and unhealthy. The population had increased to the point where the churchyards in which most Christians had hoped and were entitled to be buried were hideously over-crowded. And so were the interiors of the churches, below the floors of which parishioners had from time to time been laid. A House of Commons Report published in the 1840s established that some 44,000 bodies were buried each year in London churchyards totalling little more than 200 acres. Periodically some bodies had to be removed to make room for the newcomers.

Private burial outside the churchyard could be arranged, but all too often the contractors threw the bodies into the shallowest of excavations with the results that the decaying bodies could be smelt if not seen. Thus it was natural for the Forsytes to arrange a family tomb of their own. They chose Highgate which had been established in 1838 under the management of a joint stock company, the London Cemetery Company.

The cemetery was divided into two sectors known as the old ground and the new ground, and the chapel was notable for the mechanism which made it possible for the bier to be lowered through the floor of the chapel to an underground passage and taken from there to any part of either ground. One of the main features of the cemetery was its Egyptian Avenue entered through a rectangular archway designed perhaps with the pharaohs in mind. It led to a magnificent cedar of Lebanon with catacombs (subterranean vaults) and columbaria (underground 'dovecots' containing niches for ashes – cremation had been legalized in 1885) around it. On either side of the avenue were mausolea – family tombs above ground, protected by cast iron doors. Each consisted of a compartment with stone shelves for receiving coffins, a worthy resting-place for Forsytes.

Yet Soames realized that neither he nor any Forsyte beyond his own generation would use it, or even visit it. People's views on the celebration of death were changing, as if prompted or even decreed by the dead Queen herself.

'It was not entirely tribal snobbism that led the Forsytes to have a family tomb of their own'

16

Edwardian Revels

The Edwardian era was the period least understood by the Forsytes and the most neglected in the story of their struggles. And, in so far as King Edward VII was the symbol of his times, this disregard is easily explained. Good Queen Victoria had shaped her life according to a code of strict morality with which was coupled the desire for self-improvement displayed in so exemplary a manner by Albert, the Prince Consort. The new King, however, showed no signs of wanting to better himself or even to accede to his mother's wish to call himself King Albert Edward. His very appearance, his pear-shaped figure and his flashy, boulevardier style of dress – which led his nephew, Kaiser Wilhelm, to dub him 'the old peacock' – all betokened self-indulgence rather than frugality; and the royal eyes, heavy-lidded and pouched beneath, cast a disconcertingly worldly gaze upon his subjects and especially on his married women subjects.

There were other changes, too. The individuals who had been permitted to frequent Queen Victoria's Court at Windsor or Balmoral were notable for their unchallengeable integrity and their irreproachable respectability. But the same could not be said of the friends and acquaintances of her son, either as bachelor Prince of Wales or as a married monarch. For Edward preferred to have around him men of wealth and achievement, international financiers such as Sir Ernest Cassel, Baron Maurice de Hirsch, old Sir Anthony de Rothschild, his nephew Nathaniel

and the various Sassoons. He liked men who were personalities in their own right and not necessarily so by birth: cosmopolitans who were sophisticated and if possible witty, and above all he liked women who were beauteous, fun-loving and accessible. There was a general relaxation of etiquette outside Court circles and even staid old *Punch* suggested in 1907 that the formality of paying calls had become so meaningless that it would really be better if ladies should be out on a certain specified day of the week rather than at home, to allow cards to be left on them then.

The Forsytes could never have fitted into the Prince of Wales's set at Marlborough House or even Buckingham Palace. Forsyte achievements were solid but limited. They were well off but not nearly rich enough to entertain the King, his friends and the hordes of servants who accompanied them. They were not amusing and they neither sailed at Cowes, shot grouse in Scotland, gambled at Baden-Baden or Marienbad, nor, with one or two exceptions, raced horses. They were not even practical jokers.

Nevertheless, their conduct was by no means irreproachable; for though they might disapprove of the morals of the Court and despise its trivialities, yet they shared, in so far as the family means allowed, in the extravagance and ostentation of which Queen Victoria had complained so frequently, believing that it would bring nearer the day of revolution. They inherited traditional shopping customs. Those houses of affluence – Asprey, the Army and Navy, John Barker, Debenham and Freebody, Derry and Toms, D. H. Evans, Harrods, John Lewis (not yet a partnership), Liberty, Lilley and Skinner, Maples, Mappin and Webb, Peter Jones, Swan and Edgar (about to go public) and Woollands – had already been established before the Forsyte story opened in 1886.

The Valhalla of the Forsyte family, the treasure-house from which its wants were most frequently supplied, was probably Harrods. In the index to the Harrods' catalogue of 1895 – the oldest to survive the years – we see Prayer Books in between Prawns and Precipitated Rice, Haricot Beans next to Harmonium Voluntaries, and Cremation next to Crème de Riz. Tree Guards follow Treacle, and Hymns Ancient and Modern come after Hydrogen Peroxide.

The delivery system, 'Free within six miles by our own carts', was impressive for its frequency. Brook Street in the heart of Mayfair could depend on four deliveries a day at 9 a.m., 11.30 a.m., 2.30 p.m. and 4.30 p.m. and Bayswater only one less – the 2.30 call being omitted. Chelsea was well covered, having the same attention as Brook Street. But so also had Earls Court Road. Even Munster Road and Coniger Road, which had so recently served as cottages for workmen, received two calls a day, and Deptford had three deliveries a week. The Dispensing Department delivered medicines by Express Tricycle.

Banking, insurance, removals and warehousing were undertaken, and governesses, lady helps and all classes of male and female domestic servants were on the books.

Harrods had a restaurant on the ground floor adjoining the Floral Hall, with a Ladies' Reading Room attached. Hot luncheons were served from noon till three and a loin chop cost 10d; poached eggs on toast were 6d and muffins 2d, with Best Whitstable Natives at 3s 6d a dozen. No alcoholic drinks were served – a licence

The new King

having been refused lest the restaurant should become a place of assignation, but there was tea, coffee, cocoa, mineral waters and a speciality was made of American Ice Drinks.

The vocabulary used in Harrods was, no doubt, readily understood by the customers who patronized the store, but is less familiar today. For example, what we might call deck chairs are shown as 'hammock chairs'; cigarette holders are 'cigarette tubes', shoe horns are 'shoe lifts', coal scuttles with lids and removable linings are 'coal vases', sugar casters are 'dredgers', pince-nez, useful because they could be easily worn inside a veil, are 'eye folders', and 'overmantels' are the mirrors and shelves placed over the mantelshelf of a fireplace.

Undoubtedly we are less well versed in the vocabulary which would have been used by the Forsyte family in their normal intercourse with tradespeople. For example, Aunt Ann would have been well aware that goffering irons were used for crimping, that a mousquetaire was a lady's glove, long-armed and loose, but not slit, at the top. Also that passementerie was a kind of trimming and pilch a kind of flannel cloth used in the nursery for wrapping the baby.

She would have been aware that a jagger was a wheel with a notched edge used for cutting dough, that a muffineer was a holder from which you sprinkled salt on to muffins rather than the dish which kept them hot. A salamander was a metal plate on which meat could be browned over a flame. A pull-over was a silk or felt cover or nap drawn over the body of a hat, or a hat made in this way. 'Pier glass' was not a mis-spelling for 'peer glass' but was the term for a tall, narrow mirror suitable for putting in the piers, or spaces between windows. A bottle-jack was an object shaped like a bottle on which meat would be roasted. Door porters were door-stops.

Kid reviver was of course for kid gloves not children; Scotch hands were for shaping

butter; small signals were diminutive flags; storm glasses were barometers; forfars were a kind of towelling; mahogany loo tables, round, with three legs, were for card-players, and chimney glasses were mirrors that could be installed against the chimney over the mantel-shelf in small sitting-rooms or bedrooms – they led to many a dress catching fire. French terms were much in use – for instance: basinette (a basket with a hood), or jardinière (a vessel for displaying flowers or ferns).

The spirit of extravagance in the middle classes continued to flourish even more exuberantly after Queen Victoria's fin-de-siècle warnings had ceased; and the fire and brimstone denunciations delivered by the Jesuit priest, Father Bernard Vaughan, from his pulpit in Farm Street, almost round the corner from Winifred Dartie's house, apparently had little effect.

'I see at the counters people on whose foreheads it is written that they know themselves to be the salt of the earth', Arnold Bennett wrote in 1909:

Their assured, curt voices, their proud carriage, their clothes, the similarity of their manners, all show that they belong to a caste and that the caste has been successful in the struggle for life. It is called the middle class, but it ought to be called the upper class, for nearly everything is below it. I go to Stores, to Harrods Stores, to Barker's, to Rumpelmayer's, to the Royal Academy, and to a dozen clubs in Albemarle Street and Dover Street, and I see again just the same crowd, well-fed, well-dressed, completely free from the cares which beset at least five-sixths of the English race. They have worries; they take taxis because they must not indulge in motor cars, hansoms because taxis are an extravagance, and omnibuses because they really must economize. But they never look twice at twopence. They curse the injustice of their fate, but secretly, they are aware of their luck. When they have nothing to do, they say, in effect: 'Let's go out and spend something.' And they go out. They spend their lives in spending. They deliberately gaze into shop windows in order to discover an outlet for their money. You catch them at it every day.

Certainly they would have found plenty to interest them not merely in Knightsbridge but even in Victoria Street, where the Army and Navy Co-operative Society held more or less undisputed sway. Here the customers of 1907 were able to buy gramophones fitted with 'the new Morning-Glory horn'; disc records had been available for nearly ten years but were usually single-sided. One hundred and twenty different kinds of bag were for sale, mink capes, diamond tiaras and fifty different sorts of glove, including one specially designed for washing dogs. And there were five kinds of American cocktail including the Manhattan and the Martini (perhaps because 123 Victoria Street was the U.S. Embassy's earlier address.)

The new Morning-Glory horn

The Society was ready to install American skittle and bowling alleys; it offered portable Turkish baths heated by spirit lamp and 'self-acting roasters', 'self-opening book-markers', 'self-registering croquet-targets', 'self-righting lamps', and a 'Norwegian self-acting cooking apparatus'.

For women who already had almost everything, there were trifles such as 'In Haste' cream-laid writing paper which, when folded and stuck along one edge, provided three-cornered sealed missives. Fans of lace on mother-of-pearl sticks – almost certain to break if dropped – cost £10.

Fans of lace on mother-of-pearl sticks

Luminous match-boxes inscribed, as required, with their appointed station, were available for the library, dining-room, drawing-room, bathroom, kitchen or study. A veil-case was to be had; and chased silver perfume flasks, also a notebook with 'Whose "At Home" Day is This?' on the cover.

A woman who took her shopping at the Army and Navy with sufficient seriousness could spend the best part of an afternoon looking at the choice embroidered materials which included Bikhaneer dhurries, Guipure linen, Yarkhand numdahs, djidjims, and Lhoodiana work.

Men could choose between a patent golf-hole cutter, a stalking telescope, or a De Sausmarez hat-case which could accommodate a top hat, bowler, soft felt hat, straw boater and an opera hat all at once. There was also a cane walking-stick fitted with a blow tube and dart which was said to be 'useful for collecting small birds'.

A De Sausmarez hat-case

'To travel hopefully is better than to arrive, And true success is labour'; H. Gordon Selfridge at his desk

There was a fresh wave of bargain hunting when H. Gordon Selfridge opened his emporium of 130 departments (colour-scheme: olive green with dark mahogany fixtures) in Oxford Street in March 1909. The affair was ostentatiously uncommercial. 'Come and spend the day at Selfridge's', he invited, and he hoped that the customers would regard the store as their own so much so that he did not even put its name over the entry doors. Selfridge wanted women in particular to look on his premises as an idealized extension of their own homes. Customers were not to be harassed by shopwalkers but were to be allowed to browse freely, without being pressed to buy. Inside, the store was airy and well lit. Selfridge rejected the ancient practice of crowding shop windows with items bearing price tickets – and hiding the goods inside the shop away, in drawers. He preferred to show only a few objects in his window displays, items that would stimulate women in particular to wonder what might be inside the store behind the windows. The displays were kept illuminated after closing time.

To attract customers to the store Selfridge installed a roof garden and, on that day in July 1909 when Blériot flew the Channel, Selfridge drove straight to Dover, to ensure that the wonder-'plane would subsequently be put on display in his store.

Private party-giving was on a grand scale too. In 1905 Mr George Kessler, the promoter, amongst other things of Moët et Chandon champagne, gave a 'gondola' birthday party at the Savoy Hotel. For this purpose the forecourt of the hotel was specially flooded and the waters dyed blue to represent a Venetian lagoon, with replicas of St Mark's and the Palace of the Doges as background. The waiters were dressed as gondoliers, a baby elephant brought in the birthday cake on its back, by gondola naturally, and, as a surprise at the end of the evening, Caruso sang.

At home, the public cult of beauty, which had begun with the dawn of mass photography in Queen Victoria's day and had been officially blessed in 1893 when the Shaftesbury Memorial Fountain ('Eros') was unveiled in Piccadilly Circus, continued. Studios such as Bassano, Downey, and Window and Grove, who displayed in their windows portraits of actors and actresses, and of society beauties dressed as maidens in the hayfield, Greek goddesses or wood-nymphs stretched out romantically in hammocks, promoted a minor industry by selling 'pin-up' photographs of Lady Randolph Churchill, Mrs Luke Wheeler and Mrs Clara Rousby, the actress about whom Wybrow Robertson, who at one time ran the Westminster Aquarium, came to blows with Henry Labouchère. After the turn of the century the picture postcard sellers took up the trade.

Marriages of actresses to peers were not unknown in Victoria's time but the pace hotted up very considerably in the early years of the new century. The Prince's penchant for Lillie Langtry and, later, for Sarah Bernhardt had blurred the distinctions between 'Society' and the Stage, and, when the King and Queen Alexandra attended the opening of the new Gaiety Theatre in October 1903, they afforded considerable assistance to George Edwardes' efforts to glorify musical comedy. Soon, the Gaiety Girls were demanding coronets from the peerage in return for their favours.

Rosie Boote from Tipperary – her hit song was 'Maisie Gets Right There' – married the 4th Marquis of Headfort, whom she had met

'Mr George Kessler gave a "gondola" birthday party at the Savoy'

Miss Olive May

Mrs Clara
Rousby

the shoulders, or linked to them only by token shoulder-straps. The waist was constricted to give an hour-glass effect exaggerating the size of the hips below, and of the bosom above, and, although the latter was somewhat constrained by the new, so-called 'straight front corset', the upper half of the Gibson Girl reminded some observers of a ship's figurehead. Camille secretly married the Hon. Henry Lyndhurst Bruce, the eldest son of the 2nd Baron Aberdare in the same year. (There were ructions in the family when the secret leaked out.)

Miss Jessie Smither, who had appeared under the stage name of Denise Orme at Daly's in *The Little Michus*, married the Hon. John Reginald Yarde-Buller, the 2nd Baron Churston's heir, in April 1907. She reappeared at the Gaiety in 1909 in *Our Miss Gibbs* (in which the heroine was a shop-girl) but retired the following year, when her husband came into the title. Sylvia Storey, Fred's daughter, who

(*left*) Miss Rosie Boote
(*opposite*) Lady Randolph Church

at a garden party, in April 1901: the first such alliance to take place in the new century. The wedding was held in great secrecy at Saltwood, a village near Hythe, Kent. Next, there was Eva Chandler, who appeared under the stage name of Eva Carrington. She met the 25th Lord de Clifford in 1904 when she was playing on tour at the Gaiety Theatre, Dublin, in *The Catch of the Season*, the play which also 'made' Zena Dare. His Lordship returned from Cairo in 1906 to marry his beloved by special licence at the Holborn Town Hall.

Then there was Miss Camille Clifford who, in 1904, had been christened the Gibson Girl because she came nearest to the conception of the perfect woman as seen by the American artist, Charles Dana Gibson. The Gibson Girl was a statuesque goddess, her hair piled up in three enormous billows, with, perhaps, an oyster-shell hat on top, skewered on with pins. Her dress would be worn either completely off

Miss Camille
Clifford

Miss Denise Orme

Miss Sylvia Storey

period less changeable in their style of dress than men, for whom dress reform had begun well before King Edward VII's coronation. Men wearing straw hats and unbuttoned coats without any waistcoats had been seen in Hyde Park itself during the hot summer of 1893; and some even wore coloured shirts.

In 1897, the year which celebrated the centenary of the top hat, improper suggestions were made that it should no longer be used except by scarecrows and conjurors. Gilbert Parker, the novelist who had won the seat of Gravesend from the Tories in the 1900 'Khaki' election, was observed wearing soft silk shirts even in the House of Commons, and in 1903 it was noted that evening dress was no longer obligatory in the more expensive theatre seats.

'We are becoming rather negligent in dress', R. D. Blumenfeld noted in his diary in February 1908. 'Down in the city today, where I talked with the Hon. Claude Hay, MP, I noticed that he wore a soft collar, such as golfing men often wear, and brown boots. Also, he had no gloves. Many men, more than usual, go about in the City in bowler hats nowadays which shows the trend of the times.' Blumenfeld could truthfully have added that shoes were beginning to overtake boots. And double-fold collars for use at home or in the country had been introduced in 1906 by Sir George Alexander, the actor-manager, who appeared in them in the play *John Chilcote*, MP. Men were wearing wrist watches and using fountain pens, descendants of the 1884 prototype. The new models, it was claimed, could now be carried in any position, which was just as well since by no means all were yet fitted with a pocket clip.

King Edward, in his role of avant-garde trendsetter, had already approved the dinner jacket in 1876 when he was travelling to India with a mixed retinue of civil and military attendants who had to dine every evening at the same table aboard the adapted troopship *Serapis*. Pleated dress shirts came in around

had acted since she was six years old, married the 7th Earl Poulett at St James's, Piccadilly, in September 1908, while she was still in the cast of *Havana* at the Gaiety, and Olive May, whose real name was Meatyard, married Lord Victor Paget, younger brother of the 6th Marquess of Anglesey, in January 1913. May Etheridge married the future Duke of Leinster in the same year.

We cannot suppose that the majority of Forsytes – who disapproved both of the Aristocracy and the Stage – would have seen anything to be commended in these nuptials.

Apart from the Gibson affair and the hobble skirt, which did not girdle the ankles until after 1909, women, except perhaps in regard to their underwear, seemed at this particular

1889. Edward also helped to popularize another kind of jacket, the Norfolk, and wore something very close to plus fours when shooting. When he left undone the bottom button of his waistcoat the world copied his negligence. His was the Tyrolean hat with the shaving brush at the back and the green velour Homburg which led the irreverent to say in 1900 that it looked as though somebody had been trying to scoop out Bertie's brains and had given up in despair.

At official functions, however, he insisted that the proprieties were observed. To Lord Rosebery, who turned up to an evening party at Buckingham Palace wearing trousers instead of knee breeches, he remarked, 'I presume that you have come in the suite of the American Ambassador'. And when Viscount Haldane, who had been educated at Göttingen in Germany, arrived at a garden party in a shabby soft hat, the King turned to the ladies near him and exclaimed, 'See my War Minister approach in the hat which he inherited from Goethe'. He had to discipline even his Assistant Private Secretary, Sir Frederick Ponsonby, who had presumed to accompany him before luncheon to an exhibition of paintings, wearing a tail coat. 'I had thought', the monarch observed, 'that everyone must know

that a short jacket is always worn with a silk hat at a private view in the morning.' He also reproved an official in the Foreign Service for coming aboard *Victoria and Albert* in knee breeches instead of in trousers which, he pointed out, were always worn aboard ship.

When Lord Harris arrived at Royal Ascot wearing a tweed suit, the King asked whether he was going ratting – a gibe that pinned the term 'ratcatcher' to a tweed coat worn out hunting in place of the more normal black or pink.

King Edward wearing a Tyrolean hat, Vienna, 1903

Edward VII was no less punctilious on the subject of women's dress. 'The Princess', he said, as Prince of Wales, to the Duchess of Marlborough who was sitting next to him at dinner, 'has taken the trouble to wear a tiara. Why haven't you?'

Ladies who were considering attending their Majesties' Court in 1908 were made aware of the fact that high-necked dresses might be worn only by 'ladies to whom, from illness, infirmity, or advancing age, the present low [cut] Court dress is inappropriate'. And even those luckless ones had first to get permission from the Lord Chamberlain. So presumably they knew what they were doing when they went racing at Ascot for the first time after King Edward's death dressed from head to foot in black.

Back in London the appearance of the streets of London through which the Forsytes moved changed more during the short Edwardian period than perhaps in any other decade before or since. Piccadilly was widened considerably in 1901 and Kingsway, one hundred feet across, was carved through the territory known as The Rookery, ruled in Oliver Twist's day by Bill Sikes; the new thoroughfare was declared open in 1905, and the nearby Aldwych was conjured up about the same time after a competition between architects.

A new *caravanserai*, the Strand Palace Hotel, opened in 1908. It was the only London hotel where you could find hot and cold water and a lavatory with every room, no tips, no charge for a bath and a second helping of every dish without extra charge. A room, bath and breakfast cost six shillings, lunch 1s 6d, tea 6d and dinner 2s 6d, totalling 10s 6d a day for full board.

The horse-bus began to vanish from the streets. In 1903 all but thirteen of London's 3600 omnibuses were horse-drawn and gave good service, even though some of the best

(*right*) 'The horse-bus began to vanish from the streets'

'Taxi-cabs' in Knightsbridge, 1907

animals had been commandeered for use in the Boer War. Six years later, 980 out of 2950 omnibuses were petrol driven. By the end of 1911 the London General Omnibus Company had taken out of service all of the 343 horse omnibuses it had been running the previous year.

By 1913 the number of hansoms had fallen from 7600 at the turn of the century to fewer than 400. Taxi-cabs, only one of which had been licensed in 1903, were compelled in 1907 to install meters, by which time their numbers had risen to 723. The fare was one shilling for the first two miles and 6d a mile thereafter – the same as for horse cabs. Taxis could not be compelled to take passengers further than six miles from Charing Cross and could charge double fare outside a four-mile radius. The 1907 edition of Baedeker's *Guide to London* contained, however, a special warning to visitors hiring taxis by the hour. They were advised to negotiate specially with the driver if a speed of more than four miles per hour was required. A bonus of an extra shilling for each

mile per hour of extra speed was usual, the guide said.

The underground railway was continually spreading. The Piccadilly and Bakerloo lines were opened in 1906 and the Northern tube line, launched the following year, gave 127,500 free rides to passengers during its first afternoon and evening. The last regular steam train had been taken off the District and Inner Circle lines in 1904. The steam tram first tried in London in 1859 was already obsolete.

Electric trams were exploring outer London in 1901, and the London County Council, which was seeking to run a unified service, succeeded in 1906 in extending its tram lines across Westminster Bridge and along the embankment, despite the protests of those who declared that they would ruin the landscape, slow down traffic, and land the council with a loss. A trolley bus was tried as an experiment in 1909.

Private motoring was becoming as fashionable as the ice-skating rink had been ten years earlier. In 1896 even while Parliament was still debating the Act which would among other things raise the speed limit for self-propelled vehicles (originally steam cars) to twelve miles per hour (thus putting automobiles on all fours – so to speak – with horse traffic), an International Exhibition of 'Motors, Self-propelled Cycles, and Horseless Carriages', Britain's first motor show, was held at the Imperial Institute. The *Amateur Wheelman*, a cycle paper, which, in May 1896, had become *The Wheelman and Motor Car Weekly*, published a supplement devoted largely to the motor show.

The editor held the view that 'the most successful motor-car will be the one that has as much of the cycle and as little of the carriage as possible', and his reporter seems to have been particularly impressed by the motor cycles, some of which had 'an immense airscrew at the end'. One machine weighing only twenty-two pounds would develop two horse-power and, according to its designer, could travel a mile in fifty-eight seconds. But the reporter nevertheless also commended the Kane-Pennington Victoria and said that for two riders there was nothing to beat it. 'With pneumatic tyres, ball bearings, light, low framing, and comfortable seat, could anything be nearer cosy comfort on a Motorcar?'

In its *Hints for Engineers* the paper discussed how many cylinders a motor car should properly have. 'Two cylinders are strongly recommended,' it said,

because in case of an accident to one cylinder the other remains intact to bring the carriage to its destination. Three or four cylinders add an uncalled-for number of working parts, and increase the liability to breakage. One cylinder, on the other hand, has few parts, but has the disadvantage of exhausting a correspondingly large volume, which is found difficult to muffle.

Furthermore, the single cylinder car needed an unwieldy flywheel and despite this the vibration was 'readily noticed by those riding in the carriage'.

Soon after his accession to the throne, the King, an enthusiastic motorist himself who

King Edward about to enter his deep portwine coloured Daimler, 1904

had previously owned two Mercedes and a Renault, ordered a British Daimler. It was to hold six people with room for the footman to sit beside the chauffeur and be capable of travelling at more than sixty miles an hour. He gave orders that the royal cars should be painted a deep portwine colour.

Conditions for normal civilian car owners, however, remained rugged in the early days of motoring. As was to be expected in a land where you were still liable to meet a nervous horse round every corner, the police were eternally vigilant. Lord Carnarvon was fined in October 1900 for driving at twenty-four miles per hour, twice the speed limit, and Frank Butler, Hon. Sec. of the Automobile Club, was hauled before the magistrates of New Romney in Kent for scorching at eighteen miles per hour in his new Panhard.

The police were also endeavouring to compel motorists to carry identification numbers on their cars, and the Automobile Club said that they would not oppose this provided that the authorities would abolish the speed limit and

"Allweathers"

MOTOR CLOTHING SPECIALISTS.

Licensed Manufacturers of STRÖM'S PATENTS.

Allweathers'
LEATHER MOTOR CLOTHING
FOR LADIES.

To meet the needs of the rapidly increasing number of Lady Motorists, Messrs. ALLWEATHERS have produced a series of new garments in specially prepared leather, designed to afford comfort to the wearer and as a protection to the ordinary garments.
SEE ILLUSTRATIONS.

New Illustrated Book of every requisite for Ladies' and Gentlemen's Motoring Specialities Post Free.

Telephone: No. 2424 Gerrard.

LADIES' TAILOR-MADE LEATHER MOTORING KNICKERS, fitted with detachable flannel lining. These are made of specially prepared Leather in various shades, and are particularly adapted for ladies who drive their own motors, always ensuring perfect protection from the wind, and obviating the danger of cold from a loose or insecure apron.
(Patented.) LADIES' MOTOR LEGGINGS (as illustrated), of specially prepared black glazed kid, lined grey ripple wool. Price 23/- per pair.

"MONTAGUE."—Handsome Three quarter Coat, in specially prepared Leather, with skirt to match, combining warmth and comfort with perfect protection from dust, wind, and water; lined in various ways; coat fitted with Storm Fronts and our new patent Windguards to sleeves. Made to measure or pattern bodice in ten days.

13, New Burlington Street, London, W.; and 43, Brompton Road, S.W.

prosecute only for dangerous driving. But drivers were compelled to get number plates, and had to wait till 1903 for the speed limit to be raised marginally to twenty miles an hour, where it remained for many years afterwards.

Several of the new motor manufacturers had begun as cycle producers, changing from two wheels to four. The Humber company, which exhibited at the 1896 motor show at the Imperial Institute, was one. The first Sunbeam car was built in a cycle shed in Wolverhampton in 1899. The first Riley car was built in 1898 by the co-owners of the Riley Cycle Company. The Standard Motor Company, founded in 1903, was one of the earliest to be set up for the purpose of making cars and nothing else. The first Vauxhall car was produced in the same year. The earliest Singer car appeared in 1904 and Hillman followed suit in 1907, the same year that the Brooklands motor racing track was opened.

induced many more of the affluent to take their holidays by road, and the coal strike of March 1912, which further handicapped the railways, rammed the lesson home.

Herbert Austin who had been brought back from Australia in 1893 by his company, the Wolseley Sheep Shearing Company, to supervise the manufacture of their shearing machines, produced the first Wolseley car, a three-wheeler, in 1895. He left, ten years later, to found his own company, but the Wolseley concern continued to prosper and by 1911 came second only to Ford in the number of engines produced.

William Morris, the future Lord Nuffield, had also dabbled in cycles, motor cycles, car repair and car hire before going into production. The first Morris Oxfords (two-seater, 8.9 horsepower, four-cylinder) appeared in 1912 with the carburettor and gearbox provided by White and Poppe of Coventry, the

(*opposite*) 'Non-motorists often appeared in motoring garb as a status symbol'
(*right*) 'Irene was said to be wearing a motoring cap and scarf'; the Motor Club inaugural run to Brighton, 9 June 1907

Henry Royce had bought a second-hand French Decauville car in 1903 and had been so greatly disappointed by its ignition and cooling system that he resolved to make something better. The first Rolls Royce was ready in 1904, fifteen years before the first Bentley. The Spirit of Ecstasy mascot by Charles Sykes, which adorned Rolls Royce radiator caps, came seven years later.

The railway strike in the summer of 1911

axles from E. G. Wrigley of Birmingham and the body from Raworth of Oxford. Morris's production in the year 1919 was 387 cars.

Young Jolyon Forsyte was one of those who had taken to motoring. His eight-year-old son Jon, who was expecting him to return to Robin Hill one afternoon in July 1909, heard 'a grinding sound, a faint toot', indicating the approach of the automobile. From the grinding noise, the fact that no chauffeur was mentioned and that Bob, the groom, was down in the stables at the time, playing his concertina, we might conclude that young Jolyon, though now sixty-two, was an owner-driver.

Furthermore, Irene was said to be wearing a motoring cap and scarf, which she would not have done if she had merely been coming home from the station in a taxi, though non-motorists often appeared in motoring garb as a status symbol. Nothing is said about goggles which motorists tended to wear in open cars for protection against dust in the summer but this omission is not conclusive evidence, since the car could have been a saloon rather than an open model, or it might have been because Galsworthy did not wish to spoil Irene's glamorous image.

A good image was an essential constituent of Forsyte self-esteem which helps explain why the Forsytes, although they may not have troubled themselves about some new developments, such as the bioscope ('movies'), or for that matter about Einstein's paper on the Theory of Relativity published in 1905, were already paying reluctant attention to the popular press. Soames and Winifred were especially sensitive about the amount of publicity that might be accorded to their respective divorce proceedings. 'The papers are a pushing lot', Soames said. 'It's very difficult to keep things out. They pretend to be guarding the public's morals, and they corrupt them with their beastly reports.' They were a pushing lot in the political field, too, and encouraged people to concern themselves about topics that should properly have been left, the Forsytes believed, to people better fitted to deal with them.

Improved education had fashioned a new generation of readers: workers and business men who had no time to read the unattractive slabs of print preserved by *The Times* and other serious newspapers. Furthermore, a paper which merely recorded the events of the day was not enough. An interpretation was needed of the rapid changes which were taking place in the world and an assessment of how they would affect the average British family. Alfred Harmsworth, later Viscount Northcliffe, believed that he could provide this interpretation. The first *Daily Mail* appeared on 4 May 1896 after no less than eleven weeks of practice runs by the editorial staff, compositors and machine room. Launched with a capital of only £15,000, it made a profit of £18.5 million in its first fifty years. The first day's sales amounted to 397,215 copies, and during the Boer War, it reached a circulation of over one million a day – by far the largest in the world. Its first big campaign, launched in 1898, was in favour of equipping all police stations with telephones, and, when officials objected that this would merely lead to hoax calls, the *Daily Mail* offered to pay for the installation costs and rental for a period. The officials were compelled to give in. The paper launched its appeal for the dependants of Boer War soldiers with Kipling's poem, 'The Absent-minded Beggar', which was set to music by Sir Arthur Sullivan in one of his last compositions. In 1906 the *Daily Mail* also offered a prize of £10,000 for the first air flight from London to Manchester, four years before it was won by Louis Paulhan in a race against Claude Grahame-White.

From the start the *Daily Mail* paid particular attention to women readers, and ran a magazine section headed *Women's Realm*. The very first menu for *Today's Dinner* suggested white soup made with onions, bacon, milk and ground rice; cold lamb and mint sauce; asparagus, mashed potatoes; and marmalade pudding. When ping-pong became a craze during the early years of the century, the *Daily Mail* gave it a full page – with an illustration of the 'Crouch-smash'.

Stop Press was introduced in 1898 to keep pace with the Spanish-American war in Cuba, and a method of printing photographs using half-tone blocks on rotary machines was first used by the *Daily Mail* in 1904.

The London to Manchester air race was won by Louis Paulhan, 1910

In the early days of half-tone pictures it had taken a week to prepare each picture, but one of Harmsworth's technicians saw a way of printing them on ordinary rotary presses at the rate of 24,000 an hour, and so, in January 1904, a new paper, the 'illustrated' *Daily Mirror*, 'a paper for men and women', replaced the original *Daily Mirror* ('the First Daily Newspaper for Gentlewomen' which was written by ladies for ladies, and was at one time losing the Napoleon of Fleet Street around £500 an issue).

The *Daily Mirror*, Mark II, went off with a bang. One of its photographers, David McLellan, stationed himself on one of Swan and Edgar's balconies and tried with the help of his magnesium flash powder to take the first picture of Piccadilly Circus by night. Unfortunately the powder was incorrectly mixed. There was a sharp explosion which blasted off part of the balcony and blew in fifty-two windows. Other enterprises were more successful, and *Mirror* photographers in search of new pictures climbed Mont Blanc in winter, dropped

into the crater of Vesuvius during an eruption, and crossed the Alps in a balloon. In February 1907 the *Mirror* published a photograph of King Edward that had been sent by wire from Paris to Lyons and back to Paris.

The style of the paper was now anything but genteel. 'SAVED BY STRONG CORSET' was the headline over the story of a woman whose lover had fired three shots at her when she refused to return to him. Her defences of whalebone and steel proved impenetrable and her life was saved. Within a month of its birth the circulation of the new *Daily Mirror* increased nearly six-fold.

The *Daily Mail* remained more conservative. Its front page was devoted to advertisements, and it took the outbreak of Hitler's war to alter the routine. The *Daily Express*, founded by C. Arthur Pearson in 1900, carried news on the front page from the beginning, a decision approved by the future Lord Beaverbrook who, by 1939, had hoisted the circulation to two and a half million, as compared with the *Daily Mail*'s figure of slightly over one and a half.

But those populars which did not possess the committed readership of *The Times*, *Daily Telegraph* and *Morning Post* found that there

were no holds barred in the struggle for circulation. Alfred Harmsworth in his original publication *Answers* offered £1 a week for life to anyone who could guess the total amount of gold and silver at the Bank of England on 4 December 1889. George Newnes' *Tit-bits* offered free insurance against railway accidents. In 1890, during an influenza epidemic, *Pearson's Weekly* was printed on paper soaked in health-giving eucalyptus. In 1903 the *Daily Express* offered a prize to the owner of the first parrot taught distinctly to say, 'Your food will cost you more.' It did, of course.

Despite the Press, serious authors continued to flourish: Arnold Bennett with *The Old Wives' Tale*; Shaw with *Man and Superman, Major Barbara* and *The Doctor's Dilemma*; Joseph Conrad with *Lord Jim*; D. H. Lawrence with *Sons and Lovers*; Somerset Maugham first with his novel *Mrs Craddock* and then in 1908 with his four plays running simultaneously in London's West End.

H. G. Wells was still shocking the public, this time (1909) with his novel *Ann Veronica*, of which Canon Lambert told the Hull City Libraries Committee: 'I would just as soon send a daughter of mine to a house infected with diphtheria or typhoid fever as put that book into her hands.'

Elinor Glyn, who had already scored heavily in 1907 with her romantic novel *Three Weeks*, was getting away with it again. Her new novel *His Hour* (Duckworth, 6s), which appeared in 1910, was dedicated, with permission, to Her Imperial Highness the Grand Duchess Vladimir of Russia, and recorded the struggle of Tamara Loraine, an English widow of good

family, to retain her reputation in pre-war tsarist society by resisting the attentions of Gritzko, a half-Cossack Russian prince who had told her, 'In a little short time, you shall love me. That haughty little head shall be here on my breast without a struggle, and I shall kiss your lips until you cannot breathe.'

Yet Gritzko's days of gladness were numbered and even King Edward seems to have had his doubts about the Tsar's future. 'If only a Constitution [Russia had none] may be acceptable to the people now, and may Nicky remain firm and stick by his promises', he wrote in January 1906 in a letter preserved in the Royal Archives. But in July that year Sir Arthur Nicolson (Sir Harold's father) who was then H. M. Ambassador in the Russian capital of St Petersburg, warned the Foreign Office that the odds were even that a general upheaval was imminent, of a kind 'which will sweep away dynasty, government and much else'.

The Tsar did not come to King Edward's funeral in 1910, but eight other Heads of State were present: the Emperor William II of Germany, and the Kings of Belgium, Bulgaria, Denmark, Greece, Norway, Portugal and Spain.

Five of them – the Emperor and the Kings of Bulgaria, Greece, Portugal and Spain – were to lose their thrones. Another Edward in the procession, the late King's grandson, was to be involved, a quarter of a century later, in a romance that led to his abdication. And, with the most far-reaching consequences of all, the Archduke Franz Ferdinand of Austria-Este was assassinated at Sarajevo in 1914, an event which led to World War I.

(opposite) Ethel Barrymore (left) and Elinor Glyn

17

The Cares of Peace

The celebrations in 1918 at the end of World War I continued for at least two days after the Armistice had been signed. 'NIGHT OF PANDE-MONIUM . . . A MILLION PEOPLE OUT' wrote the *Daily Express*, recording the scenes of 13 November. At last, people were able to see each other's faces in the streets after dark. Motor lorries rushed crowds of revellers, armed with mouth-organs, paper horns and whistles, up to the West End. For the second night running, the crowd lit a bonfire in Trafalgar Square, dragged captured German guns from The Mall, tore off their wooden wheels, and threw them into the flames. A man knocked off the top of a whisky bottle against the side of a car and gulped down the contents raw. Young officers clambered on top of the lions at the foot of Nelson's Column and fired off Very Light pistols. Groups of girls, some of them wearing soldiers' hats, danced on the pavements, climbed on the roofs of cars, and threw bunches of streamers at passers-by. The ledge above the driver's seat on a London bus seemed just the right spot for a joy-ride.

It was no time to be wearing a top hat. The police stood aside discreetly in doorways. Restaurants protected themselves by letting in only those who had booked tables in advance.

Everybody – or almost everybody – believed that, now the war was over, there would soon be a return to 'normalcy'. Morale at home was still high. There had been no food rationing at all until February 1918, and, when intro-duced, it applied at first only to meat, butter

and margarine in London and the Home Counties. Bread, made with flour into which the millers released up to ninety-two per cent of the wheat berry, and sometimes some soya flour as well, may not have been appetizing, but at least it remained off the ration, even after the failure of the potato crop in 1916.

Hardly anyone realized the true costs of World War I, and some of those who did were happy to believe that Germany could be made to pay the whole bill. (The Government hoped for as much as £40,000,000,000 paid over thirty years.) But the fact remained that industries not directly geared to the war effort had been allowed to run down to a degree which made it pointless to demobilize troops before there were jobs for them to go to. And so at first the authorities released only those they regarded as 'key men' – who were often the last to have been called up.

These considerations, however, carried little weight with the troops, particularly with those officers who had volunteered to serve 'for the duration', or for that matter with the men, and Lord Byng, field-marshal-to-be, who had redeemed his military reputation in the final push of the war, had to be sent to Calais to deal with the units who had set up a species of Army Soviet at their camp.

The Government, therefore, partly as a result of these manifestations, decided to go into reverse and to let out long service men first and in rather larger quantities, although conscrip-tion was not abolished until April 1920. Yet the sequel to these releases, however welcome to the troops, was predictable. Many of those who had been promised 'a land fit for heroes to live in' found that, even after a prolonged delay in their release, their country had no work to offer them.

The personal columns of *The Times* recorded their disillusionment. On 11 November 1919, exactly a year after the end of the 'war to end all wars', 'jobs wanted' advertisements were still pouring in from ex-officers:

Ex-Artillery Major, reliable and trustworthy, age 24, single, just demobilized, offers his services anywhere in any capacity at any price. Will any Patriot communicate?

ran one inquiry.

'The celebrations in 1918 at the end of World War I continued for at least two days after the Armistice had been signed'

'Many of those who had been promised a "land fit for heroes to live in" found that their country had no work to offer them'

By no means all applicants were unqualified, for in the same issue an advertisement appeared from a naval officer:

Demobilized midshipman, age 20, two years' service in North Sea, desires post as Private Secretary or any similar position. Knowledge book keeping, type-writing, expert motor driver (R.A.C. Certificate).

Others offered languages, shorthand or accountancy qualifications or cars for hire.

Many an ex-officer had only his so-called

Victory Bounty to give him a fresh start. Some took to chicken-farming, or mushroom-grow-ing; others became cab-drivers, or hall porters; a few entertained in cabaret or danced in the chorus of Albert de Courville's revues at the Hippodrome. Ex-servicemen faced competi-tion not only from each other but also from women who had taken over their jobs in the factories for the duration but were now un-employed, from land girls no longer needed on the land, and, later, from other women demobilized from various women's auxiliary services. (It was said, by the male chauvinist pigs of the day, that there would never have been nearly as many spinsters, if women had not taken the jobs of those who would other-

THE CARES OF PEACE

wise have liked to marry and support them.) A year after the end of the war 353,000 ex-servicemen were still unplaced, and were finding the going harder rather than easier. In the army, as at school, they had formed part of a group, welded together by the same discipline, comforted by the assurance of united action. And now it was goodbye to all that.

As John Collier and Iain Lang put it in their entertaining informal history *Just the Other Day*:

The ex-Serviceman had for years had his life arranged from reveille to reveille, had been fed, clothed, and ordered to step off with the left foot. Now he was suddenly required to put his best foot forward, an indefinite and puzzling responsibility.

There was, of course, a clear division through-out the country between those who had fought in the trenches and those others – either servicemen or civilians – who had not. Front line men, according to their temperament, despised or envied the rest as shirkers. But some despised themselves as well and wondered whether they deserved to have survived when

The first woman barrister, Miss Ivy Williams, was called to the Bar in 1922

Lady Astor, the first woman to take her seat in the House of Commons

so many of their comrades were dead. They blamed the politicians for having dragged them into a senseless conflict and some agreed with the suggestion that there would be no more war if international disputes were settled by a shooting match between the political leaders of the two sides.

But, in the end, there was general agreement, for different reasons, between those who had fought and those who had not, to drop the subject of the war. It became something that nobody wished to talk about any more.

Perversely the conflict, fought and won by men, had turned out a 'victory' for the women. Married women, women householders and women university graduates who could bring themselves to confess that they were over thirty, voted for the first time in December 1918 and, four years later, helped to elect Lady Astor as the first woman to take her seat in the House of Commons. From 1918 onwards, women had been accepted as jurors and the first woman barrister, Miss Ivy Williams, was called to the Bar in 1922. Lesser women not only smoked openly in restaurants but elbowed their way into pubs. The Matrimonial Causes Act of 1923 allowed women to sue for divorce on exactly the same grounds of divorce as men, and, being now relatively well versed in methods of birth control, they were able to avoid the burdens of unwanted motherhood during their married life or even before it commenced. In fact, the enthusiastic amateur was beginning to take the place of the old-fashioned mistress who required setting up in a separate establishment. (Apart from Dr Marie Stopes – of whom more later – they could get help from Dr Norman Haire, the sandal-wearing Australian Harley-Street gynaecologist who also ran a clinic in the East End, and went nap on the Grafenberg inter-uterine ring.)

Arnold Bennett, himself no prude, noted in his Journal of 27 October 1918:

The sensual appeal is now really very marked everywhere in both speech and action on the Stage. Adultery everywhere pictured as desirable, and copulation generally ditto. Actresses play courtesan parts (small ones, often without words, but with gestures) with gusto.

No doubt those extra women who now had little chance of getting married or had no desire to do so, helped the trend.

During the war, a wide gap had grown up between the generation directly affected by the war and the younger groups less involved. The young saw a world smashed to pieces because of the follies of their elders, and many wondered whether martial valour or indeed any masculine achievements could be commendable.

In the world of the Forsytes, the changing values of the younger generations were most

Soames (Eric Porter) and Timothy (John Baskcomb)

clearly shown in the case of Timothy Forsyte, brother of James, the youngest of his generation, who had nevertheless lingered on, dying as a centenarian in 1920. Timothy was in a class of his own. When Soames went to visit him shortly before his death, he found that his devoted servants, Cook and Smither, had nursed him through the whole of the war without even telling him that it had broken out.

When Timothy at last died the diminished respect accorded to the dead in post-war years became evident, for the family, which had flocked to Fleur's wedding, stayed away from Timothy's funeral. Soames alone attended the ceremony. The absence of the others reflected a conviction on the part of some of the quick that it was high time to protect themselves from the intrusions of the dead.

The children who were still fledglings during the war were, of course, still more isolated from the older generation. Many of them had grown up in a one-parent family with their father away on active service, in an atmosphere of uncertainty and fear. Often, their education had been interfered with or even abandoned. Oxford Colleges were used as Officers' Training Centres. Well-brought-up young women faced the world untrammelled by the discipline of a Court presentation or even a formal 'coming-out' dance.

Once grown up, those who could afford it, actors, artists, boxers, old school tie men and apprentice rakes from the suburbs, sought distraction in the noise and smoke of the night clubs. There was even something a little daring about going to one during the war. The Defence of the Realm Act (DORA) had limited drinking to six and a half hours, and Whitehall officials (who knew what was best) were unwilling or afraid to relax their hold too much or too soon. Three years later, the new Licensing Act of 1921 sought to compel free Britons who wished to drink after 11 p.m. to eat a meal as well and to cease all drinking after 12.30 a.m. Those who considered these restrictions unreasonable – and most people did – crowded into the establishments run by those who were prepared to defy the law. Soon there were dozens of cosy dens in dingy alleys where whisky was drunk out of tea-cups, where the air smelt of cheap scent and stale cigarettes and you gave a false name if you were caught in the act. Mrs Kate Meyrick, the daughter of an Irish doctor, opened her famous night club, the *Forty Three*, in Gerrard Street in 1921 and, according to her account, it was visited by celebrities such as Augustus John, Joseph Conrad and Jacob Epstein, the sculptor, already notorious in 1919 in Forsyte circles for his unorthodox representation of Christ.

The *Forty Three*, well described in Evelyn Waugh's *A Handful of Dust*, was periodically raided and in 1924 Mrs Meyrick was condemned to six months' imprisonment in Holloway jail. When she came out she opened a string of new clubs, each succeeding an old one which the police had closed.

Mrs Kate Meyrick

A few of the other more ponderous establishments complied with the law; they remained genuine clubs and served drinks only to duly elected members. Most, however, found it easier and more profitable to confer membership on anyone who turned up at the entrance with sufficient cash to pay the subscription and the additional 'door money' exacted as the price of admission.

The police, in their efforts to enforce the law, made no distinction, however, between the law-abiding clubs and the others, and the fashionable *Kit-Kat* was raided the very night after the Prince of Wales had been seen there. Thus all were forced to take elaborate precautions against surprise, and to install two sets of doors each bolted and chained. And even then police sometimes forced their way in through a skylight.

It was natural that such dancing, or rather shuffling, possible in the limited space in a night club, was more intimate than ever before, and now that corsets had been abandoned body spoke directly to body. During the war there had been a violent reaction against the artificial constraints which had forced

fact, literally a girl-friend. It also proclaimed in the most unmistakable way the difference between the older generation with its ample display of bosom and bottom, and the new phenomenon, the modern girl. (It was then that slimming became respectable, nay almost obligatory for the middle aged, and it was said to be 'unforgivable' for a woman to have a figure.) In consequence the brassière came to be used by the more generously proportioned,

'The brassiere came into use in Britain from 1912 onwards'

women to resemble egg-timers or wasps. The brassière – the word originally used by the French to describe a haversack or hod secured on the back over the arms – came into use in Britain from 1912 onwards, largely because of the flimsy and diaphanous materials used for evening dresses, which made some support desirable for the breasts. It was not originally a 'bust-improver'.

With the end of the war, a slim boyish tubular figure became the rage. It proclaimed woman's new freedom from the shackles of the past, her readiness to be a comrade, a pal – in

and others too, as a means of playing-down if not constricting the breasts.

The restlessness and the craving for a distraction, which had drawn people away from private dinner tables into fashionable semi-public night clubs, were evident also in the sensational and impromptu character of private entertainment. In the years immediately after the war few girls of good family were expected to earn their own living or do anything other than amuse themselves. But even this appeared to be difficult. A party needed a special theme if it was to attract smart people. 'Come dressed

(*above*) 'A party needed a
special theme if it was to
attract smart people';
Three Arts Ball at Covent
Garden, December 1922
(*left*) Lady Diana (Duff)
Cooper
(*right*) Cecil Beaton as
Princess Tecla in the
burlesque musical comedy
'The Gyp's Princess',
Cambridge, 1924

as your dearest enemy', or 'In pyjamas', or 'Come dressed as your opposite'. 'Come as a Living Celebrity', the invitations said. Or come dressed as toys, tiny tots, or savages, cowboys, Russians or as famous lovers. Or bring with you something scavenged (a live pigeon? a nosebag?), or, better still, if the party was arranged at the last minute, a bottle of champagne. And, with people of resource like Lady Diana (Duff) Cooper, Nancy Mitford, Cecil Beaton, Oliver Messel to call on, you could even stage a do-it-yourself cabaret.

'It was the dawn of the jazz age'

It was, of course, the dawn of the jazz age; the first warning vibrations, 'Ragtime', had reached Britain in 1912 with Alexander's Ragtime Band and *Hullo Rag-Time* at the London Hippodrome – a show which Rupert Brooke saw ten times. Just before and during the war the transatlantic drummer, Louis

Mitchell, did his best to acclimatize the public at the Piccadilly Restaurant and elsewhere to the rhythms of the future. In 1919 the new attack on the ear drums was led by the Original Dixieland Jazz Band (white) with music that exploded in an Albert de Courville revue at the London Hippodrome for one night (and later at the Hammersmith Palais de Danse). The band was led by Nick le Rocca (cornet) and included Tony Spargo (drums and kazoo), Larry Shields (clarinet) and Emil Christian (trombone), plus piano. 'Tiger Rag' was the Dixielanders' favourite and they never needed to look at a score.

In the post-war era the young were needed by theatrical producers as well as by manufacturers of new lines. Old-time stars, however sexy they might seem in Variety, could never last out for the whole of an all-dancing all-singing post-war musical with a plot demanding almost uninterrupted on-stage appearance. And so the leading professionals got younger and younger. Off-stage the old began to imitate and dress like the young in a belated effort to participate fully in those oh-so-exciting dancing years.

How did Fleur Forsyte, not yet nineteen when she reappears in the *Saga*, fit into this scene? The answer is nowhere very exactly. She certainly was not a jazz fiend. She was amusing, intelligent and accomplished, and apparently spoke French with ease. She was 'modern'. She calls Soames 'dear', 'darling', 'ducky', or even pityingly 'poor father'. She has a cocktail before lunch – probably mixed with gin, once the tipple of the plebs, but now acceptable in Mayfair if served with Cointreau and lemon juice to make a *White Lady*.

Fleur knew exactly how to launch a flirtation at high speed, which was understandable, for despite the chaperons that lingered on in some quarters, it was becoming much easier even

(*opposite*) 'How did Fleur Forsyte, not yet nineteen, fit into this scene?' . . .

in South Kensington for young men and women to see more of each other. Invitations to dances were often inscribed 'Miss So-and-so and Partner' which of course allowed Miss So-and-so to choose her own escort. And when a mother gave a dance for her daughter, it gradually became the custom for friends of the family to invite half a dozen young couples to dine with them first. All of which helped to promote what was known as 'the party spirit'. And although you could not dine alone with a young man in a public restaurant, when you danced with him it was no longer necessary to wear gloves.

Fleur was attractive enough to profit from such opportunities. She was

'The fashion was for smaller furniture in smaller rooms in smaller houses' – (*above*) a tiled bathroom with composition flooring of 1925 (*opposite above*) The latest in kitchens in 1925 (*opposite below*) A dining-room of 1925

of medium height and colour, with short, dark-chestnut hair; her wide-apart brown eyes were set in whites so clear that they glinted when they moved, and yet in repose were almost dreamy under very white, black-lashed lids, held over them in a sort of suspense. She had a charming profile, and nothing of her father in her face save a decided chin.

But Soames, Annette and Fleur lived in Soames's house at Mapledurham, near Pangbourne, forty-five miles outside London, so Fleur would not normally give or receive invitations to smart parties. Within the family network she was free to make her own arrangements and probably stayed with one or other of her relatives on occasions when she was asked to private dances in London.

Outside the Forsyte circle the Age of the Common Man had dawned. It was in the spirit of the times that the Revd David Railton, a former chaplain at the Front and later Vicar of Margate, suggested that the body of an Unknown Warrior should be taken by gun carriage from the Cenotaph and buried in Westminster Abbey; and, in 1920, King George V, a plain man's king, without either the panache of his father or the imperious ways

of Queen Victoria, was glad to follow the coffin on foot.

'Curiously symptomatic – that thing', said Sir Lawrence [Mont to his son Michael as they passed the Cenotaph]; 'monument to the dread of swank – most characteristic. And the dread of swank –'

'Go on, Bart,' said Michael.

'The fine, the large, the florid – all off! No far-sighted views, no big schemes, no great principles, no great religion, or great art – aestheticism in cliques and backwaters, small men in small hats.'

And certainly Lloyd George, the Prime Minister, though his manner with time became more and more that of a company promoter and less and less that of a revivalist preacher, was neither fine, large nor florid.

From now on, the fashion was for smaller furniture in smaller rooms in smaller houses. Out of doors, the daylight-saving routine, first discussed in 1908 and introduced as a wartime measure, became the law of the land in 1925 to give zest to the increased leisure of the office and factory workers. With the war out of mind, the desires of the Common Man became paramount in the field. The camera,

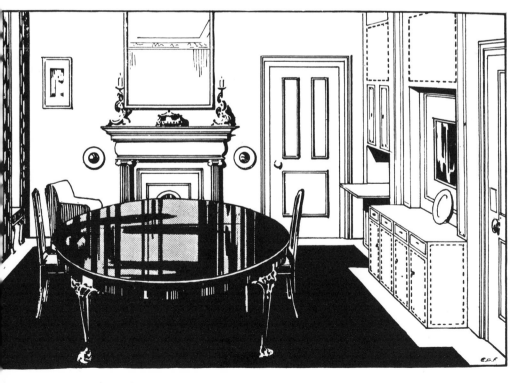

(*right*) Mademoiselle Lenglen
(*below*) The first time the cup final was played at Wembley
was in 1923
(*bottom*) Miss Gertrude Ederle

which once glamorized Mrs Langtry, now made heroines out of Mademoiselle Lenglen, the tennis player, and Miss Gertrude Ederle, the Channel swimmer. And every schoolboy on the cricket field could fancy himself as Jack Hobbs.

The ritual of the people's sport was inaugurated in 1923 when the Cup Final (between Bolton Wanderers and West Ham) was played for the first time at Wembley. Permission to play games in Hyde Park on Sunday had already been accorded in 1922. And ice cream blocks – ugh! – were being served now even in the theatres.

It was difficult for a Forsyte to reconcile himself to such disasters.

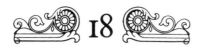

Forsytes Credulous and Incredulous

Feelings of insecurity, such as had assailed the elder Forsytes in the 1890s, possessed the minds of succeeding generations in the 1920s. The immovable landmarks by which they could have hoped to steer a course had become inconstant in position and fleeting in appearance. Lloyd George's plan to 'make Victory the motive power to link the old land up in such measure that it will be nearer the sunshine than ever before' lacked definition. Bolshevism was still endemic in Russia although Sir Paul Dukes, *The Times* newspaper's acknowledged expert, had written an article in November 1919 headed 'Bolshevism at Close Quarters: A Tremendous Failure'.

In the materialist world of science it appeared that elements which had once been considered immutable and indestructible could, in fact, be decomposed to form other elements; that the atom, which had formerly been considered the smallest known unit of matter, could itself be split. Moreover, it now appeared, there was no absolute difference between matter and energy. Einstein had furthermore declared that rays of light were not necessarily straight but could be bent. Even the universe was not finite, but continually expanding.

Then again, the philosophers appeared to have abolished the sequence of cause and effect – and the certainty that one thing would, by natural law, lead to another. Only probabilities, or as some would say, the laws of chance, remained.

Nor was there certainty as to why people acted the way they did, since they were controlled by a mind of which they were not conscious. 'There was a thing they called psycho-analysis', ruminated Soames in 1922, which, so far as he could understand attributed people's actions not to what they ate at breakfast, or the leg they got out of bed with, as in the good old days, but to some shock they had received in the remote past and entirely forgotten. The subconscious mind! Fads! Fads and microbes! The fact was this generation had no digestion. His father and his uncles had all complained of liver, but they had never had anything the matter with them – no need of any of these vitamins, false teeth, mental healing, newspapers, psycho-analysis, spiritualism, birth control, osteopathy, broadcasting, and what not.

In short, Soames's views (and, if we are to judge by one or two of his pronouncements, Galsworthy's too), had not changed much since the days when it was usual to treat hysteria, from which a good many Victorian women suffered, by pouring cold water on the patient's head.

In fact, although Soames obviously knew nothing about it, Sigmund Freud had taken the decision to study diseases of the nervous system in 1886, that year so fateful to the history of the Forsytes. Freud noticed that almost all patients tended to resist the uncovering of repressed experiences. It was not, therefore, to be wondered at that the elder generation who in Victorian days had suppressed so much, and had regarded dreams themselves as 'unhealthy', should have distrusted the psycho-analysts. It would have been still more worrying for them to have to admit that those angelic pinafored Victorian and Edwardian children were not only sexually inclined long before the age of puberty, but faced an unavoidable psychological conflict in their relationship with parents.

Those who came after, however, welcomed the psycho-analyst, who could absolve the young from their feelings of guilt, act as a father-confessor to the middle-aged and perhaps even alleviate the horrors of 'shell-shock'. After four years during which Christian slaughtered Christian with greatly improved

weapons, each claiming God to be on his side, the influence of the Church began to decline as rapidly as that of the psycho-analyst increased, and in post-war years many believed self-guidance to be an effective substitute for religion. Some sought control of body and mind alike through the discipline of Yoga, which aimed at achieving a state of ecstasy by withdrawing the attention of the disciple from all earthly objects, training him to see without looking, to hear without listening, and to fix the mind ultimately on the contemplation of a single object.

Then in 1921 appeared Emile Coué, sharp-eyed, balding but with a professional-looking beard and moustache, a pharmacist from Nancy who claimed that those who wished could induce organic changes in themselves by intoning at least twenty times at daybreak and nightfall: 'Every day, in every way, I am getting better and better.'

And Soames paid heed, though only for a time. Spiritualism came next to psycho-analysis on Soames's list of hates. But in Britain the cult got a further boost as a result of the war. Some turned to it because they preferred to receive independent corroboration of

'Spiritualism came next to psycho-analysis on Soames's list of hates'; Mrs Emma Mable Field, a noted spiritualist, May 1922

the Church's account of the life hereafter. Others wished to get in touch with relatives or loved ones who had perished in the war. And Fleur was thinking of throwing a lights-out spiritualist party just for a lark. Unfortunately there was a shortage of reliable mediums, the human intermediaries allegedly needed to establish contact between the living and the dead. But the less reliable practitioners were ready to oblige by providing what their clients wished to hear, in the form of rapping sounds, trumpet calls or explicit messages. There could be visions too: virgin film provided by the client could be sealed in the camera and developed independently after, unknown to the audience, it had been exposed to x-rays during the séance. Images, said to consist of 'ectoplasm', a substance emanating from the body of the medium, were seen, and photographed, though some prints suggested a kind of muslin cheese cloth and, at times, even luminous paint might have been used to provide the true after-life atmosphere.

Hannen Swaffer, the newspaper columnist, who, because of his pseudo-ecclesiastical appearance and his weakness for making categorical pronouncements, was nicknamed the Pope of Fleet Street, was a devotee of spiritualism. It allowed him to converse with, if not to weary, the man who had influenced him strongly in his formative years (he would have put it the other way round), Alfred Harmsworth, Lord Northcliffe.

Northcliffe, after his death in 1922, was allowed a rest-period of two years before 'Swaff' got in touch. Northcliffe's secretary and former mistress, Miss Louise Owen, had received a message from her chief, telling her, amongst other things, that he was not floating about in flowing robes but was wearing a grey flannel suit, soft collar and soft shirt, that he was paid in kind for work and that he was the happy possessor of conservatories for his flowers. Northcliffe's message from beyond the grave was accepted by Swaffer and pub-

lished on 14 September 1924 in *The People* which, for a suitable consideration, passed on the Chief's words through its syndication department to non-competitive newspapers in other parts of the globe.

Soames remained deaf to the spirit world but he did get out of his depth in the world of finance. He had been persuaded by Fleur's father-in-law, Sir Lawrence Mont, to become a director of the Providential Premium Reassurance Society. For Soames this proved to be a bitter experience, as Elderson, the old Wykehamist General Manager of the Society, happened to be a villain. He had been accepting secret commissions as an inducement to commit the Society to high-risk foreign contracts, and, when the German mark became worthless, the company was saddled with enormous losses. Alone among the directors, Soames had expressed misgivings, both about the foreign commitments, and about Elderson, but, when the manager finally decamped, it was Soames who got the blame for not having taken further action in the light of his suspicions. Soames got off lightly. He resigned together with Sir Lawrence after a fighting speech at a special meeting of the shareholders, and from then on, the shareholders seemed disinclined to proceed against the Board for malpractice or negligence.

The City shark whose real-life case came closest to Elderson's was Gerard Lee Bevan, senior partner of Ellis and Company, well known stockbrokers, and a director of the City Equitable Fire Insurance Company, of which Lord Ribblesdale, the Earl of March and Sir Douglas Dawson, the State Chamberlain, were also directors. Bevan was an old Etonian, a man of culture who collected paintings. The City Equitable was outwardly highly profitable and its shilling shares at one time changed hands at over £12. It was therefore with astonishment that the City fathers learned one day that Ellis and Company had closed its doors and that Bevan had

departed for France, taking with him a French woman as travelling companion. The police hunted for him all over Europe. He was nearly caught in Naples. The Belgian sleuths missed him in Brussels by minutes. Finally the police arrested him in Vienna, disguised as 'Léon Vernier', a luxuriously bearded French artist. The company's crash caused acute discomfort in the City. Bevan, it turned out, had used City Equitable money to bolster up Ellis and Company and, in addition, shareholders in City Equitable had to find an extra £300,000 for capital not previously called up.

Horatio Bottomley was another artist at the game. His technique was simple. His practice was to raise capital for a company, spend the money on champagne, chorus girls, and in later years, race horses, and then, when the company failed, to 'reconstruct' it under a new name, offering shares in the new concern to those who had lost money in the old. From time to time additional working capital was called for to allow for substantial dividends to be paid. Shareholders' meetings were packed with supporters guaranteed to stifle the opposition. Sometimes duplicate certificates were issued, doubling the company's liabilities, and the share registers were kept permanently in disarray so that it was almost impossible to discover what had happened. If any companies were to be acquired, Bottomley bought them first on his own account through a nominee, then sold them at a handsome profit to his own company. In ten years he issued shares nominally worth £25 million. A typical case was that of the Anglo-Austrian Printing Union of which an unfriendly investigator reported in 1891: 'The Company has acquired no business in Vienna or elsewhere, has no property whatsoever, and its whole capital appears to be lost.' Of the original capital of

Horatio Bottomley

£93,022, £88,500 had been paid to Bottomley.

Bottomley was an expert at paying money to phantom winners, and his 1914 Derby Sweepstake had been won by Helen Gluckman, billed in *John Bull* as 'the blind widow of Toulouse', who, it was said, kept a general shop there. She was in fact the sister-in-law of Saul Cooper, one of Bottomley's cronies, and had never visited Toulouse before she went there to collect the prize money.

Soames, as we know, never offered prizes and escaped trouble, but the very thought of being associated in the public mind with any financial irregularities was bad enough (and not to have known about Elderson's misdeeds merely made things worse). After the Elderson affair, Soames resolved to take up no more directorships and resigned from the management of almost all the family trusts for which he still acted.

(*opposite left*) 'Northcliffe's message from beyond the grave'
(*opposite right*) Hannen Swaffer

167

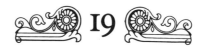

19

The Forsytes take Professional Advice

It was a sound move on Galsworthy's part to introduce a libel action into the plot of *A Modern Comedy*. British newspaper readers could be relied on to manifest sustained interest in those non-violent attempted character-assassinations in which important reputations are publicly torn to shreds and self-esteemed personalities shorn of their dignity.

One outstanding example occurred in 1923 when Dr (of Philosophy) Marie Stopes, who had also achieved academic distinction for her work on plant fossils, and popular acclaim through her bestseller *Married Love*, brought an action for libel against Dr Halliday Sutherland. Dr Sutherland claimed that the birth-control clinic which Marie Stopes had set up in Marlborough Road, Holloway, was being used for experiments on the families who came to it and that at least one of the methods advocated there for birth control was highly dangerous. Marie Stopes lost her case on appeal to the House of Lords partly because of an original misdirection of the jury by Lord Chief Justice Hewart.

Another highly sensational case came up in 1918 when the Hon. Violet Blanche Douglas-Pennant, ex-commandant in the Women's Auxiliary Service of the Royal Flying Corps, alleged before a Government Select Committee, with Lord Wrenbury, an ex-judge, as its chairman, that Lieutenant Colonel Bersey, the officer responsible for the training accommodation, was a party to immorality which

occurred at Hurst Park to which both men and women were posted as well as at other camps. Here, Mr Patrick Hastings – who also appeared in the Marie Stopes case – provided a lively piece of cross-examination, as reported in H. Montgomery Hyde's biography:

'Now, Miss Pennant,' Hastings asked, 'are you prepared to tell the court on your oath that there is plenty of evidence that Colonel Bersey desired to keep these camps open for the purpose of immorality?'

'I desire to tell the court that I charge Colonel Bersey with being a party to those matters.'

The Chairman (interposing): 'Let us have it in plain terms. You accuse Colonel Bersey of being a party to the immorality that was going on?'

'The immorality that was going on in certain camps', Miss Douglas-Pennant replied. 'By party, of course, I only mean that he was allowing it to continue. I do not mean, and I have no knowledge, that he himself was taking a direct part.'

'We know that you have given your opinion that Colonel Bersey is the lowest thing that walks?', Hastings suggested.

'No: I have not said that.'

'Surely he is, according to you, scheming to continue this immorality at these camps. You cannot think of anything lower than that, can you?'

'People take different views about that, do they not?'

'Do they?'

'I think so.'

'Do you think', Hastings asked, 'that it is possible that there can be two views about a man who deliberately enters into a conspiracy to permit immorality to go on in camps?'

The committee had no doubt there could be but one view about such a conspiracy if it existed. However, they found that Miss Douglas-Pennant's dismissal from her post of commandant had been justified and she was not thereafter offered any further Government employment.

The libel action brought by Marjorie Ferrar against Fleur Forsyte, in the spring of 1925, was perhaps of less moment but nevertheless made equally compulsive reading. Marjorie, a guest at one of Fleur's evening parties, had been overheard by Soames describing Fleur as 'a born little snob' and, in effect, a lion-huntress, and Fleur, in a letter to a friend (who turned out not to be one), had referred to Marjorie as 'a snake of the first water . . . who hasn't a moral about her'. After various overtures and rejections on both sides for a settlement out of court, the case eventually came up before Mr Justice Brane.

In preparing the defence, Soames set about matters in rather the same way that the Marquis of Queensberry had adopted in the Oscar Wilde case thirty years earlier. That is, detectives were employed to discover as much information as possible to the discredit of Marjorie Ferrar – the books she read, the friends she had and when she saw them, the advanced plays she was ready to appear in, unpaid. And the cross-examination to which she had to submit, as in Wilde's case, would be plentifully loaded with sneers.

The advocates of the 1920s could be broadly divided into two classes. On the one hand there were those who, through the use of their special legal acumen, aimed at influencing the minds of the judges, and on the other hand there were those who concentrated on the emotions of the jury. The most effective legal tear-jerker in the mid-twenties was Edward Marshall Hall who once said of himself:

My profession and that of an actor are somewhat akin, except that I have no scenes to help me, and no words

The Hon. Violet Blanche Douglas-Pennant

Edward Marshall Hall

are written for me to say. There is no backcloth to increase the illusion. There is no curtain. But, out of the living dreams of somebody else's life, I have to create an atmosphere – for that is advocacy.

Marshall Hall was not above saying, as he did in the case of Mrs Marie Hermann, accused of murdering Henry Stephens, a cab-driver, with a poker: 'Look at her, gentlemen of the jury. Look at her. God never gave her a chance – won't you?' They did, too. She was acquitted.

Another case handled by Marshall Hall, and one far more in tune with the atmosphere of *The Forsyte Saga*, was the libel action brought in 1924 by Lady Terrington against the *Daily Express*. The article to which Lady Terrington objected had appeared during the General Election campaign of December 1923, when she was contesting the seat of Wycombe, Buckinghamshire, as a Liberal candidate against the Conservatives who were supported by the *Daily Express*. She won the seat but was defeated in the General Election of October 1924. Lady Terrington complained that the article represented her to be an extravagant and frivolous woman, given to ostentation and boastful about the luxurious character of her establishment. It was headed: 'The best-dressed woman MP: Lady Terrington's aim if elected. Furs and Pearls.'

Edward Marjoribanks, Marshall Hall's biographer, recorded that the great advocate imperilled his cause on this occasion by reducing Lady Terrington to tears (a point overlooked in both the *Daily Express* and *The Times* reports) and that he saved the day only by contrasting the solemnity of the two minutes' Armistice silence, which occurred during his address to the members of the jury, with the triviality of the issues before them.

Soames for his part also wished for a leading King's Counsel whose advocacy would concentrate on the prejudices of the jury. Soames hoped that the jury would be sufficiently

Foskisson (Richard Pearson) and Marjorie Ferrar (Caroline Blakiston)

shocked by the kind of life that Marjorie Ferrar led without it being necessary to establish – a far more dangerous undertaking – that she had in fact taken a lover before becoming engaged to her current fiancé, Sir Alexander MacGowan. He therefore chose Sir James Foskisson, noted for his air of scrupulous trustworthiness, as leading counsel for the defence. ('At close quarters his whiskers seemed to give him an intensive respectability –

difficult to imagine him dancing, dicing or in bed.') He would be the right man to make the most to the jury of anything unbecoming about the conduct of Miss Ferrar without going into charges which, if not fully proven, might turn both judge and jury against Fleur.

Sir James did not benefit from any such opportunities as had been offered on Armistice Day to Marshall Hall, but, by threatening to widen the scope of his questions, he bluffed Miss Ferrar into a tactical error when she refused to answer whether or not she had had 'a liaison'. That refusal lost Marjorie Ferrar the case, which was settled on the basis of each side paying its own costs. But 'Society' sympathized with her and thought Fleur far too self-righteous.

The Forsytes as a family showed rather less faith in their doctors than in Counsel's opinion.

Two reasons could help to account for this lack of faith on the part of the Forsytes. One possibility was that they were born hypochondriacs. No doctor could heal them because nothing was really wrong with them. The other possibility was that the Forsytes, who were perspicacious if not perceptive, were not satisfied by the generalizations pronounced by doctors in the days when it was still possible for a not-specially-talented practitioner to have at least a nodding acquaintanceship with all branches of medicine (or, to put it another way, to possess only a severely limited knowledge of the workings of the human body).

In 1855 when Soames was born, it was still believed that putrefaction was the source of bacteria and not the other way round. Malaria, the cause of which remained undiscovered till 1900, was still prevalent in certain areas of Britain, notably the Fen country in East Anglia, the Thames estuary, and the parts of Kent and Sussex around Romney Marsh.

At the time of Soames's marriage to Irene in 1883, hypodermic syringes had been invented but there were no local anaesthetics. Blood transfusions had been given, but no one guessed that there might be different blood groups. There was no easy way the ordinary doctor could take a patient's blood pressure. No one yet had ventured to open up an abdomen specifically for the removal of an appendix. Surgeons were able with the aid of chloroform to do their work more deliberately and with less gore, and some wore white jackets, but rubber gloves and the 'no-touch' technique were refinements for the future; dressings were not yet steam-sterilized. No x-rays could be taken of broken bones. No one

had isolated the bacilli of diphtheria, tetanus or typhoid. It would be sixteen years before the virtues of salicyclic acid, the main constituent of Aspirin, were discovered.

But why in 1901 should a careful man like Soames have allowed the position to arise where he had to choose between a delivery which would put Annette's life at risk and an operation which would assure her survival but preclude that of the child, with no time left to summon a specialist for a second opinion?

Apparently there was no question of a Caesarean delivery though this might have been possible. Somerset Maugham, who attended sixty-three confinements during his period as obstetric clerk at St Thomas's Hospital, went in 1897 to see a Caesarean performed there because, he tells us in *A Writer's Notebook*, it was rarely done. The hospital surgeon said that the operation was seldom successful and told the mother she had only an even chance of surviving. She did not, in fact, pull through.

To explain Soames's apparent folly, a glance at the history of medical practice and the position of specialists at the time of Annette's confinement is needed. Up to the end of the eighteenth century there had been little chance for the young doctor in a general hospital who wanted to specialize to do so; for the teaching in these establishments was controlled by non-specialists who preferred to keep it that way. Promotion, of course, was by seniority, and posts were handed on if not bequeathed only to those who conformed. As time went by, however, specialist hospitals began to spring up: Moorfields Eye Hospital founded in 1804 was one of the earliest. And general Hospitals began to feel the need for specialists, particularly after the appearance of the ophthalmoscope in 1851 and the laryngoscope four years later, since special training was needed for the use of either of these instruments.

The practice of calling in a specialist for

patients at home caught on more quickly in the big cities where specialists abounded than in the countryside to which they were relative strangers. To summon a specialist from London or elsewhere was a major step for a country doctor to take, and some no doubt still regarded it as a reflection on their own competence.

In addition, an unusual state of affairs still existed in the field of gynaecology, because, until the latter part of the nineteenth century, it was not regarded as 'doctor's work', and was left largely in the hands of the midwife. Not until 1888 did the surgeons and physicians of the General Medical Council insist that candidates for a degree must have attended a dozen confinements before they could practise. We do not know whether Soames's doctor was sufficiently young to have been forced to undergo such rigorous training. But either he was unobservant or overconfident and neither Soames nor Annette appears to have questioned his judgment sufficiently to insist on calling in a specialist from the start for the birth of Annette's first child.

Medical imprudence, however, was not confined to the Forsyte family and was to be seen, as they might themselves have said, in all walks of life. The fact that, except for the sick poor, there was no free medical service in Victorian times and, until 1919, no Ministry of Health, led many to put their trust in patent medicines and surgical devices. In 1909 the British Medical Association published a stiff-covered pocket-size booklet, entitled *Secret Remedies*, which analysed some of the most widely advertised 'cures' of the day. The investigators established, amongst other things, that the ingredients in Dr Lane's Catarrh Cure, sold at a shilling a bottle, could be bought for one-thirtieth of a farthing.

Investigators also discovered an added danger for those women who swallowed Mrs Seegrave's Pills in the hope of promoting an abortion: at least one customer who wrote for the pills was afterwards blackmailed. They further proclaimed that Derk P. Yonkerman, the progenitor of Yonkerman's Tuberculozyne, a widely advertised remedy for tuberculosis, was a veterinary surgeon in Michigan.

Then there were the wines which, if substances such as quinine hydrochloride were added, became tax-free 'medical wine'. Some of them were very potent. Lydia E. Pinkham's Vegetable Compound, for instance, contained twenty per cent alcohol – more than twice as much as claret. Bovril Wine had the same strength, whereas Vin Mariani, a wine warmly commended by the Pope, had a mere sixteen per cent (two less than the eighteen per cent which a Government Select Committee attributed to sherry). But the public remained stiff-necked and unrepentant. As late as 1924 a product called Yadil was widely advertised as a cure for sufferers from consumption, cancer, bronchitis, pleurisy, pneumonia, malaria, scarlet fever, measles, diphtheria and pernicious anaemia.

Soames was not easily imposed on. Thus although Sir Frederick Gowland Hopkins had deduced as early as 1906 that certain diseases such as scurvy and rickets were due to deficiencies in the diet of certain unknown substances, and although Casimir Funk, who was working at the Lister Institute in London, suggested in 1912 that these unknown substances should be called 'vitamines' – the 'e' was dropped later – in 1926 we find Soames still unconvinced: 'You want some sun after that canteen', he told Fleur. 'They talk about these ultra-violet rays. Plain sunshine used to be good enough. The doctors'll be finding something extra-pink before long. If only they'd let things alone!'

Whether Soames knew it or not, ultra-violet rays had been discovered in 1801 more than fifty years before he was born, and portable quartz mercury vapour 'sun lamps' had been used for treating skin complaints, tubercular joints and the like from 1904 onwards. Auguste Rollier, a tuberculosis specialist, set up his clinic at Leysin in the High Alps for treating tuberculosis by exposure to natural sunlight before World War I and similar methods were used from 1908 by Sir Henry Gauvain at Lord Mayor Treloar's Cripples' Hospital at Hayling Island, Hampshire.

But like many a man in his seventies, Soames found it far more satisfying to preserve memories of the deprivations he had had to survive in his youth rather than accept the view that such hardships were now patently fruitless and unprofitable.

'Soames was not easily imposed on'; Soames (Eric Porter)

Twentieth-Century Communicators

Few expressed the changes that had come over Britain during the war more effectively than the so-called War Poets, one of whom, the Hon. Wilfrid Desert, was in love with Fleur. When first the trumpets blew, most of the bards were in a romantic mood. 'And he is dead who will not fight', wrote Julian Grenfell, son of Lord Desborough, in his poem 'Into Battle'. (He died of wounds the following year, after winning the DSO for gallantry.) 'Now in thy splendour go before us, spirit of England, ardent-eyed', urged Laurence Binyon in 'The Fourth of August'. 'If I should die, think only this of me', wrote Rupert Brooke, happy to give his life for the land that had mothered him. (He died at Skyros in 1915 of acute blood-poisoning, following sunstroke.)

But as the war dragged on, a jarring note of realism became noticeable. Binyon, whose 'Requiem for the Fallen' still glorified death, began to write also of the squalor at the Front. And the lines he wrote on the 'Men of Verdun' are all the more macabre for being set to a polka-like measure:

> There are five men in the moonlight
> That by their shadows stand.
> Three hobble, humped on crutches,
> And two lack each a hand.

Edmund Blunden, who was awarded the Military Cross and survived to become Professor of Poetry at Oxford in 1966, was no less disenchanted in his lines on the third battle of Ypres as he describes how:

> . . . the clay dances
> In founts of clods around the concrete sties
> Where still the brain devises some last armour
> To live out the poor limbs. . . .

Wilfred Owen, who was killed at the age of twenty-five just a week before the Armistice, as he helped his men across the Sambre and Oise canal, had still fewer illusions:

> With him they buried the muzzle his teeth had kissed,
> And truthfully wrote the Mother, 'Tim died smiling.'

The most bitter, perhaps, of all the poets was Siegfried Sassoon (also awarded the MC for bravery) who specially mentioned in his despatches the quality of the Allied military leadership:

> Good morning; good morning! the General said
> When we met him last week on the way to the Line.
> Now the soldiers he smiled at are most of 'em dead.
> And we're cursing his Staff for incompetent swine.
> 'He's a cheery old card,' grunted Harry to Jack
> As they slogged up to Arras with rifle and pack.
> But he did for them both with his plan of attack.

Sassoon, like Owen, whom he befriended, also had something to say about post-war prospects in 'Does it Matter?', one verse of which ran:

> Does it matter? – losing your sight?
> There's such splendid work for the blind;
> And people will always be kind,
> As you sit on the terrace remembering
> And turning your face to the light.

Wilfrid Desert, Fleur's suitor, was as handsome – and as travelled – as Brooke, as aristocratic as Grenfell and as cynical as Owen or Sassoon. He had served both in the air force and the front line. But,

Desert never spoke of the war, it was not possible to learn from his own mouth an effect which he might have summed up thus: 'I lived so long with horror and death; I saw men so in the raw; I put hope of anything out of my mind so utterly, that I can never more have the faintest respect for theories, promises, conventions, moralities, and principles. I have hated too much the men who wallowed in them while I was wallowing in mud and blood. Illusion is off. No religion and no philosophy will satisfy me – words, all words. . . . The war's done one thing for me – converted life to comedy. Laugh at it – there's nothing else to do!'

Wilfrid had met Michael Mont in hospital and their friendship was renewed when Michael joined Winter and Danby, the publishers, in 1920. Michael encouraged Desert to write and persuaded his firm to publish his first book of poems, and when Michael married Fleur, Wilfrid was his best man.

He found himself attracted to Fleur, in love with her and unable to break away. Fleur tantalized him; she refused to have an affair with him and yet hated to lose him. He was very handsome. But she did drop him after he had confessed his feelings to Michael. And so Wilfrid went abroad again to write more poems, and retain his reputation as a migrant.

The War Poets, even when writing about the most harrowing events seemed to be able to avoid vulgarity of style. And vulgarity was what Soames and his like objected to in the prose they read most frequently in public: advertising copy. Most advertisers, in the Forsyte view, had no discretion. They assumed that they were addressing a mass audience and made no special distinction between the Forsytes and other potential clients. Furthermore the advertisements that had been most familiar to the Forsytes in their formative years dealt with mundane products such as Sapolio Linoleum Polish, Bumsted's Royal British Table Salt and Warren's Nubian Blacking (illustrated with a picture of a negro grinning at his own reflection in a Wellington boot that he has just polished).

Advertisements showed *photographs* of young women in their underclothes instead of the more discreet *sketches*. And then there had been that suggestive warning printed beneath a picture of a hansom drawn up outside a private house: 'BEFORE STARTING', it said in large capitals, 'on a journey to visit friends, to the sea-side, or the Continent, ladies should take care to provide themselves with a supply of Southalls' Improved Sanitary Towels – the greatest invention of the century for increasing women's comfort at the cost of washing only.' Some advertisements might even be considered to be subversive of propriety. As far back as 1890 Players ran advertisements showing young women smoking, or at least with cigarettes between their lips.

Advertisers were also far too pushing. Already, in 1894, the Parisians had been using powerful searchlights to beam slogans on to convenient clouds, and that very year the British went even further by projecting advertisements for watches, pills and blacking on to the base of Nelson's Column. In the first year of the new century, hoardings were to be seen above the white cliffs of Dover, publicizing the product of an American oat company. Neon lighting, indispensable for after-dark displays, had been invented by the Parisian George Claude in 1910.

The presumption of advertisers was almost incredible. For example, *The Queen* magazine on 2 August 1884 had shown a sketch of Queen Victoria seated at table in the royal dining-car – the outlines of Windsor Castle could be seen in the distance through the far

(*opposite*) Bovril advertisement of 1926

carriage window. Before her on the table is a cup of something with the spoon in it. And in the steam over the top of the carriage we read 'Drink Cadbury's Cocoa'. On the outside of the carriage: a large 'By Appointment' shield.

The Prince of Wales was fair game, too, for the advertisers. An advertisement in the *Illustrated London News* of 7 August 1889 shows an artist's impression of the Prince talking to the Shah of Persia. The Prince, bottle in one hand, glass in the other, is offering royal counsel: 'Try a glass of old Bushmills Whiskey, Your Majesty', he advises, pouring it out. 'It is the whiskey all connoisseurs drink.' (This assurance came, understandably, directly from the Bushmills Distillery, of Bushmills, Co. Antrim.)

Pope Leo XIII was not involved in hard liquor advertising, but might well have needed a hot cup of something to prevent that sinking feeling if he had happened to read *The Illustrated Sporting and Dramatic News* of 1 March 1890 which proclaimed: 'Two Infallible Powers: the Pope and Bovril.' He was also alleged by the producer of Mariani Wine ('Hastens convalescence especially after influenza') to have declared in writing that he 'fully appreciated the beneficent effects of this tonic wine'. The advertisement added that, in token of his gratitude, he had forwarded a gold medal bearing his effigy to M. Mariani.

And an unusual conference took place during the Prime Ministership of Mr Gladstone in 1893, according to an advertisement which appeared in the *Illustrated London News* of 18 February that year. 'A Cabinet Council. Matter under Discussion: Avoncherra Tea' appears over an artist's impression of a Cabinet meeting. The face of each minister is meticulously shown, and each is identified by a china cup bearing his name. Lord Kimberley, at that time Secretary for India and Lord

(*opposite*) Eno's Fruit Salts advertisement of 1924, by E. McKnight Kauffer

'Advertisements showed *photographs* of young women in their underclothes'

President of the Council, is quoted as saying, 'Yes, and the price is extraordinarily low.'

In many other respects advertisers did not display the tact and discretion that a Forsyte like Soames might have hoped for. Originally they seemed to think that it was sufficient for them to buy half a column in a newspaper and repeat in it the name of their product – and nothing more – twenty or so times, as if Soames would not have got the message the first time. Or they thought he would be impressed by a testimonial from Lillie Langtry or, later, from George Robey, the comedian, who was to be seen almost simultaneously drinking health salts, shaving, pumping up a motor tyre, and listening to the gramophone.

(*left*) 'As far back as 1890 Players ran advertisements showing young women smoking, or at least with cigarettes
between their lips'; women motor cyclists, 1925
(*above*) 'Avoncherra' tea advertisement of 1893

On occasion advertisers showed poor psy-
chology: Harness' Electropathic Belt was
advertised in 1891 under the superscription
'An Invitation to Weak Men'.

But the Forsytes were probably more
influenced by advertising than they themselves
realized. Certainly some old favourites were
household words well before Fleur or Michael
Mont were born. In particular they included
the products of Cadbury and Schweppes – not
yet married – Callard and Bowser whose
butterscotch had then no connection with
Guinness, Spratt's Dog Biscuits, Brown and
Polson's Cornflour, Eno's Fruit Salts, Allen
and Hanbury's Glycerine Jujubes, Ovaltine,
Jeyes' Fluid, Keating's Powder, Scott's Emulsion, Angier's Emulsion, Fry's Chocolate,
Bovril, Elliman's Embrocation, Friar's Balsam,
Scrubb's Ammonia, Parrish's Chemical Food,
Colman's Mustard, McVitie and Price's

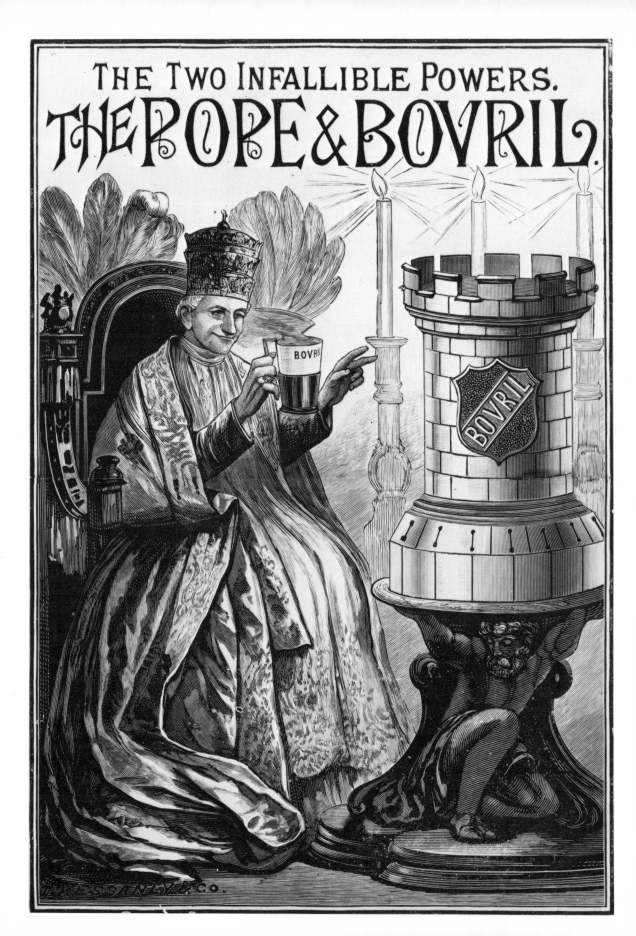

Biscuits, Huntley and Palmer's Biscuits, Reckitt's Blue, Bird's Custard, Rose's Lime Juice, Crosse and Blackwell's Marmalade, Bryant and May's Matches, Gentleman's Relish, Cerebos Salt, Yardley's Soap, Wright's Coal Tar Soap, and many others. Despite head-tossing, the Forsytes had probably been seduced into what advertising men call 'brand loyalty'.

The telephone, like advertising, was an invasion of Forsyte privacy. Of course, it was very nice to be able to ring up one's friends instead of sending a note by a servant without knowing whether the person addressed would be at home to read it. But, on the other hand, there was always the possibility that the operator who put through a telephone call from one Forsyte to another would find the conversation sufficiently interesting to listen to it. The first mechanized exchange, allowing calls to be dialled, was established in Epsom in 1912 but the London exchanges, which needed to be converted, had to wait. Holborn (1927) was the earliest to be mechanized.

Furthermore, the original 'candle-stick' telephone, not superseded in Soames's lifetime, required two hands, one to position the mouthpiece and the other to hold the ear-piece to your ear; it was of unsurpassed ugliness and when not in use had to be concealed, either in a 'cosy' or telephone dolly or in the nearest convenient cupboard. Fleur kept hers in a Chinese tea-chest. This arrangement raised a further social problem. When Fleur telephoned to Wilfrid Desert, the poet (which she should not have done), the telephone had to be fetched out of its cupboard, ready for all to see. And no sudden replacement of the receiver would conceal the fact that the instrument had been in use.

Meanwhile the wireless had begun to shrink distances even more than the telephone. Soames, as we shall see later, deeply distrusted the wireless, being of one mind with the Post Office itself, whose Chief Engineer, Sir William Preece, declared unequivocally on 5 October 1900 that 'wireless telegraphy is not and cannot be a commercial success'.

In time for the New Year of 1927 – too late to worry Soames – a Royal Charter was issued to the British Broadcasting Corporation. But there were troubles enough before then.

The original 'candle-stick' telephone

21

The Forsytes in the Twenties

Even the Forsytes were not averse to dancing. At least not all of them. There was, first of all, Roger Forsyte's dance in Prince's Gardens at which Francie Forsyte's 'lovers' 'bounded, twirling their partners at great pace, without pedantic attention to the rhythm of the music'. June Forsyte was there, too, and would also have liked to dance, but Irene had already pre-empted her fiancé and she had to return home by herself in the carriage with her grandfather.

Soames had once had dancing lessons:

He remembered the academy of dancing where he had been instructed as a small boy in the polka, the mazurka, deportment and calisthenics. And a pale grin spread over his chaps – that little old Miss Shears, who had taught him and Winifred, what wouldn't she have died of, if she had lived to see these modern dances!

At Mapledurham Soames had a pianola – that piece of mechanism, worked in his case by electricity and compressed air, which would play tunes on the piano according to the perforations made in a moving band of paper.

Dancing, often apparently for the sake of dancing, had become very popular among Fleur's contemporaries. It was not always thus. In fact, at the end of the nineteenth century some young men were beginning to follow the example of the Tenth Lancers who boasted that they never danced. One reason was that, although the dances of the time – the

Quadrille, the Valse Cotillon and the Valeta – were by no means intricate, they required some application and previous knowledge, without which a novice who took to the floor could expose himself to ridicule and contempt.

This also applied to the Boston – a kind of side by side (and side to side) – promenade, performed to waltz time, which became fashionable about 1909, as well as to the Tango which came to London two years later via the bordellos of Buenos Aires and the cabarets of Paris. It was said that the original steps were especially suited to the Gauchos of the Argentine who danced in boots and spurs, but in spur-less London there were so many different steps that only those who had learned them together could dance together.

A fundamental change in the social character of dancing was, however, already taking place. From about 1910 onwards the newer dances which reached the general public through the stage rather than through dancing academies were based not, as formerly, on the artificial postures of the ballet but, instead, on the movements of the natural walk. Thus the Two-Step appeared in 1910, the One-Step a year later, and the Fox Trot in the summer of 1914, the latter being featured in such shows as *Push and Go!* at the Hippodrome, *Watch Your Step* at the Empire and *Tonight's the Night* at the Gaiety.

This new do-as-you-please arrangement

(*overleaf*) 'At Mapledurham Soames had a pianola'

*Those gypsies' souls sang and floated on mag—
waves to him who listened, transfixed and silent —
the dark.*

The Duo-Art

THE STORY OF THE SECOND HUNGARIAN RHAPSODY

IT is an old story now, begun three-quarters of a century ago, when a band of gypsies sat before a fire in a placid valley in old Roumania ; they laughed, they chattered, they sang, their wild, dark faces and tawdry tinsel gleaming in the firelight.

Slightly apart sat a man, pale and ascetic looking. He was the great Franz Liszt, come to share the gypsies' thoughts and lives and to learn the magic secret of their songs. Lower and lower sank the sun, out from the fire's red glow floated a song that had within it the mournful wistfulness of a child, then held a burst of passion vivid as a flower. Those gypsies' souls sang and floated on magic waves to him who listened, transfixed and silent in the dark.

That day was born the vision of an immortal beauty of music which will never fade while music beauty lives upon the earth.

THE GYPSY SONG IMMORTALISED

Three years later a great audience sat breathless whilst the master played. His mind went back to that peaceful Roumanian valley, to the gypsy folk whose voices had sounded those age-old songs. That music lived again, infinitely beautified, infinitely adorned.

Suddenly, almost abruptly, he ceased ; the master had completed the playing of his masterpiece. Liszt, the great musical genius, had translated the spirit of a people, had given to the world the priceless gift of his Second Hungarian Rhapsody.

Unfortunately the wonders of the 'Duo-Art' Reproducing Piano were unknown in the great master's time and, consequently, the genius of his playing can only live in the imagination, but the world's greatest pianists have made 'Duo-Art' Music Rolls of his wonderful works which are available to every owner of a 'Duo-Art' Reproducing Piano.

FRANZ LISZT,
the great pianist-composer, whose wonderful works have been recorded by, the world's greatest pianists for the 'Duo-Art' Reproducing Piano. It is of the greatest importance and interest to know that one of these artists, namely, Arthur Friedheim, was a pupil of this great master ; his 'Duo-Art' records of these works are, therefore, not only beautiful contributions to the art of music, but set for all time an authoritative standard of Liszt's own genius.

By Appointment

THE AEOLIAN COMPANY, LIMITED

The Spirit of Franz Liszt lives again in the great pianists who have recorded his masterpieces for the 'Duo-Art' Reproducing Piano.

eproducing piano

FAMOUS PIANISTS WHO HAVE RECORDED THE LISZT RHAPSODIES FOR THE 'DUO-ART'

O those who are fortunate enough to own the 'Duo-Art' Reproducing Piano, Liszt Rhapsodies are a source of almost unlimited enjoyment. Not only the Second, but the almost equally wonderful Twelfth, the Sixth, Eighth, Tenth and others of the series that Liszt composed, are available in the form of 'Duo-Art' Rolls that are practically priceless.

These rolls alone record the interpretations of the following group of pianists whose names head the list of the world's great musicians of to-day :—

IGNACE JAN PADEREWSKI, ALFRED CORTOT, JOSEPH HOFMANN, RUDOLPH GANZ, ARTHUR FRIEDHEIM, DAVID STEIN, ALEXANDER RAAB, MICHAEL ZADORA, BERYL RUBINSTEIN, ERNEST SCHELLING.

ough the Hungarian Rhapsodies are but a small fraction of the instrument's repertoire, nothing could forcibly illustrate the value of the 'Duo-Art' Reproducing Piano, both to musical art and the lover usic, than this wonderful group and the illustrious names of those who have interpreted them.

tically all the great pianists of to-day are making records of the world's best music for this derful instrument, and its possession brings music of all classes, popular and dance, as well as ic, directly into the home.

THE THREE-FOLD VALUE OF THE
"DUO-ART" REPRODUCING PIANO

'DUO-ART' IS, FIRSTLY, A PIANO OF EXQUISITE TONE FOR HAND-PLAYING, hree instruments with which it is combined—the famous Steinway, Weber, and Steck—being e front rank of their respective classes.

ONDLY, IT IS A 'PIANOLA' PIANO with all that instrument's exclusive devices for ling one to play ordinary music rolls with the fullest degree of individual expression.

RDLY, IT IS A MEDIUM THROUGH WHICH ONE CAN HEAR AT WILL THE ARACTERISTIC PLAYING OF THE GREAT MASTERS. Special music rolls, made by pianists while actually playing, reproduce their performances with absolute fidelity in every detail. subtlety of touch, no element of individuality is lost. As the Pianist plays, the 'Duo-Art' s ; there is no difference.

'Duo-Art' Piano is obtainable by a liberal exchange and convenient payment em, which makes its purchase a simple proposition and a sound investment.

If you have not yet heard the 'Duo-Art' Reproducing Piano we invite you to call at Aeolian Hall to hear your favourite composer interpreted by your favourite pianist through the medium of this wonderful instrument. If unable to call, write for 'Duo-Art' Recital Tickets and fully illustrated and descriptive Catalogue Z.

COLIAN HALL, NEW BOND STREET, LONDON, W.1

ARTHUR FRIEDHEIM, one of the most famous of Franz Liszt's pupils. An invitation is extended to you to call at Aeolian Hall to hear Mr. Friedheim's wonderful interpretation of his master's Hungarian Rhapsody No. 2, played by the 'Duo-Art' Reproducing Piano.

STECK GRAND 'DUO-ART' PIANO. A wide variety of Grand and Upright Models of the 'Duo-Art,' either Electric or Foot-operated, is always on view at Aeolian Hall.

(*below*) 'There were so many different steps that
only those who had learned them together could dance together';
Gertie Miller and Raymond Lauzerte dancing the Tango

(*opposite*) 'A fundamental change in the social character of
dancing was already taking place'

exactly suited the needs of the officers and men of the World War I who were to come on leave from the trenches without either the time or the inclination to learn the involved routines of the old 'processional' dances. They progressed after their own fashion and preferred steps that allowed them to advance steadily round the room without side-steps, reverses, or sudden halts that could lead to embarrassing collisions with couples following them. In·the early days of the war, before fuel shortages made themselves felt, officers and men were allowed to dance in uniform provided that they remained 'properly dressed'. (The Military Police pounced on any officer who discarded his Sam Browne, the leather belt with a diagonal strap across the shoulder to which a sword and many other objects could be attached.) *Thé dansant*s which had been in vogue for a year or two before the war were revived, and outlasted the war.

The select dance club to which Fleur

(*left*) 'The Charleston was introduced to London in the spring of 1925 in *Midnight Follies*'
(*below*) The Fox Trot was featured in *Push and Go*

belonged in the twenties was equally not a post-war development. The earliest pre-war dance clubs had no premises of their own, and hired halls such as the Grafton Galleries or the Connaught Rooms or the Hampstead Drill Hall or (more ambitious) Prince's for organized dances. But there were also fairly exclusive clubs with their own premises: Ciro's, for example, in Orange Street, the Lotus in Garrick Street, and the Four Hundred, which, in pre-war times, used the premises in Old Bond Street afterwards occupied by the Embassy Club.

When Fleur and Michael visited their highly respectable dance club one night after the theatre, they found a Charleston in progress and 'seven couples wobbling weak knees at each other in various corners of the room'. First fully publicized in New York in the negro musical *Runnin' Wild* in 1923, the Charleston was introduced to London in the spring of 1925 in *Midnight Follies* at the Hotel Metropole in Northumberland Avenue. But in the ballroom the Charleston required too much elbow (and ankle) room. It was in the more successful night clubs and in restaurants which could not afford to clear too much of their floor space that post-war 'crush-dancing' first began. Here there were no steps, no reversing, or side-stepping and very little progress even forwards.

But communications between the two partners were far, far better than ever before. When the Waltz first came to Britain in 1812, it was considered fairly revolutionary to hold one's partner round the waist. But at least in the case of the Waltz there was the excuse that one needed to do so in order to keep one's balance. That applied also to the Polka, which became so popular in the 1840s. In crush dancing, however, no such pretext was advanced. The man danced without gloves and the woman was no longer afforded the protection of a corset. 'Say it while dancing' became a piece of sound advice much honoured in the observance. However, night clubs were by no means entirely informal. For example, a cartoon published in September 1915 of the Fifty-Fifty night club, which was said to have included a mixture of the stage with Bohemia, showed fourteen men in white ties, four in street clothes and only one man – Leslie Henson – in a black tie and dinner jacket.

Of course those who danced for the sake of dancing could still do so, and, surprisingly enough, Marjorie Ferrar – fast-living granddaughter of the Marquis of Shropshire – was one of those, as Francis Wilmot, an unwilling admirer, discovered as he sat in the lounge of the Cosmopolis Hotel:

In the middle of the parquet floor, sliding and lunging, backing and filling, twisting and turning in the arms of a man with a face like a mask, was she, to avoid whom, out of loyalty to Fleur and Michael, he had decided to go to Paris. Fate! For he could hardly know that she came there most afternoons during the dancing hours. She and her partner were easily the show couple; and, fond of dancing, Francis Wilmot knew he was looking at something special.

It rather sounds as though Miss Ferrar's style was old-fashioned display stuff, resembling the glides and swoops of modern ballroom dancing rather than the shoulder-shaking Shimmy which had already appeared in the last months of the war or the later jerky and rhythmic Charleston. But the object was the same – to blot out the past, the present and perhaps the future as well.

The man with the face like a mask could have been a 'lounge lizard', a type already despised in the twenties (although it was not yet considered anti-social to be of independent private means).

For the not-so-well-off and the less self-assured there was the Palais de Danse, the first of which, at Hammersmith, was opened in 1919. Arnold Bennett went there and found the place intensely respectable. He formed the opinion that the instructresses – you still had to encourage the bashful – had a certain *chic*.

The elderly, if they were incapable of improvisation, or if they had seldom danced before, still took private dancing lessons – Lord Reading met his future wife at a dancing class and Arnold Bennett took daily dancing lessons to be told: 'What you want is courage, decision. Don't be afraid of 'em [women]. Remember they have got to do what you want. You've got 'em, and it's the only time you *have* got 'em.' But often the steps that they had learned with so much diligence quickly became unfashionable as soon as they were seen performing them in public.

Tunes seemed to last longer in the days when Fleur went dancing. There were the dreamy waltzes like *I'm Forever Blowing Bubbles* (1919), *Alice Blue Gown* (1920) and, later (1925), *Always*, the tune to which Fleur and Jon floated past together at the fancy dress ball. There were the cosy numbers such as *Whispering* (1920), *Last Night on the Back Porch* (1923) and, in 1925, *Tea for Two*. There were 'cheery' tunes such as *Ain't We Got Fun* (1921), *Look for the Silver Lining* (1921) *Say it with Music* (1921) and *I Want to be Happy* (1925). There were one or two – but many fewer – laments such as *What'll I do* and *All Alone* (both 1924), and comic turns, such as *And Her Mother Came Too* (1921), *Yes, We have no Bananas* (1923) and *It Ain't Gonna Rain No Mo' (No Mo')* (1924).

The melodies that lingered on longest through the Dancing Years were those directly connected with dancing itself, particularly because they were traditionally played as the last or next to last dance of the evening – or dawn – like *Three O'Clock in the Morning* (1922) and, in 1925, *Show Me the Way to Go Home*.

The year 1925 when Fleur herself was, to some extent, 'runnin' wild', was the most characteristic of any in the twenties.

Clothes were exaggerated. Some men wore suede shoes though at first they were thought to be chichi; others appeared in white buckskin shoes with brown toe-caps which were believed to be favoured by the kind of people cited in divorce cases. Oxford 'bags' in lavender or even lime shades with trouser-legs as wide as a sailor's were only just going out of fashion. The young progressives sympathized with the philosophy of the Weimar Republic in general, and in particular with the permissive atmosphere of Berlin. But, for the conventional, the clean-shaven, Prince-of-Wales, well-brushed look, with well-brilliantined hair, was still almost imperative. It was still almost obligatory, too, to carry a cigarette case of silver or even gold. Both men and women favoured long cigarette holders to give them poise and distinction. Women wore 'Russian Boots' – high boots of soft leather, wrinkling round the calves, and for more formal occasions high (two to two and half inches) heels.

The skirt which had dropped nearer the ground just after the war had risen in 1925 to

Fashion of 1925

E.M.L.

SAY IT WITH MUSIC

Song- Fox- Trot.
by

Irving Berlin

2/ NET

LONDON: FRANCIS, DAY & HUNTER.

'Tunes seemed to last longer'

just below the knees and was to go higher yet. Bosoms, which suggested motherhood and the emotions associated with it, were taboo among people whose feelings had been continually overworked during the war years. Women now made up their faces in public and had their eyebrows plucked in private. Evening dresses were at times almost backless, and cut very low in front. The waist moved downwards towards the rising hemline of the skirt.

Bobbed hair and permanent waving were very much in the news by 1924

There was a revolution in women's hair styles. Feminists of the nineteenth century had cut off their tresses as a symbol of revolt. (Annie Besant was one of those whom the style particularly suited.) Bobbed hair was featured in the early days of the war by Irene Castle, the dancer, and during the war, factory workers were encouraged to bob their hair to keep it out of the machines. A bitter struggle followed after the war between those who

hoped that hair styles would return to 'normality', that is, what they had been before the war, and those who were determined never again to endure the burdens of long hair. But, once having plumped for short hair, the younger woman had to decide whether to stay with the bob, with the hair forming a hard pudding-basin line round the head, or whether to go for the shingle with the hair sloping gradually into the nape of the neck.

In hair-styles, if not in dancing, Fleur was up-to-date. Thus in *The Silver Spoon*, dealing with the years 1924 and 1925, we learn that Fleur ('already dressed for the evening, she had little on') had had her hair shingled.

'My dear girl,' Michael had said, when shingling came in, 'to please me, don't! Your *nuque* will be too bristly for kisses.'

'My dear boy,' she had answered, 'as if one could help it! You're always the same with any new fashion!'

She had been one of the first twelve to shingle, and was just feeling that without care she would miss being one of the first twelve to grow some hair again. Marjorie Ferrar, 'the Pet of the Panjoys', as Michael called her, already had more than an inch. Somehow, one hated being outdistanced by Marjorie Ferrar.

What made it impossible for Fleur to help it was the fashion for the helmet-type cloche hat, a type of tight, almost brimless paper-bag hat which left all too little room at the back for any un-shingled hair.

But you could never be absolutely sure. For already in January 1924, before shortened hair was taken for granted, there was talk of growing it again in order – however illogical this might seem – to show the ears.

An article in *Hairdressing Fashions* for that month read:

With the New Year our thoughts turn to the new Spring fashions. As regards hair there is a tendancy

(*opposite*) 'Clothes were exaggerated'

VOGUE

HELEN DRYDEN

Early September 1922   CONDÉ NAST & CO LTD
LONDON   One Shilling & Six Pence Net

(*above*) Erté *Harper's Bazaar* dress of 1925
(*opposite*) 'Women made up their faces in public
and had their eyebrows plucked in private';
'The Ear-ring', 1924, by K. K. Forbes

towards a higher angle which will presumably show the ears once more. These delightful appendages, which have been buried for such a long time, will once more be brought to light, and I feel sure that the rediscovery of the beauties of this almost forgotten feature will fill us with as much admiration as those wonderful and mysterious works of art which are being unearthed in Egypt from the tomb of Tutenkhamen. . . .

Now, of course, most of my readers will have short hair at the sides of the head, and this change of fashion will be extremely difficult to negotiate. But somehow we find Dame Fashion usually chooses the most inopportune moment to bring in a change. The signs of bobbing becoming extinct are rapidly increasing. And I think this will mean that those who have the sides bobbed will very soon be following their more venturesome sisters and letting them grow.

The writer adds that the new fashion of showing the ears is all the more desirable since so many young women 'listen-in' to broadcasts on headphones which tear and break the hair.

The older woman had a particularly difficult time. Thus in 1926,

the future – according to Annette – was dark. Were skirts to be longer or shorter by the autumn? If shorter, she herself would pay no attention; it might be all very well for Fleur, but she had reached the limit – at her age she would *not* go above the knee. As to the size of hats – again there was no definite indication. The most distinguished cocotte in Paris was said to be in favour of larger hats, but forces were working in the dark against her – motoring and Madame de Michel-Ange '*qui est toute pour la vieille cloche*'. . . .

Annette, who was not yet shingled, but whose neck for a long time had trembled on the block, confessed herself '*désespérée*'. Everything now depended on the Basque cap. If women took to them, shingling would stay; if not, hair might come in again. In any case the new tint would be pure gold; '*Et cela sera impossible. Ton père aurait une apoplexie.*' In any case Annette feared that she was condemned to long hair till the day of judgement. Perhaps, the good God would give her a good mark for it.

'If you want to shingle, Mother, I should. It's just father's conservatism – he really doesn't know what he likes. It would be a new sensation for him.'

Annette grimaced. '*Ma chère; je n'en sais rien.* Your father is capable of anything.'

A fashion exhibition at Holland Park Hall, 1925

The Revolution
that Wasn't

The Forsytes were not a politically-minded family of the kind that felt compelled to haunt the Palace of Westminster, and Soames told Sir Lawrence Mont in 1924 that he had never been inside the House of Commons since Gladstone died. Michael Mont decided, however, on the eve of Fleur's twenty-second birthday, to 'chuck publishing' and 'go into Parliament'.

He was able, through his father's Tory connections, to secure a nomination to the constituency of Mid-Bucks and was duly elected; and we must assume – since Galsworthy was a realist – that, in those days, it was considerably easier than it would be today to find a safe seat; we must also assume that the seat, if safe, could be won by someone without previous experience of political work either at party headquarters or in the constituency. Moreover the seat must have been quite exceptionally safe, since in the election in which Mont first stood – that of December 1923 – the Tories did extremely poorly and lost eighty-eight seats. The final result gave the Tories 258 seats, Labour 191 and the Liberals 158, and, six days after Michael took his seat, Mr Baldwin's Government was defeated and resigned.

Without the formality of a further election, King George V asked Ramsay MacDonald to form Britain's first Labour Government, an administration which remained in power till October 1924. MacDonald's Government fell partly because the Prime Minister was believed to have intervened to halt the prosecution of Mr J. R. Campbell, Acting Editor of *The Workers' Weekly*, who had been arrested and charged under the Mutiny Act of 1795 for having published an article inciting the military not to obey orders when instructed to go into action against strikers. Neither the Tories nor the Liberals were prepared to stand for that. The Government lost a vote of confidence and a General Election followed.

Four days before polling day the famous Zinoviev letter was published, addressed, apparently, to the Central Committee of the British Communist Party by Zinoviev, Chairman of the Presidium of the Communist International. It urged the British Party to mobilize the 'army of the unemployed proletarians', to form Communist cells in the armed forces, to organize insurrections in the colonies and Ireland and to establish good relations with the Soviet Union in the run-up to a revolution in Britain. Moreover, the Foreign Office, by delivering an official protest to Rakovsky, the Russian Chargé d'Affaires in London, appeared to regard the letter as genuine. The Zinoviev affair tipped the balance heavily against Labour, and the Conservatives achieved an overall majority at the polls.

So this time there need have been no surprise among the Forsytes or anywhere else at Michael's winning the seat. But we may perhaps pause to notice another aspect of parliamentary life, which, for better or worse,

becomes evident as we read the *Saga*. It happened that Michael Mont was by no means a true-blue Tory, but harboured in his mind independent policies for which he had not received the backing of his own party. He had derived them from a book by Sir James Foggart, published by Danby and Winter, the firm in which he had worked. Sir James Foggart was, of course, a mythical character but his views were somewhat akin to those of Rider Haggard and his 'Back to the Land' movement. 'His [Foggart's] eyes are fixed on 1944,' Michael explained, 'and his policy's according. Safety in the Air, the Land and Child Immigration; adjustment of Supply and Demand within the Empire; cut our losses in Europe; and endure a worse Present for the sake of a better Future.' The plan got nowhere for, as Michael's father pointed out, 'Half the Party won't like it because they've never thought of it; and the other half won't like it because they have.'

The affair is mentioned here only to illustrate the difficulties which, even in those days, faced politicians who wished to make their own independent contribution to the political life of their country. The Liberal Party did not offer a way out. It was being ground to pieces between the upper and nether millstones. Patrick Hastings, though Liberal in his views, had felt obliged to join the Labour Party and took the post of Attorney General. Winston Churchill, formerly a declared Liberal, stood for Epping in 1924 as a Constitutionalist.

The polarization which preceded, and followed, the Zinoviev Letter election helped to set the scene for the General Strike of 1926, though it was not its sole cause. The real trouble was that there could be no return to 'normalcy' as long as Britain relied on pre-war markets which she had since lost.

Furthermore, while Germany's reparations, made partly in kind at cut rates, made exporting more difficult, Britain's return to the gold standard was to raise the value of the pound to a level which made her own exports even more uncompetitive. There were riots once more in Trafalgar Square, and an earlier general strike was only narrowly averted the same year when the railway and transport workers, who had cemented their Triple Alliance with the mineworkers in 1919, decided not to make their support unconditional.

1921 saw the introduction of the dole (cursed alike by them that gave and them that took), and also the foundation of the Communist

Grigory Zinoviev

(*opposite*) 'Michael Mont decided on the eve of Fleur's twenty-second birthday, to "chuck publishing" and "go into Parliament"'; 'Ramsay MacDonald addressing the House of Commons', 1923, by Sir John Lavery

The Paisley hunger marchers, February 1923

Party of Great Britain; 1922 witnessed the first hunger march demonstration from Glasgow to London.

The nine-day General Strike of 1926 in which Fleur Forsyte ran a canteen for strike-breaking railway workers and Jon Forsyte stoked a railway engine, arose, once again, out of the troubles of the coalminers.

On 1 May, at a crucial meeting in the Memorial Hall, Farringdon Street, London, the Executive Committees of 141 Trades Unions had agreed to delegate their powers to the General Council of the Trades Union Congress, and to carry out its instructions regarding 'the conduct of the dispute and its financial assistance'. The miners' representatives too agreed to hand over the issue to the General Council, leaving the Council free to pursue negotiations, provided that the miners were consulted during the negotiations and particularly before any terms were accepted.

Later that same day the TUC informed the Government that, from then on, its Council would be handling the negotiations for the miners, and, on this basis, they received an invitation to send delegates to Downing Street at 6 p.m. that same evening. During the discussions at Number Ten, a promising formula emerged, and the TUC undertook to put it to the miners' representatives, and to give the Government an answer by lunchtime the following day (Sunday). But unknown (apparently) to the TUC, the miners, believing that no pre-strike negotiations were now possible, had left town. They had to be recalled by telegram.

Equally ignorant of this turn of events, the Cabinet met at noon the next morning to await the promised reply from the TUC. It did not arrive. Nor was the Cabinet given any explanation for the delay. It was not until 9 p.m. that the TUC representatives met again with those of the Government, and Arthur Pugh, their leader, sensed that in the meantime there had been a hardening of the Government attitude. Perhaps some members of the Cabinet detected intentional discourtesy on the part of the Trades Unionists or lack of good faith or ability to carry out their obligations. Or possibly it was becoming clear that the Government was not, as it had been told, negotiating merely with the TUC but with the TUC *and* the miners (whose belated arrival interrupted the resumed talks between the Government and the TUC). Anyway the fact remained that, with the minutes still ticking away towards the strike deadline, half a day had been lost without the Government receiving a reply to its proposal of Saturday.

Nevertheless on that Sunday evening the Trades Union delegates were still working on a paper of proposals to place before the Cabinet, when a new development occurred. The Prime Minister received news that the machine men of NATSOPA (the National Society of Operative Printers and Assistants) had refused to print the Monday issue of the *Daily Mail* unless its 'leader' was altered to

their satisfaction. Giving way, perhaps unwillingly, to the 'hawks' in the Cabinet, Baldwin summoned the TUC delegates and informed them that 'overt acts' including 'gross interference with the freedom of the Press' had now taken place, and that this constituted 'a challenge to the constitutional rights and freedom of the nation'. Accordingly, the Government could not continue negotiations unless the Trades Union Committee both repudiated the actions referred to and immediately and unconditionally withdrew their instructions for a general strike. The Cabinet then dispersed to bed, leaving the next move up to the TUC.

And so the General Strike, which the TUC preferred to describe first as 'co-ordinated action' and later as the National Strike, began at midnight on Monday 3 May. From then on there were three, by no means co-ordinated, struggles. One was in the streets between the Government and the pickets; the second was within the Labour movement between the moderates and the militants; and the third was between the General Council of the TUC and the miners.

Hyde Park, at that time still securely surrounded by high iron railings, became the Government fortress and nerve centre – the national larder and dairy, the headquarters of the transport system, with its own special water supply and telephone exchanges.

But in the field of communications, the Forsytes and many other people learned for the first time of a new force. Even Soames appreciated the importance of listening-in:

Having finished dinner, Soames lighted the second of his daily cigars and took up the ear-pieces of the wireless. He had resisted this invention as long as he could – but in times like these! 'London Calling!' Yes, and the British Isles listening! Trouble in Glasgow? There would be – lot of Irish there. More 'specials' wanted? There'd soon be plenty of those. He must tell that fellow Riggs to enlist. This butler chap, too, could well be spared. . . . After listening with some attention to the Home Secretary, Soames put the earpieces down and took up the *British Gazette*. It was his first sustained look at this tenuous production, and he hoped it would be his last.

The BBC with its repeated news bulletins – at least five a day – was certainly more objective than the *British Gazette*. While Churchill admitted that he 'could not claim to be impartial as between the fire brigade and the fire', the BBC announced from the first that it had no opinions of its own and would do its best to be fair to both sides. Accordingly it broadcast announcements of the TUC General Council, and summaries of speeches by Labour leaders, as well as announcements by the Government, and, when it refused to put out a broadcast by Ramsay MacDonald, it did so for fear that Winston Churchill might demand the right of reply, rather than because of any prejudice against Labour politicians.

There were, however, several other obstacles to the success of the strike – and they were far more serious than the attacks of the press.

In the first place, the TUC faced great organizational problems. In those days it was possible for the Government to take advance measures for its security without being accused of being 'provocative'. Labour, however, was not in the same fortunate position, and its organization was sketchy. There was little two-way communication between London and the provincial centres, and no definite ruling was given on whether Government lorries and, equally important, Government dispatch riders, should be stopped by the pickets or not. Sometimes different unions in the same city received conflicting instructions.

The strikers also suffered from the fact that Post Office staff continued to work during the strike, thus enabling the Government to tap messages and learn in advance of TUC plans. Yet if the Post Office had shut down, the TUC would have been still less able to keep in touch with the local strike committees.

The TUC insisted that it must retain control over all propaganda and that none was to be undertaken in the provinces without its prior approval. In addition, local representatives were ordered not to move outside their own districts.

There was a strongly held desire in Trades Union circles to keep the movement 'respectable' and the TUC General Council was acutely embarrassed when a cheque for two million roubles arrived from well-wishers in the Soviet Union. (It was returned with thanks.)

Reports of the General Strike have emphasized the gentlemanly fashion in which it was conducted and the good relations which existed between the strikers and the stricken. One probable explanation was that, in London at any rate, the bourgeoisie, although they faced greater difficulties in getting to work than their provincial counterparts, did not consider themselves directly involved in the dispute. It was the miners' strike, they thought, and miners were people who lived in the coalfields a long way away and worked underground. Let them settle their own affair.

But occasionally there were incidents that warned the TUC that they might yet find themselves, after all, leading a rebellion. The *Flying Scotsman* was derailed near Newcastle on the seventh day of the strike, and an attempt was made to burn down *The Times* by pouring petrol into the machine room. Special Constables were attacked, especially if they wore bourgeois-style 'Plus Fours' and stockings kept up with tasselled garters, and no witnesses could be found willing to give evidence of such assaults. Local Councils, if of Labour complexion, placed the Town Halls and other municipal resources at the disposal of the strikers. Workers' ('unarmed') Defence Corps for strengthening 'mass pickets' and for ensuring that strikers did not enter unprepared into conflict with the police were recruited in many cities. There were clashes with the

'There were several other obstacles to the success of the strike' – wiring the bonnets of the buses to stop strikers getting at the engines

police in Newcastle, Gateshead, Glasgow, Edinburgh, Wolverhampton and Nottingham, and Raymond Postgate in *A Workers' History of the Great Strike*, which he wrote with Ellen Wilkinson and J. F. Horrabin, recorded that in London no black-leg driver dared go east of Aldgate.

Nevertheless strike solidarity began to crumble at the top after unofficial negotiations, to which the miners were not originally invited, began between TUC leaders and Herbert Samuel (of the Samuel Commission which had previously inquired into the efficiency of the Coal Industry). Samuel, making clear that he was acting without official authority, came up with fresh proposals for linking the reform of the coal industry with wage reductions which might nevertheless have to be made.

But the miners, resentful at not having been consulted at the outset, and uncertain whether the Government could be relied on to approve the Samuel proposals once the strike had ended, were not prepared to take the responsibility of agreeing to a return to work. Neither was the TUC prepared to leave both its own future and that of the negotiations in the hands of the miners. Possibly the General Council felt that the solidarity and the relatively speaking unruffled tempers of the participants could not last much longer and that their own position as leaders could only become weaker as time went by. But they did not drive a very good bargain. The General Strike, with the miners still in vigorous opposition, was called off unconditionally on 12 May. 'The Movement came out in order to ensure a fair deal for the Miners'. 'The General Council is satisfied that this can now be achieved,' the TUC official announcement said. But since the miners had not accepted the Samuel proposals, the Government was likewise absolved from doing so.

The Saga summed up the reaction of the middle classes, in which Galsworthy moved, to the end of the strike, but could only conjecture the feelings of the strikers:

The news of the General Strike's collapse caught him [Michael Mont] as he was going home after driving Fleur to the canteen. A fizz and bustle in the streets, and the words: 'Strike Over' scrawled extempore at street corners, preceded 'End of Strike – Official' of the hurrying newsvendors. Michael stopped his car against the kerb and bought a news-sheet. There it was! For a minute he sat motionless with a choky feeling, such as he had felt when the news of the Armistice came through. A sword lifted from over the head of England! A source of pleasure to her enemies dried up! People passed and passed him, each with a news-sheet, or a look in the eye. They were taking it almost as soberly as they had taken the strike itself. 'Good old England! We're a great people when we're up against it!' he thought, driving his car slowly on into Trafalgar Square. A group of men, who had obviously been strikers, stood leaning against the parapet. He tried to read their faces. Glad, sorry, ashamed, resentful, relieved? . . . Some defensive joke seemed to be going the round of them.

It has sometimes been assumed that the collapse of the General Strike was due largely to the success with which amateurs from universities, medical schools, the Stock Exchange, Lloyds and elsewhere took over and ran essential services. And certainly many of the well-to-do found the strike a bit of fun, with all the excitement of war and only a small percentage of its dangers. Lady Mountbatten manned the switchboard of the *Daily Express* and remained well informed. Duff Cooper, a future Minister of Information, worked in the dispatch room of *The Times*, folding copies of the paper, and was presented with a silver matchbox for his trouble. C. E. Pitman, the Oxford Rowing Blue, drove a Great Western Railway train from Bristol to Gloucester, and many others fulfilled their childhood ambition to be engine drivers. (The fashionable Café de Paris did its bit by admitting patrons who were not wearing evening dress.)

Jon Forsyte was delighted to be back in London as a stoker; Fleur enjoyed running the canteen he patronized – a coincidence which led to their final affair. Val Dartie piloted a lorry and Marjorie Ferrar (that girl proved to have the right stuff in her after all once she realized the country was in danger) drove for the Downing Street car pool. At least two more of the Forsyte family were 'Specials'.

It has been argued that, if one judges by statistics, the value of these self-sacrifices was marginal. Many of the jobs which the volunteers hoped to take over were beyond their capabilities. Guards and signalmen are made, not born. Handling packing cases or sacks in the docks without dropping them or straining a muscle requires a knack given to few medical students or Stock Exchange clerks. And Jon Forsyte, no doubt, found out that a stoker needs not only to move coal from the tender to the fire box, but must do so at a rate suited to the capacity of the engine, with the coal distributed evenly so that the heat from it reaches all parts of the boiler. Expensive machines can easily be wrecked beyond repair by a novice who does not know how to use them.

Even in London, where the concentration of Forsytes was at its greatest, public transport, notwithstanding the numbers of volunteer drivers, was patchy. Bus routes where driving was dangerous were readily abandoned. The London General Omnibus Company did not move any of its three thousand buses out of their garages on the first day of the strike and the total number of buses operating (including 'pirate' services) reached only 529 out of a total of 4400 by the fifth day, and 959 by 11 May. The bus windows had eventually to be protected with wire netting and two special constables were needed, one to guard the driver and the other the conductor. There was no driving after dark.

Trams were still more vulnerable because it was easy for the strikers to tear up the track or interfere with the points. At times about a quarter of the Underground trains ran, but the trains did not always reach the right stations.

Yet perhaps in the end the volunteers' attitude was decisive. If the bicycles, the pony traps and the small cars of the middle classes had stayed immobilized at home, who can say whether the Government's nerve would have held? And how would it have turned out if the students had been *for* the strikers instead of mostly *against* them? (The Oxford University Debating Society, The Union, actually did pass a vote criticizing the Cabinet for breaking off negotiations.)

Soames would probably never have asked himself such questions and the strike once over, with the miners and railwaymen brought to heel, he was able to devote himself once more to the pursuit of riverside happiness.

Stanley Baldwin acknowledging cheers at the
end of the Strike

The Passing of Soames

Soames had a garden among his fifteen acres of land at Mapledurham.

In this bright weather, the leaves just full, the may-flower in bloom, bulbs not yet quite over, and the river re-learning its summer smile, the beauty of the prospect was not to be sneezed at. Soames on his green lawn walked a little and thought of why gardeners seemed always on the move from one place to another. He couldn't seem to remember ever having seen an English gardener otherwise than about to work. That was, he supposed, why people so often had Scotch gardeners.

Soames was paying out 'a pretty penny' in wages (did any Forsyte consider servants a bargain?). He could still afford to keep a head-gardener, and therefore by implication an under-gardener as well. Furthermore, although Soames remonstrated over the possibility of an extra boy being taken on to create the third asparagus bed, he was not appalled at the idea. On the other hand, the difficulty of finding reliable labour suggests, as Soames did, that the younger generation was already moving to London, if not to 'play instruments in the streets', as Soames appeared to think, at least to seek work there.

It is clear that Soames had not, even after his retirement, become an amateur flower-grower. Nor may we assume Annette to be one of those owner-gardeners who delight to put on a battered sun-hat and gardening gloves to go round the flowerbeds snipping off dead-heads, weeding or staking.

We are not told much about the design of the garden at Mapledurham except that there was a flower border under the kitchen wall with hollyhocks and sunflowers in bloom, and a summerhouse. And that the roses were in little round beds. This would make Soames's garden a compromise affair – showing both Victorian and twentieth-century features.

The rose-beds suggest a Victorian garden with a profusion of geometrical figures – diamonds, crescents, rondels, and gravel paths edged with miniature box edging, together with terraces, parapets, balustrades, statues and other 'garden furniture' which would help to turn the whole into part of an architectural scheme.

But the border of hollyhocks and sunflowers 'under the kitchen wall' suggests a different picture. This could have been either an unauthorized reversion by the staff to the kind of cottage gardens they would have known in their childhood; or more probably a reflection of the counter-revolution in garden design which had already begun in 1883 with the publication of William Robinson's famous work *The English Flower Garden*, which ran through fifteen editions during the next half century. Robinson's philosophy called for a return to nature and to the unpretentious charm of the English cottage garden.

He wanted each and every corner of the garden to mirror the flower garden of the world outside. Walls he considered should be covered with flowering climbers. He not only rejected geometrically designed beds (which he described as 'pastry-cooks' work') and artificial pleasances ('railway embankment gardening') but also abhorred any elaborate topiary and 'fountain-mongery'. Above all he denounced the invasion of open-air flowerbeds by garish bedded-out greenhouse plants as a shameful imposture.

Yew trees festooned with white clematis appealed to him and Chinese peonies against a background of grass.

In *The Wild Garden* he called for hardy exotic plants to be introduced into British gardens where they could flourish without needing further care or attention. He was lucky in as much as explorers, acting on behalf of private collectors and go-ahead nurserymen, were able, during the latter part of the century, and after, to collect and send home scores of new hardy plants – magnolias, camellias, azaleas, lilies, rhododendrons, viburnums, clematis, and the like, from Western China, Japan, the Himalayas, Vietnam and elsewhere.

Robinson's views were strongly supported by Miss Gertrude Jekyll, though she differed from him in designing new gardens rather than reconstructing old ones. To her as much as anyone we owe the herbaceous border and the conception that the garden should subordinate itself to the landscape – should be a fringe of the countryside extending up to the house, rather than an appendage of the dwelling itself. Her layouts were neither pseudo-rustic on the one hand nor over-dramatic on the other. She could best be described as a gardener's gardener whose designs were planned to show off the flowers and shrubs – and their colours – to the best. Photographs of many of her gardens were to be seen in *Country Life* which first appeared in 1897 and no doubt strongly influenced amateurs and professionals alike.

In 1870, after a walking tour in Switzerland, William Robinson published *Alpine Flowers for British Gardens* and an artificial rock garden was built at Kew in the eighties, a spin-off, perhaps, of the increasingly popular amateur sport of mountaineering. But, generally speaking, the rock garden was an Edwardian rather than a Victorian novelty and, even then, the essentials were often lacking. Many of the early examples were crude adaptations of earlier grottos and ferneries, and were not constructed according to geological principles. Reginald Farrer, whose book *My Rock Garden* published in 1907 became a standard work, had to fight hard against nurserymen's 'rockeries' which looked, he said, like almond puddings or even dogs' graves. Some rascals even used clinkers or conglomerate bricks for their moraines.

World War I forced a good many changes on gardeners and gardening. Headmen and underlings alike volunteered or were called up and could not be replaced. Hothouses had to be shut down to save fuel, and when peace came, few private owners could afford to re-establish what they had lost.

But for the nurserymen there were compensations. *Amateur Gardening*, first published in 1884, had built up a new market for sure-fire seeds and seedlings for the city back garden, and for the cold greenhouses in which the favoured 'Chrysanths' could be grown side by side with a tomato or two – with the help, now that horses were out of favour, of artificial fertilizer.

The Royal Horticultural Society, through their gardens at Wisley, and their shows at Vincent Square and Chelsea, continued to keep nurserymen and amateurs alike in touch with new cultivars and species. Mendel's laws of heredity, first published in 1865, had been fortunately rediscovered at the turn of the century and helped plant breeders in the search for new strains and varieties.

The eclipse of the private hot-house and the success of the herbaceous border meant that (with a few exceptions) cut flowers rather than pot plants were used for indoor decorations. So, in one way, Soames should have been glad that his head-gardener specialized in roses, however unwilling the gardener might be for them to be cut and brought into the house. On the other hand so many other plants had been successfully 'specialized' that it was a pity to ignore them.

The sweet pea, originally grown in Britain in 1700 by Dr Uvedale at Enfield from seeds sent to him by a Sicilian monk, had been developed by Henry Eckford, formerly head-gardener to the Earl of Radnor. His first big success, 'Bronze Prince', came in 1882 and, at the Sweet Pea Exhibition held in 1900 to celebrate the bicentenary of the species, he had raised 115 out of the 264 varieties shown.

A Cambridge physiology don, Michael Foster, later knighted, had evolved the modern bearded iris between 1880 and 1890 in his small garden at Shelford. Another breakthrough came in 1898 when the Revd George Engleheart, Vicar of Chute Forest in Wiltshire, working on strains classified by Peter Barr, produced six bulbs of 'Will Scarlett', a daffodil with an orange-red cup. He sold three to a nurseryman for £100. By 1900 the Revd William Wilks, working in his garden, The Wilderness at Shirley, Surrey, transmuted the wild field poppy into the delicately coloured Shirley Poppy and was giving the seeds away generously. George Russell, an allotment holder of York, had been experimenting successfully with new types of lupin well before World War I. The famous yellow Malmaison carnation had first been produced in 1904, and, from 1910 onwards, Montagu Allwood was presenting exciting crosses between the perpetual flowering carnation and the pink-fringed dianthus.

However, as in most prosperous families, the gardener rather than the master decided what was to be grown in any given garden and what flourished there, and Soames probably had the good sense to realize this.

When Soames left the gardener after his discussion of the third asparagus bed, he went for a walk with the Golden Retriever that had belonged to Fleur as a girl. Soames and the dog now had a common bond of sympathy in so far as they felt neglected. Fleur's special confidant was now Ting-a-ling, a tawny Pekingese which Michael had bought out of a Bond Street shop window as a four-month-old puppy for her twentieth birthday. The animal settled down well in the Mont mansion in South Square, Westminster (four bathrooms), despite the fact that Fleur had a 'Spanish Room' as well as a Chinese, and so the present was a great success.

Galsworthy originally christened the dog Confucius but altered the name following an official Chinese protest.

'Oh!' said Fleur. 'There's Ting and a cat!' Ting-a-ling, out for a breath of air, and tethered by a lead in the hands of a maid, was snuffling horribly and trying to climb a railing whereon was perched a black cat, all hunch and eyes.

'Give him to me, Ellen. Come with Mother, darling!'

Ting-a-ling came, indeed, but only because he couldn't go, bristling and snuffling and turning his head back.

'I like to see him natural,' said Fleur.

'Waste of money, a dog like that,' Soames commented. 'You should have had a bull-dog and let him sleep in the hall. No end of burglaries. Your aunt had her knocker stolen.'

'I wouldn't part with Ting for a hundred knockers.'

'One of these days you'll be having *him* stolen – fashionable breed.'

And the Pekingese was indeed a fashionable breed, having, by 1925, convincingly outnumbered the Pomeranians at Crufts. Once there had been only five Pekingese in Britain. The British had found them in 1860 when they captured Peking and burned the Summer Palace. The Emperor's aunt committed suicide and the animals were discovered in her apartments in the Yuen Ming Yuan Pavilion on the edge of the city. They were of the species that had appeared repeatedly on the Imperial scrolls since the middle of the seventeenth century. Imperial edicts had specified that they should be small enough to be carried in the sleeve of a court robe, and that only animals coloured in one of four colours – sable, red, black or white – to suit the Imperial Wardrobe, should be bred. The dogs' feet must also be tufted plentifully with hair to allow them to pad noiselessly along the corridors of power. Four of the five Pekingese were taken by Admiral of the Fleet Lord Hay, and the smallest, a fawn-and-white bitch, by Lieutenant, later General, Dunne who presented it to Queen Victoria. A true palace dog, it survived for twelve years.

'Fleur's special confidant was now Ting-a-ling, a tawny Pekingese'

At least four more Pekingese were imported to Britain in the 1890s, but, until 1898, when the Kennel Club officially recognized the breed, they had to be shown in the 'Any Other Varieties' class.

The value of all show-dogs, Pekingese included, increased steadily from 1904 when the Kennel Club made it compulsory for owners to register all dogs to be shown at recognized shows. Then, in the later years of the Kaiser's war, when pedigree breeding was suspended (to save dog food), values rose still higher.

Paintings, however, were more profitable and Soames had always been personally involved in them.

It had long been his custom on Sunday afternoons to retire to his 'gallery' to gaze at them, and dealers knew that it was worth letting him know when they had a rarity for sale – at the right price. But his attitudes were not fully understood throughout the Forsyte family. At tea one day Juley asked:

'Have you bought any pictures lately, Soames?'
Her incomparable instinct for the wrong subject had not failed her. Soames flushed. To disclose the name of his latest purchases would be like walking into the jaws of disdain. For somehow they all knew of June's predilection for 'genius' not yet on its legs, and her contempt for 'success' unless she had had a finger in securing it.
'One or two,' he muttered.
But June's face had changed; the Forsyte within her was seeing its chance. Why should not Soames buy some of the pictures of Eric Cobbley – her last lame duck? And she promptly opened her attack: Did Soames know his work? It was so wonderful. He was the coming man.
Oh yes, Soames knew his work. It was in his view 'splashy', and would never get hold of the public.
June blazed up.
'Of course it won't; that's the last thing one would wish for. I thought you were a connoisseur, not a picture-dealer.'

June was right. For though it was Soames's delight to gaze at pictures and to learn as much as he could of their history, yet it is clear that he was a trader rather than a collector. Thus:

Lunch was over and Soames mounted to the picture-gallery in his house near Mapledurham. . . . He stood before his Gauguin – sorest point of his collection.

He had bought the great ugly thing with two early Matisses before the War, because there was such a fuss about those Post-Impressionist chaps. He was wondering whether Profond would take them off his hands – the fellow seemed not to know what to do with his money – when he heard his sister's voice say: 'I think that's a horrid thing, Soames,' and saw that Winifred had followed him up.

'Oh you *do*?' he said drily; 'I gave five hundred for it.'

'Fancy! Women aren't made like that even if they are black.'

Both saw the flat two-dimensional slabs of colour in which Gauguin revealed the women of Mataiea and Tahiti as a challenge to the values of Western civilization, though Soames refused to admit it, and eventually declined to sell the picture.

But his attitude towards conventional painters was equally suspect. Thus we find him musing over Fred Walker, the Victorian artist whose paintings of the romantic peasantry showed every girl as a madonna and every man a Greek hero.

Fred Walker! [Soames ruminated] The fellow was old-fashioned; he and Mason had been succeeded by a dozen movements. But – like old fiddles, with the same agreeable glow – there they were, very good curiosities such as would always command a price.

(Even more of a curiosity was the Fred Walker picture never shown in an art gallery – the first modern-style British poster which he produced in 1861 as an advertisement for Wilkie Collins' thriller, *The Woman in White*.)

Then:

Having detached a Courbet, early and about ripe [the implication here is that Soames behaved towards his paintings like a market gardener], he was standing in his shirt-sleeves with a coil of wire in his hand, when Michael entered.

'Where have you sprung from?' he said, surprised.

'I happened to be passing, sir, on my old bike. I see you've kept your word about the English School.'

Soames attached the wire.

'I shan't be happy,' he said, 'till I've got an old Crome – best of the English landscapists.'

'Awfully rare, isn't he, old Crome?' [John Crome's first known picture was not painted until the artist was well into his thirties.]

'Yes, that's why I want him.'

The smile on Michael's face, as if he were thinking: 'You mean that's why you consider him the best,' was lost on Soames giving the wire a final twist.

Soames's collection at Mapledurham, which he believed to be worth £100,000 at 1926 values and which he planned to bequeath to the nation, was a hotch-potch assembly, more appropriate to a museum which wants to show the public a specimen or two of this 'school' and an example or two of that. It lacked the distinctive personal style which one would have hoped to find in the gallery of a private connoisseur.

One would like to think that Soames believed, as Oscar Wilde once postulated, that to talk of the English (or French) school of painting is as meaningless as it would be to talk of English (or French) mathematics: that all good work looks perfectly modern and that the artist is not the mouthpiece of his century but the master of eternity. It would have been a strange, yet not inconceivable meeting of minds, and would have accounted for the fact that he had not specialized in any one group of artists.

Yet the more likely explanation is that Soames did not want to put all his eggs in one basket. He was not the man to trust his own judgment of the artistic worth of a painting, as distinct from its likely commercial value. One does not feel that Soames would ever have agreed with the Post-Impressionist suggestion that a running horse has twenty legs. One doubts whether, when the fire broke out at his home, he made a special effort to save those paintings by Gustave Courbet and Honoré Daumier, the apostles of realism, because they triumphed over the ugliness and vulgarity of the scenes they painted. More likely it was because in the years since their deaths in the 1870s they had become established and therefore worth more than Soames had paid for them.

Living in London, Soames could be excused for lagging about a generation behind art development in Paris, where the original Impressionists, Renoir, Pissarro, Monet and others made their début in 1874. But we do not find Soames buying English moderns either. He believed that he would outlive their reputations.

True collectors today are concerned when the value of their pictures increases. It adds to the difficulty of guarding their treasures and the expense of insuring them. We are not told that this problem worried Soames or that he grumbled about paying the premiums. But

neither do we hear of him keeping a picture once its value had increased and was unlikely to go any higher.

It was sad that, in the end, it all went up in smoke.

In 1926 when fire broke out in Soames's picture gallery on the second floor of The Shelter at Mapledurham, the fire service, taking the country as a whole, left much to be desired. There was, for example, despite the recommendation of a Royal Commission in 1923, no national fire service, and the Government had imposed no obligation for fire stations to arrange pacts of mutual assistance with stations in the surrounding areas. (That was not to come until 1938.) Indeed for many years fire services had been operated by insurance companies who on principle sent engines only to those houses bearing a leaden plaque or fire mark certifying that the building was duly insured.

'Soames showed his usual good sense when he gave orders "to telephone Reading for the engines"'

In 1908, the year when the London Fire Brigade received its first petrol-driven pump, there were, according to *Fire*, the journal of the British fire services, only 1469 public fire brigades in the whole of the United Kingdom. Fewer than one hundred 'motor appliances' were in commission. There were 700 'steamers' (that is, the fire-pump was powered by steam from a boiler which had to be stoked up during the journey from the station to the fire) and 1307 manuals. There were only 1209 mobile

fire-escapes. Breathing apparatus was still worked with the aid of hand bellows.

Thirteen years later *Fire* declared that the number of public fire brigades was 'now about fifteen hundred', that is about thirty-one more than in 1908. And around one-third of these were still either steamers or manual.

As late as 1928 Pangbourne, which is only two miles from Mapledurham as the crow flies, depended on a horse-drawn steamer. A small manual fire engine is preserved at Mapledurham itself. It had a supply-trough in the middle into which the water was poured, and its two reciprocating pumps were manned

'It was Fleur, the person Soames loved most, who started the fire'; Fleur (Susan Hampshire)

by groups of men standing at either end of a long beam, mounted like a see-saw. When one group pulled down their end of the beam, the pump on their side expelled water through a hose made of leather strips joined together with copper rivets.

Soames, therefore, showed his usual good sense when he gave orders 'to telephone to Reading for the engines'. The town is only four miles away on a more direct route than Pangbourne. Reading, at the time, had two fire engines both with three-stage petrol driven turbine pumps. Each engine had attachment points for two independent hoses and could deliver 350 gallons of water per minute; and each had its own fire escape. The engines had been in use in Reading since 1912. But Soames would have been luckier if his fire had occurred two years later. For in 1928 Reading invested in a new Dennis engine with pumps for three hoses.

As it was, the fire was confined almost entirely to one wall of Soames's gallery, and from that he himself saved amongst others a Constable, a Gauguin, a Corot, a Monet, a Turner, a Morland, a Courbet, and his favourite, a Daumier. In the end, however, it was the powerful jet of the Reading fire engine that dislodged another picture, a Goya copy, standing on the window sill, which fatally injured Soames as it fell to the ground.

It was Fleur, the person Soames loved most, who started the fire that destroyed the possessions he loved most. After the end of her affair with Jon she felt so exhausted that she had not even the strength to undress, and the cigarette she was smoking dropped to the carpet.

At this point one loves her least. But somehow she never becomes despicable. Susan Hampshire, who played Fleur in the BBC's television production of *The Forsyte Saga*, studied Fleur till she saw her almost as clearly as Galsworthy himself must have, and a great deal more clearly than most of Galsworthy's readers. Her verdict:

I didn't feel I was a bit like Fleur, and so I didn't identify myself with her. But I loved her dearly with every fault that she had, and some of them were enormous. I mean I really cared about her, which was surprising because one would not have expected that the actual person who was playing an unsympathetic character would have liked her so much. I think that Fleur was extremely selfish. But she was very true to life and this was why she was attractive to so many people: all her faults were such human ones. . . .

Like her father, she felt the need for the affair of a lifetime – the 'grand amour', and was ready to cross the world to get it, just as if she were blindly following a star. . . .

I don't really think she was particularly highly sexed; or that she particularly wanted to be surrounded by men all the time. She only wanted one person in the world. She had a flirtation with the poet, Wilfrid Desert, but this was because he was entertaining and she had so little to do. She should have taken a regular job. She should have worked. Then she would have had so much less time to waste. . . .

In the end she was rather warm to her husband, and realized that he had more to offer than Jon, who, I personally thought, was a fool and rather a weak person.

It wouldn't have worked for them, although she believed that it would.

When Fleur first lost Jon she was very bitter against Soames. When you are as young as she was, you think you are suffering more than anyone else in the world. It is not till you are older that you see everybody else is going through the same sort of trials.

The second time round was different from the first.

If you're not married and you're denied the thing you desperately want, there's the feeling that there might still have been an opportunity for it to come right. But by the time you're married and you've got a child, if you get to the point where you're prepared to risk everything and, perhaps, both of you are ready to get divorced and run off together, and then it doesn't work out, then there must be a voice in you that says, as it must have said to Fleur: 'Well, I suppose I *am* married already, and we have a child, and Michael is not such a bad chap. In fact he's rather nice.' And so you become reconciled to things as they are, as Fleur seems to have been at the end of the *Saga*.

*   *   *

'You know me, darling?' [Fleur asked as she came into Soames's bedroom, and saw him for the last time.]

His eyes said: 'Yes.'

'You remember?'

Again his eyes said: 'Yes.'

His lips were twitching all the time, as if rehearsing for speech, and the look in his eyes deepening. She saw his brows frown faintly, as if her face were too close; drew back a little and the frown relaxed.

'Darling, you are going to be all right.'

His eyes said: 'No'; and his lips moved, but she could not distinguish the sound. For a moment she lost control, and said with a sob:

'Dad, forgive me!'

His eyes softened; and this time she caught what sounded like:

'Forgive? Nonsense!'

'I love you so.'

He seemed to abandon the effort to speak then, and centred all the life of him in his eyes. Deeper and deeper grew the colour and the form and the meaning in them, as if to compel something from her. And suddenly, like a little girl, she said:

'Yes, Dad, I will be good!'

A tremor from his finger passed into her palm; his lips seemed trying to smile, his head moved as if he had meant to nod, and always that look deepened in his eyes.

'Gradman is here, darling, and Mother, and Aunt Winifred, and Kit and Michael. Is there anyone you would like to see?'

His lips shaped: 'No – you!'

'I am here all the time.' Again she felt the tremor from his fingers, saw his lips whispering:

'That's all.'

And suddenly, his eyes went out. There was nothing there! For some time longer he breathed, but before 'that fellow' came, he had lost hold – was gone.

Soames never saw a talking picture; never pulled up at a traffic light; never dialled a telephone number, or listened to an automatic record-player. He had never watched a television show or been to the dogs at the White City; never heard King George V broadcast a

Soames in his seventies (Eric Porter)

Christmas message, or seen a backless bathing-dress. In his day there were no tennis shorts; there was no penicillin. The speed limit was still twenty miles per hour. And London still had its choking fogs. So, to this extent, we may look on him as under-privileged (though he did escape the Great Depression, Munich and Hitler's war).

Should we therefore conclude that the World of the Forsytes ended with Soames's death? In one sense: Yes.

Who could imagine, half a century later, that a modern Irene would have accepted Soames as her only suitor, and would have married him not knowing whether he was sexually eligible? And after Irene's escapade with Bosinney, would Soames Mark II have held back from a divorce through fear of scandal? Clearly the whole plot of the *Saga* would need to be revised.

Even the characters in it would have, today, a diminished significance; for, as Galsworthy pointed out, the period of which he wrote was especially favourable to the inflorescence of the upper-middle classes. Its members were relatively wealthier than their descendants today, and the family as a unit was more influential, since the parents did not yet depend on the State for the education of their children, the protection of their health, or the solace of their old age. Perhaps this explains why no family in contemporary literature looks like taking the place of the Forsytes.

Nevertheless the appeal of the Forsyte family is persistent rather than perishable. The spectacle of a family group disintegrating as it did provokes nostalgia among all who have loved their parents and been loved by them.

The frustrations of Soames, the gaiety and the grief of Fleur, and the regrets of old Jolyon draw us back, too willingly perhaps, into a world which, with its remoteness, becomes more and more attractive to those who could have frequented it – a world which almost certainly none of us will ever see again.

Forsyte Family Tree

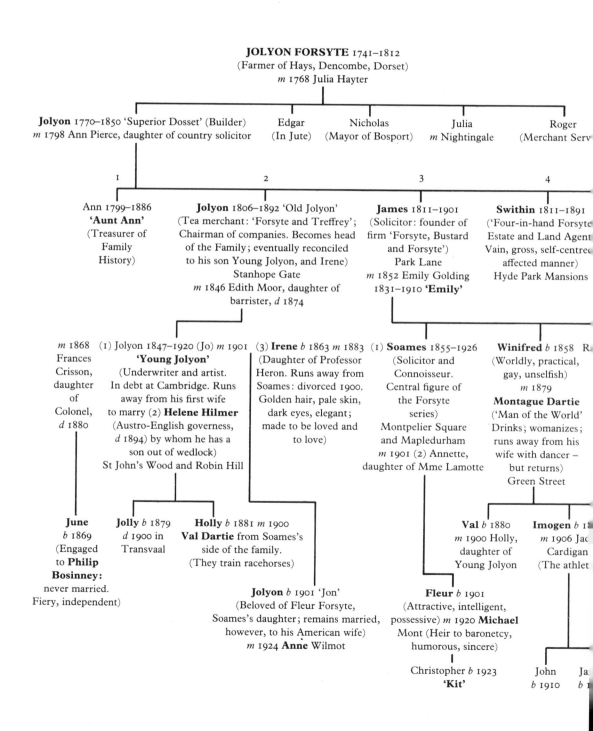

JOLYON FORSYTE 1741–1812
(Farmer of Hays, Dencombe, Dorset)
m 1768 Julia Hayter

Jolyon 1770–1850 'Superior Dosset' (Builder)
m 1798 Ann Pierce, daughter of country solicitor

Edgar
(In Jute)

Nicholas
(Mayor of Bosport)

Julia
m Nightingale

Roger
(Merchant Serv

1   2   3   4

Ann 1799–1886
'Aunt Ann'
(Treasurer of
Family
History)

Jolyon 1806–1892 'Old Jolyon'
(Tea merchant: 'Forsyte and Treffrey';
Chairman of companies. Becomes head
of the Family; eventually reconciled
to his son Young Jolyon, and Irene)
Stanhope Gate
m 1846 Edith Moor, daughter of
barrister, *d* 1874

James 1811–1901
(Solicitor: founder of
firm 'Forsyte, Bustard
and Forsyte')
Park Lane
m 1852 Emily Golding
1831–1910 **'Emily'**

Swithin 1811–1891
('Four-in-hand Forsyte
Estate and Land Agent
Vain, gross, self-centre
affected manner)
Hyde Park Mansions

m 1868
Frances
Crisson,
daughter
of
Colonel,
d 1880

(1) Jolyon 1847–1920 (Jo) *m* 1901
'Young Jolyon'
(Underwriter and artist.
In debt at Cambridge. Runs
away from his first wife
to marry (2) **Helene Hilmer**
(Austro-English governess,
d 1894) by whom he has a
son out of wedlock)
St John's Wood and Robin Hill

(3) **Irene** *b* 1863 *m* 1883
(Daughter of Professor
Heron. Runs away from
Soames: divorced 1900.
Golden hair, pale skin,
dark eyes, elegant;
made to be loved and
to love)

(1) **Soames** 1855–1926
(Solicitor and
Connoisseur.
Central figure of
the Forsyte
series)
Montpelier Square
and Mapledurham
m 1901 (2) Annette,
daughter of Mme Lamotte

Winifred *b* 1858 R
(Worldly, practical,
gay, unselfish)
m 1879
Montague Dartie
('Man of the World'
Drinks; womanizes;
runs away from his
wife with dancer –
but returns)
Green Street

June
b 1869
(Engaged
to **Philip
Bosinney**:
never married.
Fiery, independent)

Jolly *b* 1879
d 1900 in
Transvaal

Holly *b* 1881 *m* 1900
Val Dartie from Soames's
side of the family.
(They train racehorses)

Jolyon *b* 1901 'Jon'
(Beloved of Fleur Forsyte,
Soames's daughter; remains married,
however, to his American wife)
m 1924 **Anne** Wilmot

Val *b* 1880
m 1900 Holly,
daughter of
Young Jolyon

Imogen *b* 1
m 1906 Jac
Cardigan
(The athlet

Fleur *b* 1901
(Attractive, intelligent,
possessive) *m* 1920 **Michael**
Mont (Heir to baronetcy,
humorous, sincere)

Christopher *b* 1923
'Kit'

John
b 1910

Ja
b 1

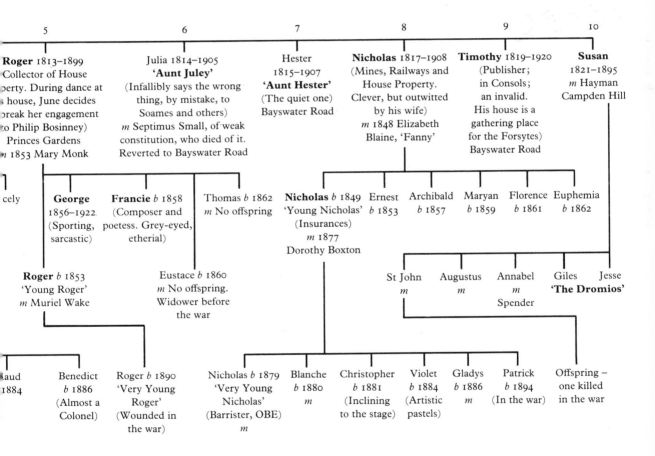

5   6   7   8   9   10

Roger 1813–1899
Collector of House
Property. During dance at
his house, June decides
break her engagement
to Philip Bosinney)
Princes Gardens
m 1853 Mary Monk

Julia 1814–1905
'Aunt Juley'
(Infallibly says the wrong
thing, by mistake, to
Soames and others)
m Septimus Small, of weak
constitution, who died of it.
Reverted to Bayswater Road

Hester
1815–1907
'Aunt Hester'
(The quiet one)
Bayswater Road

Nicholas 1817–1908
(Mines, Railways and
House Property.
Clever, but outwitted
by his wife)
m 1848 Elizabeth
Blaine, 'Fanny'

Timothy 1819–1920
(Publisher;
in Consols;
an invalid.
His house is a
gathering place
for the Forsytes)
Bayswater Road

Susan
1821–1895
m Hayman
Campden Hill

cely

George
1856–1922
(Sporting,
sarcastic)

Francie b 1858
(Composer and
poetess. Grey-eyed,
etherial)

Thomas b 1862
m No offspring

Nicholas b 1849
'Young Nicholas'
(Insurances)
m 1877
Dorothy Boxton

Ernest
b 1853

Archibald
b 1857

Maryan
b 1859

Florence
b 1861

Euphemia
b 1862

Roger b 1853
'Young Roger'
m Muriel Wake

Eustace b 1860
m No offspring.
Widower before
the war

St John
m

Augustus
m

Annabel
m
Spender

Giles
'The Dromios'

Jesse

aud
1884

Benedict
b 1886
(Almost a
Colonel)

Roger b 1890
'Very Young
Roger'
(Wounded in
the war)

Nicholas b 1879
'Very Young
Nicholas'
(Barrister, OBE)
m

Blanche
b 1880
m

Christopher
b 1881
(Inclining
to the stage)

Violet
b 1884
(Artistic
pastels)

Gladys
b 1886
m

Patrick
b 1894
(In the war)

Offspring –
one killed
in the war

Select Bibliography

ADBURGHAM, ALISON. *Shops and Shopping 1800–1914*. George Allen & Unwin, London, 1964

—ed. *Victorian Shopping: Harrods' 1895 Catalogue*. David & Charles Reprints, Newton Abbot, 1972

—ed. *Yesterday's Shopping: Army & Navy Stores Catalogue, 1907*. David & Charles Reprints, Newton Abbot, 1969

ANDERSON, RACHEL. *The Purple Heart Throbs: The Sub-Literature of Love*. Hodder & Stoughton, London, 1974

ANONYMOUS: 'A Member of the Aristocracy'. *Society Small Talk or What to Say and When to Say It*. Frederick Warne, London, 1879

—'The Author of *Manners and Tone of Good Society*'. *Party-Giving on Every Scale*. Frederick Warne, London, 1882

ASSOCIATED NEWSPAPERS, London. *News in Our Time: Golden Jubilee Book of the 'Daily Mail'*.

BARKER, SIR ERNEST. *Father of the Man*. National Council of Social Service, London, 1948

BARKER, T. C., and ROBBINS, MICHAEL. *A History of London Transport*. George Allen & Unwin, London, 1974

BARNICOAT, JOHN. *A Concise History of Posters*. Thames & Hudson, London, 1972; Abrams, New York, 1972

BEER, M. *A History of British Socialism*. G. Bell, London, 1919

BELL, CLIVE. *Since Cézanne*. Chatto & Windus, London, 1922

BELL, E. H. C. MOBERLY. *Josephine Butler*. Constable, London, 1962

BENNETT, ARNOLD. *Books and Persons 1908–1911*. Chatto & Windus, London, 1917

—*The Journals of Arnold Bennett*. Cassell & Co., London; Vol I (1896–1910), 1932; Vol. II (1911–21), 1932; Vol. III (1921–8), 1933

BENSON, E. F. *As We Were*. Longmans, London, 1930

BIRD, ANTHONY. *Roads and Vehicles*. Longmans, London, 1969

BLUMENFELD, R. D. *R. D. B.'s Diary 1887–1914*. William Heinemann, London, 1930

BOOTH, J. B. *The Days We Knew*. T. Werner Laurie, London, 1943

BORER, MARY CATHCART. *The British Hotel Through the Ages*. Lutterworth Press, London, 1972

BOTT, ALAN. *Our Fathers: 1870–1900*. William Heinemann, London, 1931

BRENT, PETER. *The Edwardians*. BBC Publications, London, 1972

BRIANT, KEITH. *Marie Stopes*. Hogarth Press, London, 1962

BRITISH MEDICAL ASSOCIATION. *Secret Remedies*. London, 1909

—*More Secret Remedies*. London, 1910

BULLOCK, ALAN. *The Life and Times of Ernest Bevin*. William Heinemann, London, 1960

CALDER-MARSHALL, ARTHUR. *Havelock Ellis*. Rupert Hart-Davis, London, 1959

CARR, JOHN DICKSON. *The Life of Sir Arthur Conan Doyle*. John Murray, London, 1949

CARTLAND, BARBARA. *We Danced All Night*. Hutchinson, London, 1970; Pyramid, New York, 1972

CLARKE, SIR EDWARD. *The Story of My Life*. John Murray, London, 1918

CLEPHANE, IRENE. *Our Mothers*. Edited by Alan Bott. Victor Gollancz, London, 1932

CLOUD, YVONNE, ed. *Beside the Seaside*. Stanley Nott, London, 1934

CLUNN, HAROLD. *London Rebuilt: 1897–1927*. John Murray, London, 1927

COLLIER, JOHN, and LANG, IAIN. *Just the Other Day: An Informal History of Great Britain since the War*. Hamish Hamilton, London, 1932

COOPER, LADY DIANA. *The Light of Common Day*. Rupert Hart-Davis, London, 1959

—*The Rainbow Comes and Goes*. Rupert Hart-Davis, London, 1958

COWLES, VIRGINIA. *Edward VII and His Circle*. Hamish Hamilton, London, 1956

CRUIKSHANK, R. J. *Roaring Century*. Hamish Hamilton, London, 1946

CUDLIPP, HUGH. *Publish and Be Damned: The Astonishing Story of the Daily Mirror*. Andrew Dakers, London, 1953

CUNNINGTON, PHILLIS, and LUCAS, CATHERINE. *Costume for Births, Marriages and Deaths*. A. & C. Black, London, 1972; B. & N., New York, 1972

CUNNINGTON, WILLETT, and CUNNINGTON, PHILLIS. *Handbook of English Costume in the Nineteenth Century*. Faber & Faber, London, 1959; Plays, New York, 1972

—*The History of Underclothes*. Michael Joseph, London, 1951

CURL, JAMES STEVENS. *The Victorian Celebration of Death*. David & Charles, Newton Abbot, 1972; Gale, New York, 1972

DELGADO, ALAN. *Have You Forgotten Yet?* David & Charles, Newton Abbot, 1973

—*Victorian Entertainment*. David & Charles, Newton Abbot, 1971; McGraw-Hill, New York, 1971

DISHER, MAURICE WILSON. *Victorian Song: From Dive to Drawing Room*. Phoenix House, London, 1955

DONALDSON, FRANCES. *King Edward VIII*. Weidenfeld & Nicolson, London, 1974

DRIBERG, TOM. *Swaff: The Life and Times of Hannen Swaffer*. Macdonald, London, 1974

DRUMMOND, J. C., and WILBRAHAM, ANNE. *The Englishman's Food*. Jonathan Cape, London, 1939

DUDLEY, ERNEST. *The Gilded Lily: The Life and Loves of the Fabulous Lillie Langtry*. Odhams, London, 1958

EDIS, ROBERT. *Decoration and Furniture of Town Houses*. Kegan Paul, London, 1881; E.P. Publishing, London, 1972; British Book Center, New York, 1973

ELTON, LORD. *The Life of James Ramsay MacDonald*. Collins, London, 1939

FLETCHER, HAROLD R. *The Story of the Royal Horticultural Society 1804–1968*. Oxford University Press, London and New York, 1969

FRANCATELLI, CHARLES ELMÉ. *The Cook's Guide and Housekeeper's and Butler's Assistant*. Richard Bentley, London, 1888

FRASER, ANTONIA. *A History of Toys*. Weidenfeld & Nicolson, London, 1966

FYFE, HAMILTON. *Behind the Scenes of the Great Strike*. Labour Publishing Co., London, 1926

GARNER, PHILIPPE. *The World of Edwardians*. Hamlyn, Feltham, 1974

GARNETT, EDWARD, ed. *Letters from John Galsworthy*. Jonathan Cape, London, 1934

GATHORNE-HARDY, JONATHAN. *The Rise and Fall of the British Nanny*. Hodder & Stoughton, London, 1972; Dial, New York, 1973

GIBBS-SMITH, C. H. *A History of Flying*. Batsford, London, 1953

GIROUARD, MARK. *The Victorian Country House*. Oxford University Press, London and New York, 1971

GLOAG, JOHN. *Victorian Comfort*. A. & C. Black, London, 1961

—*Victorian Taste*. A. & C. Black, London, 1962; B. & N., New York, 1973

GRAVES, CHARLES. *Champagne and Chandeliers: The Story of the Café de Paris*. Odhams, London, 1958

—*Leather Arm Chairs*. Cassell, London, 1963

—*Mr Punch's History of Modern England*. 4 vols. Cassell, London, 1921–2

GRAVES, ROBERT and HODGE, ALAN. *The Long Week-End*. Faber & Faber, London, 1940

GREVILLE, LADY. *The Gentlewoman in Society*. Henry & Co., London, 1892

GRIERSON, HERBERT, and SMITH, J. C. *A Critical History of English Poetry.* Chatto & Windus, London, 1970

GROSVENOR, LOELIA, DUCHESS OF WESTMINSTER. *Grace and Favour.* Weidenfeld & Nicolson, London, 1961

HADFIELD, JOHN, ed. *The Saturday Book (vide* Russell, Leonard). Hutchinson, London, yearly editions from 1952

HADFIELD, MILES. *Gardening in Britain.* Hutchinson, London, 1960

HERBERT, A. KENNEY. *Fifty Dinners.* 2nd ed. Edward Arnold, London and New York, 1895

HIRST, FRANCIS W. *In the Golden Days.* Frederick Muller, London, 1947

HOWE, BEA. *Antiques from the Victorian Home.* Batsford, London, 1973; Scribner, New York, 1973

HUDSON, W. H. *Hampshire Days.* Longmans, London, 1903

HUEFFER, FORD HERMANN. *The Soul of London.* Alston Rivers, London, 1905

HUSSEY, CHRISTOPHER. *The Life of Sir Edwin Lutyens.* Country Life Books, Feltham, 1973

HYDE, H. MONTGOMERY. *Carson.* William Heinemann, London, 1953

—*Sir Patrick Hastings.* William Heinemann, London, 1960

JEFFERIES, RICHARD. *Life of the Fields.* Chatto & Windus, London, 1884

JENKINS, ALAN. *The Twenties.* William Heinemann, London, 1974; Universe Books, New York, 1974

JONCOURT, MARIE DE. *Wholesome Cookery.* 6th ed. Kegan Paul, London, 1895

LAVER, JAMES. *The Age of Optimism: Manners and Morals 1848–1914.* Weidenfeld & Nicolson, London, 1966

—*Between the Wars.* Vista Books, London, 1961

—*Edwardian Promenade.* Edward Hulton, London, 1958

—*Victorian Advertisements.* John Murray, London, 1968

—*Victorian Vista.* Hulton Press, London, 1954

LAYTON, T. B. *Sir William Arbuthnot Lane.* E. & S. Livingstone, London and Edinburgh, 1956

LESLIE, ANITA. *The Edwardians in Love.* Hutchinson, London, 1972

LEWIS, ROY, and MAUDE, ANGUS. *The English Middle Classes.* Phoenix House, London, 1949

LILLY, MARJORIE. *Sickert: the Painter and his Circle.* Elek, London, 1971; Noyes Press, New York, 1973

LODGE, SIR OLIVER. *Why I Believe in Immortality.* Cassell, London, 1928

LOW, RACHEL, and MANVELL, ROGER. *The History of the British Film: 1896–1906.* George Allen & Unwin, London, 1948

—*The History of the British Film: 1906–1914.* George Allen & Unwin, London, 1949

MAGNUS, PHILIP. *King Edward the Seventh.* John Murray, London, 1964

MANDER, RAYMOND, and MITCHENSON, JOE. *The Theatres of London.* Rupert Hart-Davis, London, 1961

MANNIN, ETHEL. *All Experience.* Jarrolds, London, 1932

—*Confessions and Impressions.* Jarrolds, London, 1930

—*Young in the Twenties.* Hutchinson, London, 1971

MANSFIELD, ALAN, and CUNNINGTON, PHILLIS. *Handbook of English Costume in the Twentieth Century.* Faber & Faber, London, 1973; Plays, New York, 1973

MARGETSON, STELLA. *Fifty Years of Victorian London.* MacDonald, London, 1969

MARJORIBANKS, EDWARD. *Life of Sir Edward Marshall Hall.* Victor Gollancz, London, 1930

MARROT, H. V. *Life and Letters of John Galsworthy.* William Heinemann, London, 1935

MASTERMAN, C. F. G. *The Condition of England.* Methuen, London, 1909

METCALFE, CRANSTOUN. *Peeresses of the Stage.* Andrew Melrose, London, 1913

MONTGOMERY, JOHN. *The Twenties.* George Allen & Unwin, 1957

MORRIS, MARGARET. *My Galsworthy Story.* Peter Owen, London, 1967; Humanities, New York, 1967

MOTTRAM, R. H. *For Some We Loved: An Intimate Portrait of Ada and John Galsworthy.* Hutchinson, London, 1956

MOWAT, CHARLES LOCH. *Britain Between the Wars 1918–1940.* Methuen, London, 1955

MUIR, PERCY. *Children's Books 1600–1900.* Batsford, London, 1954

MURRAY, SIR EVELYN. *The Post Office.* G. P. Putnam's Sons, London and New York, 1927

NEVILL, RALPH. *London Clubs.* Chatto & Windus, London, 1911

NORBURY, JAMES. *The World of Victoriana.* Hamlyn, Feltham, 1972

OGILVIE, VIVIAN. *Our Times: A Social History.* Batsford, London, 1953

OMAN, SIR CHARLES. *Memories of Victorian Oxford.* Methuen, London, 1941

PACKARD, VANCE. *The Hidden Persuaders.* Longmans, London, 1957; David McKay, New York, 1957

PEARSALL, RONALD. *The Worm in the Bud: The World of Victorian Sexuality.* Weidenfeld & Nicolson, London, 1969

—*Victorian Popular Music.* David & Charles, Newton Abbot, 1973; Gale, New York, 1973

PEARSON, MICHAEL. *The Age of Consent.* David & Charles, Newton Abbot, 1972

PEVSNER, NIKOLAUS. *London.* Penguin Books, Harmondsworth, 1973

PIKE, E. ROYSTON, ed. *Human Documents of the Age of the Forsytes.* George Allen & Unwin, London, 1969; Praeger, New York, 1970

PIMLOTT, J. A. R. *The Englishman's Holiday.* Faber & Faber, London, 1947

POLLOCK, GEORGE. *Mr Justice McCardie.* John Lane, London, 1934

POSTGATE, R. W., WILKINSON, ELLEN, and HORRABIN, J. F. *A Workers' History of the Great Strike.* Plebs League, London, 1927

POYNTER, F. N. L., ed. *The Evolution of Medical Practice in Britain.* Pitman Medical and Scientific Publishing, London, 1961

PRIESTLEY, J. B. *The Edwardians.* William Heinemann, London, 1970; Harper & Row, New York, 1970

REYNOLDS, M. E. *Memories of John Galsworthy by his Sister.* Robert Hale, London, 1936

RICHARDSON, P. J. S. *A History of English Ballroom Dancing.* Herbert Jenkins, 1946

ROBERTS, CECIL. *The Years of Promise 1908–1919.* Hodder & Stoughton, London, 1968

—*The Bright Twenties.* Hodder & Stoughton, London, 1970

ROBINSON, HOWARD. *The British Post Office.* Princeton University Press, Princeton, 1948

ROWELL, GEORGE. *The Victorian Theatre.* Oxford University Press, London, 1956

RUSSELL, LEONARD, ed. *The Saturday Book (vide* Hadfield, John). Hutchinson, London, yearly editions 1941–51

SACKVILLE-WEST, V. *The Edwardians.* Leonard and Virginia Woolf, London, 1930

SAUTER, RUDOLF. *Galsworthy the Man.* Peter Owen, London, 1967

SHAW, BERNARD. *The Intelligent Woman's Guide to Socialism and Capitalism.* Constable, London, 1928

SHERRINGTON, C. E. R. *A Hundred Years of Inland Transport.* Duckworth, London, 1934

SHORT, ERNEST. *A History of British Painting.* Eyre & Spottiswoode, London, 1953

SIMS, GEORGE R. *Living London.* Cassell, London, 1902

SINGER, CHARLES, and UNDERWOOD, E. ASHWORTH. *A Short History of Medicine.* Oxford University Press, London, 1962

SMITH, A. CROXTON. *Dogs Since 1900.* Andrew Dakers, London, 1950

STEPHENS, FREDERICK G. *Sir Edwin Landseer.* Sampson Low, Marston, Searle & Rivington, London, 1880

STEVENS, ROSEMARY. *Medical Practice in Modern England.* Yale University Press, New Haven, 1966

SYMONS, JULIAN, ed. *Between the Wars in Britain.* Batsford, London, 1972

—*Horatio Bottomley.* Cresset Press, London, 1955

—*The General Strike.* Cresset Press, London, 1957

Times, The. Fifty Years: Memories and Contrasts by Twenty-Seven Contributors to The Times. Thornton Butterworth, London, 1932

TREVELYAN, G. M. *English Social History.* Longmans, London, 1942

—*Illustrated English Social History.* Longmans, 1952

TURNER, E. S. *The Shocking History of Advertising.* Penguin Books and Michael Joseph, London, 1952

TWEEDSMUIR, SUSAN. *The Edwardian Lady.* Duckworth, London, 1966

VESEY-FITZGERALD, B. *The Book of the Dog.* Nicholson & Watson, London, 1948

VRIES, LEONARD DE, ed. *Victorian Inventions.* John Murray, London, 1971

—*Little Wide-Awake: An Anthology from Victorian Children's Books.* Arthur Barker, London, 1967

VRIES, LEONARD DE, and VAN AMSTEL, ILONA. *History as Hot News 1865–1897.* John Murray, London, 1973

WALBANK, FELIX ALAN. *Queens of the Circulating Library.* Evans Brothers, London, 1950

WILLIAMS, GERTRUDE M. *The Passionate Pilgrim: A Life of Annie Besant.* John Hamilton, London, 1932

WILLIAMS, NEVILLE. *Powder and Paint: A History of the Englishwoman's Toilet.* Longmans, London, 1957

Specialist and other periodicals consulted include *The Bystander, Eve, The Lady, The Queen, The Hairdressers' Weekly Journal, Hairdressing Fashions, The Tailor and Cutter, Fire: The Journal of the British Fire Services* and *The Wheelman and Motor Car Weekly.*

Acknowledgments for Illustrations

Index

In the following Index titles of books, periodicals and plays are set in italics, the names of Forsyte and other fictional characters are in quotation marks, page numbers in italics refer to black-and-white illustrations, and page numbers in bold to colour illustrations.